A New World in the Making

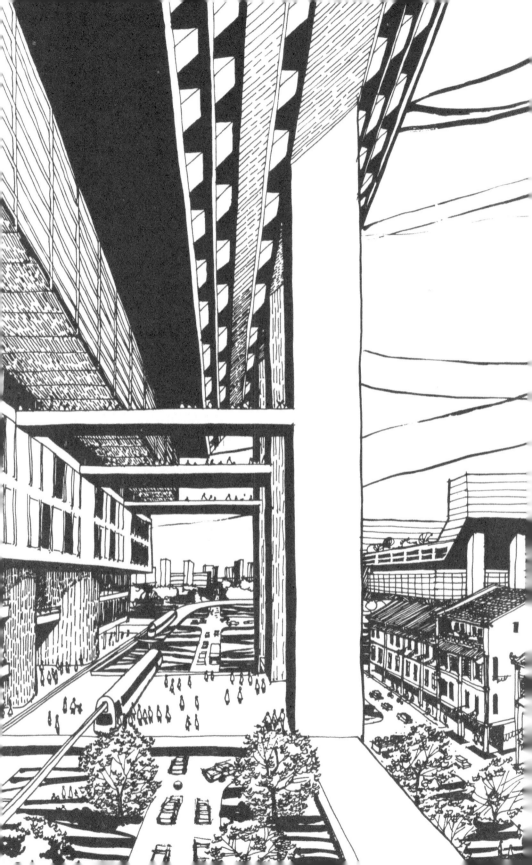

A New World in the Making
Life and Architecture in Tropical Asia

Tay Kheng Soon

RIDGE BOOKS
SINGAPORE

With thanks to Alvin Tan and Kevin Tan for the initial selection of texts.

© 2023 Tay Kheng Soon

Published under the Ridge Books imprint by:

NUS Press
National University of Singapore
AS3-01-02, 3 Arts Link
Singapore 117569
Fax: (65) 6774-0652
E-mail: nusbooks@nus.edu.sg
Website: http://nuspress.nus.edu.sg

ISBN: 978-981-325-169-4 (paper)
ISBN: 978-981-325-262-2 (case for Asia market only)
ePDF ISBN: 978-981-325-253-0
ePub ISBN: 978-981-325-254-7

All rights reserved. This book, or parts thereof, may not be reproduced in any form or by any means, electronic or mechanical, including photocopying, recording or any information storage and retrieval system now known or to be invented, without written permission from the Publisher.

National Library Board, Singapore Cataloguing in Publication Data
Name(s): Tay, Kheng Soon.
Title: A new world in the making : life and architecture in tropical Asia / by Tay Kheng Soon.
Description: Singapore : Ridge Books, [2023]
Identifier(s): ISBN 978-981-325-169-4 (paperback) | ISBN 978-981-325-262-2 (casebound) | ISBN 978-981-325-254-7 (ePub) | ISBN 978-981-325-253-0 (PDF)
Subject(s): LCSH: Tay, Kheng Soon. | Architecture--Singapore. | Architecture--Political aspects--Singapore. | Urbanization--Singapore. | Architecture--Asia. | Urbanization--Asia.
Classification: DDC 720.95957--dc23

Cover and facing title page: Sketch of a megastructure adjacent to a row of shophouses in Singapore as envisioned by the Singapore Planning and Urban Research (SPUR) Group in 1966. It was later realised in Golden Mile Complex (1972) by Design Partnership with Kheng Soon as its lead designer.

Project Editor: Justin Zhuang
Printed by: Integrated Books International

Contents

Introduction	1

Beginnings 7

- Family — 9
- Sibling Rivalry — 13

Early Years

- Second World War — 17
- The Language/Class Divide — 25
- Life in Cameron Highlands — 27
- Return to Serangoon Road — 29

Becoming 33

- Off to School — 35
- Adventures in Braddell Heights — 36
- Adolescence, Power and Purpose — 38
- Scouting Days — 39
- The 12 School Boy "Apostles" — 41
- The Spiritual Experience — 44

Early Designs

- Pursuing Architecture — 47
- Taking Charge of One's Own Learning — 62
- Trip to Java — 67

Being 73

- Malayan Architects Co-Partnership — 75
- Chong Keat versus Willie — 78
- The Rise of Local Firms — 81
- Awakening the Malayan — 83
- Singapore Planning and Urban Research Group — 85

Designs & Proposals 1960–70

- Meeting Lee Kuan Yew — 87
- To Kuala Lumpur and Back — 97
- My Explusion from Design Partnership — 101

- A Tribute to the Malayan Generation — 107

Essays · 117

The Cultural Role of Singapore City
1 June 1966 · 119

The Future of Asian Cities
May 1966 · 122

Collyer Quay's 12-Lane Coastal Superhighway
5 July 1967 · 129

Development and its Impact on Changing Values
June 1970 · 133

Singapore's Transport Dilemma
4 September 1974 · 139

Is Singapore Architecture "Obiang"?
15 March 1990 · 146

Heritage Conservation's Political and Social Implications:
The Case of Singapore
23 April 1990 · 149

Scope for the Economic and Cultural Invigoration
of the National Sector
26 July 1990 · 160

Civil Society's Contribution: Beyond Power Politics
23 March 2000 · 162

Creating Cultural Capital in Singapore
7 July 2002 · 167

Beyond Current Reality: A New Singapore, Perhaps?
4 August 2002 · 169

Interrogating Great Asian Streets
7 December 2004 · 173

Hanyu Pinyin and Singapore Street Names
12 October 2005 · 178

Singapore Colloquial Values that Strike a Chord
11 August 2005 · 183

Singapore: A Paradoxical Paradise
19 April 2006 · 184

Ideas and Proposals · 187

Proposal for "South Sea Lagoon Project" at
East Coast Reclamation
October 1968 · 189

Housing for Industrial Centres
5 October 1969 · 193

Locate Airport at Changi
23 February 1971 · 198

Low-Rise High-Density Housing: Towards a More
Sociable Housing Form
27 September 1978   201

Synopsis of Concepts of the Intelligent Tropical City
23 September 1989   217

The Kampong Bugis Case Study
23 November 1990   223

Retirement Cottages: An Option for Housing Singapore's
Elders within the Community
8 May 1999   229

Building Linear Blocks Over Roads: A Prelude to
The Singapore Management University Saga
11 August 1999   240

Proposed Indo-Pacific Cultural Centre at
Marina Bay Singapore
29 August 2005   244

Ideas for 21st Century   246

Singapore Version 2.0
27 December 2012   258

Rubanisation
13 March 2012   264

Afterword   271

List of Images   275

Index   277

01

Introduction

Some will ask why I did not write a typical architectural sort of book since I am an architect. For one, I have previously published a monograph of my architecture works in *Line Edge & Shade: The Search for a Design Language in Tropical Asia* (1997). Many people in Singapore also wonder why I do not stay within my primary field of architecture. They usually accuse me of being "political" which refers, I guess, to my ongoing concern with the dynamics of society and state power. Of course, I am interested in the dynamics of power, not least because it has such an important effect on aesthetics and the quality of the environment.

I am often asked where I stand regarding Singapore. Here is my chance to be clear. I love this land and this place. I do because it is a part of my cultural landscape. Singapore is the epicentre, but I feel expanding circles of affinity that radiate out from here. It's something like a family. Loving a family would include loving the children. And so it is in my case with Singapore. My affinity and affection for it is part of my affection for the larger region. I hold fast to the possibility of rekindling all that we share in common with our neighbours.

What does it mean to be a nationalist in today's world? A nation claims the affiliation of its citizens by virtue of its ability to exercise coercive power on their behalf. In a globalised world where economic interests and environmental effects have no regard for boundaries, "nationality" must necessarily be affected. But this is not to say that locational identification is obsolete. Territorial concepts of affiliation must now enlarge to include support for ecologies, be they natural, economic, resource-based or cultural. My Singaporean nationalism takes the form of concentric rings, reflecting my links to the global, regional and the local. It is in this context that my political affiliation must be re-defined. My affiliation is to an undivided land and a sensibility: Though I am a Singaporean, I am still a Malayan in the way I sense my Singaporeanness.

I have to constantly bridge the gap between what I am and what I imagine I can be. Intellectually, my language is also caught in this indeterminate space. I tend to adopt a terse language in clipped Malayan tones to maintain a certain neutrality and distance as well as a creative space. It is a tone that is necessarily apolitical. It is a space of possibilities. Detachment has its advantages and its flaws. Culturally, I struggle against the rising tide of the American-led North Atlantic hegemony to which Singapore is economically and culturally subordinated. It is a reality that I have to live with, but I insist on having my own creative space, nonetheless. That space is premised on the commonality of Southeast Asia.

Of Words and S. P. A. C. E.

"Winning hearts and minds" in the global establishment of hegemony is a combination of rice bowl politics and wordplay. It is also a strategy for local domination. Command of words is always the first step in the colonisation of the mind. In the Singapore context, the process has to adapt to the political culture. Words must be handled in a special way to avoid unintentionally fanning critical contention. They have to be neutralised. Management-speak is convenient. "Problems" are neutered and become "issues". "Difficulties" become "challenges". The overwhelming "master narrative" is echoed daily by the "nation-building press" and such political rhetoric drowns out almost all normal thought.

Words like modernisation take the place of modernity. Nation is equated with state. Democracy is merely elections and not a culture of open expression. Politics becomes only a contest for power instead of a contest of ideas. Free speech means only the forum pages in the press. Criticism of the state is regarded as churlish and ungrateful. Principles are but naive assertions. To be pragmatic is to be virtuous and smart. To argue based on principle is to be infantile. Government means administration and that is equal to the ruling party. To be anti-party is therefore to be anti-government and to be anti-nation. Law is equal to justice. Order is obedience to rules. Code is conformism. Anything organic is ipso facto disorderly. Chaos is the greatest dread. Progress means more consumption

Introduction

of goods and fashions. Freedom is the ability to consume. Elections are a mere changing of the guard. The opposition is the lunatic fringe. Development is building more buildings. Real estate means more land sales. Citizenship means property ownership. Ownership is leasehold. Rights are subject to law, and not inalienable. Citizenship is a privilege. To demand is to petition. Aesthetics is style. Beauty is what is published in the western media. Creativity is artful whims and fancies. Design is styling. Architecture is iconic. Foreign is desirable, local is backward. Asia-ness becomes ethnicity. Identity is a label. Urbanity is a western style. Achievement is something bagged. Love is passion and acceptable only if it is constructive. Value is cash value. Choice becomes having options. Thinking out of the box is a posture. To be critical is to be rejectionist. The good life is shopping. Public space is for entertainment. Initiative is mobilisation. Frenetic activity is regarded as vibrancy. Vibrancy is merely crowdedness. Quality is what money can buy. Talent is that which is acclaimed by others in the world. Youth are potentials to be harnessed. Pioneers are has-beens. Senior citizens are the aged. Icons are what people put up as wallpaper: decorative and harmless!

As I trawl through my scattered thoughts and experiences of my past and contrast them from the vantage point of the present, I discover things between the lines. And so, I have edited and rewritten my past writings. In so doing, I have also chanced upon forgotten ideas and eagerly brought these in. My main concern is that what I say should ring true to me, then hopefully to the reader. The content, the purpose and the integrity of narration I searched for is found in the acronym, "S. P. A. C. E.". It is this metaphorical "space" I have searched so hard for all my life. It is where I longed for in the shrinking space caused by the pragmatic "nation-building" in Singapore that reduces all to the single dimension of profit. My "S.P.A.C.E" is formed in between several words. "Singapore", the self-elected orphan of Malaya and South East Asia. "Politics", the diminution of the intellect and the sensibilities through the unrelenting use of the stick and the carrot and in its wake, the shrinking of every self. "Architecture", the hem-strung product of rules and regulations and the timid client-market that unknowingly dictate that no liminal space is left where art may dwell. Space is thus so desiccated that the ensuing "Culture", when stripped of its gloss reveals nothing but a whimpering identity crisis, desperately seeking "styling" to cope with the emptiness.

Finally, of course, there is "Education", which has meant the narrowing of the inner eye to focus on skilling, disciplining, harnessing, divesting the unruly senses and thereby numbing all aesthetics. At last, I grasp the linguistics of the whole scheme: "S. P. A. C. E.". It is a "space" that has to and is being shaped in a special way to create an obedient and productive digit, a proud product of the "patriot of the will". This book is a record of my journey through the mindscape of such a space and time.

Why I Write

While many have urged me to publish my thoughts and writings, I have resisted for several reasons. The claim on one's time is very real, but the deeper reason is my abiding sense of futility. When I have written, it is a response to some specific task, such as a conference, a request for a chapter, a reaction to something interesting or annoying. But to sit down and put it all together is quite another matter. I needed to sense that the time has come. It has. There is a feeling that things have got to change.

My place, Singapore, is at such a time. Maybe I am at such a time too. A time where the rushing waters have quelled, arrived at the delta, listless... it meets the wild, wide ocean. It is a strange moment when the two meet. And so, it dawdles at the mud flats reluctant to take the plunge. It is a hung time. What purpose would my words serve? Who do I speak to? My son recently asked why I am so obsessed with Singapore. He has been puzzled at the futility of my vexations all these years. I gave him a pat answer: "I have to scratch the itch for the sheer pleasure and need of it!" He was unconvinced, having seen me vexed too often. It is because Singapore is a puzzle that needs to be solved: How is it that it can be so productive with so little creativity among the people?

There is also a personal reason for writing. I could not do otherwise. Refusing the embrace of pragmatic reality is not a choice for me. That path is to die a little each day. My self-regard would not allow me to conform to pragmatic norms. Five decades of rapid mobilisation forced upon by the dictates of industrialisation and driven by the politics of survival has achieved for Singapore much by material progress. But it has wrought havoc on all fine sensibilities in the interest of "survival". That is pragmatism. All justifiable in retrospect, except that such progress should have left some space for new seeds to sprout when a new time comes. This is my acceptance yet regret of the past. My earnest hope for the future is that the new moment must not be lost. I feel compelled to write at this time in the belief that there are dormant seeds out there that may be prompted to grow if they can find some fertile patch in a left behind space. I feel compelled to put on record my experiences and thoughts born in the debris of times past, hopefully to encourage such new growth.

My life began after the Second World War, at a time of change that has shaped the present. My story is a small fragment in the larger narrative, a tapestry that reveals new connections and old knots. I take comfort in the thought that aside from the dominance of the master narrative, some small voices may be necessary to enrich the perspective of the human condition. In some senses, our lives are not only our own, but part of a larger story through which the "ours" become more meaningful. The lives of others enrich our own only when we know how they dealt with the issues of their time. This is community in its most important sense. Here is a thought for atomised lives that seek totally private spaces to be themselves in an increasingly incomprehensible world of silhouettes: isolation is no way to live. It offers no way to sense the richness of other lives. It is also the ultimate desired endgame of the disembodied machinery of everyday life.

A memoir is always a partial story. The human condition is such that we edit ourselves even as we live. No one can be conscious of everything all the time, much less narrate it as we live from moment to moment. To do so is to exist in a perpetual state of memorising and counting. Forgetting is necessary if one is to zoom in and out and scan the landscape of life. An ever-present memory would produce a gridlock of the mind. I freely admit that there are many things I forgot to say or do not want to say. There are many stories left to be told or not told, or never to be told.

Beginnings

My paternal grandmother (seated)
with the rest of the family, c. 1947.

02

Family

My mother, Pang Swee Keng, was born in a village outside Swatow, China, whose Teochew name is known as "Ho-lo-gou". However, her birth certificate states that she was born in Sarawak. Her family had reported so to help her obtain British subject papers more easily during the colonial times. She attended the Church of England Zenana Mission Society (CEZMS) School in Singapore, now known as St. Margaret's School. My father, Tay Meng Hock, was born in Singapore and attended St. Joseph's Institution. Both never finished school. My mother dropped out because her father's business failed due to the stock market crash of 1929. My father had to shoulder the financial burdens of the family after his father died when he was a teenager.

My father started working life in the early 1930s by selling football tickets at Jalan Besar and Anson Road stadiums while attending night classes at the Young Men's Christian Association (YMCA). He also collected, cleaned, bunched and sold scrap vegetables at the Beach Road market. To feed his family, then living in Kim Chuan Lane off Paya Lebar Road, my father collected leftovers from friends working in the kitchen of the Singapore Cricket Club. From these humble beginnings, he rose to become an accountant in the American International Assurance Company (AIA) and later a manager. During the Second World War, he saved the company's records in the Supreme Court basement with the agreement of Justice Tan Ah Tah and was later promoted for it. After the war, he went from one company to another before retiring altogether as the managing director of a local insurance company. My father was a self-made man and succeeded in most things. His talent was in organising and motivating his sales force, and he told me from young to always take the initiative in everything I do. During the recession of 1985, he was bankrupted from unrecoverable premium accounts owed by his insurance agents to him. It was beyond his control. The company folded and he set up a direct sales company even though he was in his seventies by then.

My mother quit school to look after her younger siblings when her mother moved to Sumatra to join her father to try to recoup his business. She was the youngest girl amongst six other siblings, including four brothers and two sisters. It was a miserable time for my mother as she was bullied and mistreated in a strictly hierarchical Teochew family. She developed a strong distaste for unfairness and unkindness. When she met my father, she saw in him the kind of generosity of spirit and entrepreneurial drive missing in her own siblings and fell for the dashing, young and self-made man.

There was always a strain between the two families. It was a complicated case of class and culture difference. My mother's family was Teochew and middle class. They were known in China as "middle peasants" because they owned some land and employed tenant farmers to work it. My father's family was Hokkien and probably of labouring class background. The Teochews have traditionally felt superior to the Hokkiens and our families' relationship was also mixed with personal feelings of envy, jealousy and perceived inferiority. My mother says that my father's mother was uncomfortable with her family from the beginning. In retrospect, it could have been a case of chemistry but also class antipathy. All these were present beneath the surface civility whenever the two families met, and I too felt the chill as a child.

Despite these undercurrents, my parents got married. It was a strain on both, given my paternal grandmother's antipathy towards my mother's family. They married in the then-Sun Yat Sen Memorial Library at Armenian Street. It was a popular wedding solemnisation location for modern young couples who were neither Christians nor believed in traditional Chinese religious practices. The strain between the families was evident in my parent's wedding photographs. It was the bane my mother bore throughout her life. She never fails to lament her lot but also resolve to do her duty and be kind to her mother-in-law despite the perceived injustices. I, however, remember my paternal grandmother kindly. My brother and I were her two great joys, as all grandsons are.

Beginnings

My paternal grandmother, Lim Swee Ee, wore sarong kebayas although she was a Hokkien lady through and through. But she also spoke Malay. She had a stubborn streak. When she turned twelve, she repeatedly refused to have her feet bound unlike other girls of that time who were traditionally interned in mimicry of "proper" families. She was thus relegated to a *huan*, meaning native in dialect. It was a pejorative term for the "uncivilised" and has all the horribly racist and dismissive Chinese sense of the term. My grandmother did not mind as she was a sort of tomboy in her youth. She spoke fondly of her carefree days living in a kampong in Bedok where she wandered about barefoot and rowed *koleks*, a type of small Malay fishing boat. When she was 90 years old, I brought her to find the remains of the village where she recalled an "iron" suspension bridge over a small creek. Rummaging around the tall weeds at the spot she recalled, I was pleasantly surprised to find the steel stump of the old bridge, now sawn off. It was opposite a small octagonal surau that marked the entrance to the village from the nine-mile Bedok bend.

My grandmother and father seldom spoke about their family. All I recall is grandmother telling me of her brother's *tongkang* (barge) business which ferried granite from Pulau Ubin. Alas, he was ruined when the *tongkang* sank in a storm off Changi. It was grandmother's way of telling me that her family was really not that poor. As far as I know, my paternal grandfather, Tay Cheng Kui, came from China to work in Singapore as a coolie. My father always spoke fondly of my grandfather as hardworking, honourable and having a very straight and honest character. He also remembers my grandfather's admonitions about maintaining personal reputation and honour at all costs, which my father endeavoured to remind us of on every suitable occasion. My grandfather had two sons and a daughter. There was another son whose life was snuffed out by an ignorant midwife's attempt to clear his nostril passages by sucking on them. My father was the eldest of the siblings and the only one to receive some education. After my grandfather died of typhoid, his debts fell onto my father's shoulders which led him to quit school and work. My father's sister later started a small business buying and selling war-surplus goods at the Sungei Road Thieves' Market. She eventually opened a grocery stall next to the old Tekka market. My father's brother was an odd-job labourer.

Both my parents were modern for their time. I attribute this to their exposure to Christianity in the schools they attended. But they were also in some ways the product of the in-between times they lived through. They lived within the strictures of piety, convention and traditional ideas, and within that, they exercised their autonomous spirit. My mother accommodated her mother-in-law's expectation of a compliant and servile daughter-in-law to some extent but was not prepared to be totally subservient. Over the years they lived together, she was torn between her partial acceptance of the traditional daughter-in-law role and her free spiritedness. In contrast, my parents were decidedly liberal towards my brother and me. They gave us the freedom and education they themselves did not have in their youth. Though concerned in the usual way with safety and obedience, they allowed us to develop an independent spirit and to roam on bicycles and explore the spaces around us. When we lived in Braddell Heights, there was a tall Casuarina tree at the back of the house which I climbed often to contemplate the great distances. It sparked a longing to go to those distant places to see what it was really like on the ground. My parents also encouraged us to join the scouts, to go camping, to take initiative, and to adventure. If only they knew the risks we actually took, they would have fainted!

But when we were much younger, my brother and I were cooped up in the upstairs of a row house flat at 558A Serangoon Road as my mother did not want us to mix with the ruffians downstairs. Once, my brother and I went down to the five-foot way and encountered a brood of them at the end of the block. One of them pushed my brother, but I—a mere four-year-old—caught hold of the bully and gave him a bear hug so tight that he bawled out loud. It was a sign of my natural aggressiveness and became a family legend that was retold many a time with pride. At home, we spent time with our chins on the windowsill, looking out at the passing traffic of cars as well as electric trams which made a loud "switch" sound accompanied by an electrical flash as they whined by. We also heard the sing-song recitation of the Chinese school pupils across the street as they intoned the classics of Confucius, interspersed by the tick-tock of the itinerant noodle sellers soliciting customers. We also read a lot of books. My mother used to read to us and even stopped to explain when we asked her questions. I remember my brother and I seated on the broad armrests of the lounge chair she sat in while reading to us and being mesmerised by the nursery stories. Our love of reading came from this, and I realised later that this indelible connection comes about when reading is associated with parental love.

We were only allowed to play outside of the house occasionally. There were also occasional visits to the Pillay family a few doors down. Mr Pillay was a big and rather stern Indian man, and we children were scared of him. In contrast, Mrs Pillay was a jolly, rotund Chinese woman who wore sarong kebayas. They had four kids, each one year apart, and we liked them as they were close to our age. I noticed that some of their children had darker skin and others were fairer. This was my first experience with a different race and an inter-racial family. It was unremarkable, and we played happily together. We felt quite at home with the Pillays, and English was the medium of our communication.

Sibling Rivalry

My brother Tay Eng Soon and I were both born in 1940 but 11 months apart. He was born in January and I in December. I did not know then that one year could make such a tremendous difference in school. He was seven and I had just turned six when we started attending Anglo-Chinese School (ACS) Primary. I remember parents conversing about having children born at the end of the year so that they could start going to school earlier, presumably to steal a march over others. What a mistaken notion! My brother excelled in school as he was more mature, and his brain was that much more developed. As modern research now shows, months can make big differences in cognitive development. My age-induced learning handicap was demoralising as I was an average student. My better subject was art, and I became the teacher's little helper in illustrating anything. I also cultivated wider interests in sports, drawing, photography and reading. I even started a chemistry lab at home to make gun powder. I obtained chemicals from my second uncle's Singapore Dispensary store next to the Pavilion Cinema along Orchard Road. Luckily, I failed as I could not get enough concentrated nitric acid to make nitroglycerin.

In the ACS system, "A" was the arts class, "B" was the science class, "C" was the commerce class and the "D" and "E" classes were the omnibus classes. While my brother attended the "B" class and was the top student all the way through school, I was in the "C" class and my attainments during my early years in school were disappointing to my parents. I was careless in arithmetic and therefore did not do well. It was only years later that I understood the difference between math and arithmetic. Mathematics is a conceptual-spatial capability, while arithmetic and calculation are simply diligence and accuracy in numerical computation. Knowing the difference has helped me overcome my fear of math and recognise that I do have a very powerful, intuitive spatial and mathematical sense with which to conceptualise new urban forms and cities. Sadly, schools never made the distinction. The countless number of children who have been wronged by this misconception and thus stigmatised for life will never be known! Parents did not know of such things then. They thought that underperformance was due to a lack of diligence and application. In those days, they also knew nothing of sibling rivalry and the damaging effects it has on an individual's development. I also only saw sibling rivalry from my point of view. My brother surprised me years later when he said he felt threatened by me because I was following too close to his heels. For example, he was very good at drawing when he was five years old and had a natural ability to put down on paper what he saw. I begged him to teach me, but he refused. I tried on my own and distinctly recall that something miraculously clicked in my brain when I drew my first battleship with some soldiers and a parachute. I remember the absolute elation of the moment, and I never stopped after that. There were other rivalries that ended in fisticuffs. While I always pulled my punches, he delivered his with full force and I wept whenever he hit me mercilessly. That was his character! This inbuilt taste for power and domination drove him into politics later in life and is also what kept me away. I do not have a taste for the coup de grace like him. No killer instinct as such!

We shared a room at home. Our parents made us a long worktable along the window wall, where we did our homework and worked on our hobbies. My side of the table was always in a mess whereas his was always tidy. There was an invisible line he maintained between us, and I could not cross it without rousing his ire. He had his books, tools and toys, while I had mine. We had different reading interests. He kept to himself and his friends, and I to mine. Our relationship was cordial overall. It was a different matter with our parents. They favoured the "smarter" child, and "smart" meant scoring high marks in school. I felt the discrimination. Furthermore, my brother had a prodigious memory. He could tellingly recall every detail of who said what and when, and he used it effectively in arguments. It was useless to argue with him on such terms. He always won!

After he joined the People's Action Party (PAP) and politics in 1980, we argued on every subject relevant to Singapore over a period of 15 years. As we had lunch every Sunday at our parents' house with our respective families, there would inevitably be discussions on political and social matters. The children all got a full dose of "Singaporeana"! On matters of values, the divide between us was distinct. His conservative line was at odds with mine. In many ways, our disagreements took on a good-natured discussion as we knew each other's position thoroughly. But our differences are now surfacing in the new Singapore. I was ahead of time… out of sync, as in many things I thought and did. What was clear to me in all our arguments was his inherent dim view of human nature. This may be a stance he adopted only with me because the teachers and others who dealt with him perceived him as a paragon of positiveness and humane concern. This view was entirely in line with his brand of Christianity. He had become "born again" although he had always been church-going since we started the Barker Road Methodist Church as students. While I "graduated", he continued and ultimately became an elder. His belief in the "original sin" logically implied that "evil" was ever present and had to be countered through perpetual vigilance on the part of those responsible. This of course means that it is the government that must shoulder the role of being the ultimate protector against evil and the promoter of good. I am sure this was his motive for going into politics, even to the extent that he would sacrifice himself in the process.

His values fitted well into the PAP government's working philosophy. Despite being side-lined for many years, he put considerable intelligence and knowledge into the service of the people of Singapore in his role as Minister of State for Education. This fortitude can only be explained by his dedication to duty to the Party and the good of the people. Lacking his spiritual certitude, I could never have done what he did. I would have rebelled against the injustice. I also do not believe in absolutes in human nature. The good and the evil that exist in the world reside in each of us concurrently. I therefore could not have the sort of certainty and self-righteousness he had. Evil is not out there. It is also in each and every human being. What we are is a tendency provoked by the circumstances we create or are in, exacerbated by natural as well as man-made conditions.

For me, creativity is a condition to be fostered in societies as a means of actualisation. It is a condition in which the positive tendencies of humans can be enhanced, and therefore evil and all things negative can be held back, including psychotic tendencies. Creativity is therefore a necessity, not a phase of development after the basics have been achieved. But it is also true that creativity tends to become indulgent if it is not directed at things greater than self-gratification. There is a dialectic involved to match self-interest with larger interests. It is therefore the genius of a society to craft the conditions in which individuals, while serving self, also serve the larger good imaginatively and out of free will.

Volunteerism and initiative are critical qualities in any culture. Here is where modern culture has to innovate in a given social situation to derive the conditions to bring it out. Education and empathy for the plight of others and nature are important at this time in history. Community and creativity are prerequisites of the human eco-system. Experimentation with social forces is vital to test the relevance of ideas, gain experience and understand the ecology of creativity. Authoritarian leaders are notoriously ignorant as to how to actualise conditions of creativity because they do not view human nature positively. They believe only in using the stick and the carrot to reward the positive and curb the negative. Instead of leading by inspiring positivity, they do so by fear. The PAP government tried very hard through campaigns and disincentives. But it failed and has since changed tactics. However, the government needs a different insight into human nature to really change. There is a tentativeness and a timidity in their recent moves aimed at invoking the new spirit needed. Our political leaders need more courage and creativity to turn the old Singapore into a new one. A strong government now needs strong people more than ever, and to do so, it must have a strong belief in the people.

The PAP government justifies the legitimate retention of the moral right to be guardians of society. However, there never was any guarantee in human history that moral righteousness did not, in the end, turn upon itself and negate the very virtues it originally espoused. To say that people can vote out the government, in a "nominally democratic" society like Singapore, is nothing more than a convenient argument to fob off critics. True democracy has to be founded on a positive attitude towards human beings risking power in the belief in peoples' goodness. Thus, no one can be sanguine about the prospects of societies based on the PAP's dim view of society becoming democratic except the thoroughly ignorant and deluded. Such is the politics I am against, and what my brother and I often argued over. I absolutely accept the sincerity of his convictions. What I fear is the results of those like him who take it upon themselves to be the guardians of truth and decency, especially those who act out what they perceive to be the will of God. Too many atrocities have been committed by people against others in the name of God and the good.

While editing this memoir, I realised another thing. My father was a passionate person, very brave, innovative, pro-active and an entrepreneur. My mother is the typical micro-managing person socialised into the female role by society and circumstances. But she was unusually intelligent, had a prodigious memory and was capable of thinking the unthinkable. I am an amalgam of them both, with a bias towards my father's nature. I can be coolly analytical and passionate in what I do and think too. My choice of career therefore fitted my nature perfectly. However, as the conditions of architecture practice seldom supported my passion and my rationality, I struggled to overcome this. My nature is therefore the source of my creativity and my temper. It is strange that it takes time to really understand one's own nature. It takes a certain cool hard look at oneself to do this.

My brother was more like my mother. He kept his passions strictly under control. Another tendency of his was to seek approbation from people in authority. This is part of the socialisation of the first born and it is exacerbated by a traditional Chinese upbringing. His God-fearing nature also derives from this, I think. It is the psychological lot of the first born to shoulder the family values. In the end, we agreed to disagree. He was basically a decent human being, and in some ways my alter ego. He and I shared an intense dislike for bluff and insincerity. His passing left a void in me. As the second born, I revelled in my freedom. While I made many mistakes and blundered into many situations, the consolation was that I also made many discoveries in understanding the complexities of reality. This memoir, for want of a better word, is my scrap book of this journey... In some ways, it is my story of the other Singapore, outside of the persuasions of the current master narrative.

Second World War

I remember the whine of bombs as they fell and the dull thud on impact. The scent of gunny sack sandbags in the makeshift air raid shelter where

Early Years

My parent's wedding portrait, c. 1938. (across) I was born in Serangoon Road, until the family moved to the Cameron Highlands during the Second World War where we stayed in a house at the base of the Boh Tea estate near Ringlet (below). We returned to Singapore in 1945. In 1949, we moved into a new home in Braddell Heights (left).

Scouting Days

Scouting was very important in teaching me initiative and a sense of adventure (above). Through building bamboo kitchen gadgets as a scout, I learnt about knots and the nature of materials (across). My brother and I joined the Wolf Cubs at the Anglo-Chinese School Primary in Coleman Street (right).

the family hid under the concrete staircase of 558A Serangoon Road. I was exactly one year old on the day the Imperial Japanese Army Air Service bombed Singapore on 8 December 1941. It could be a case of retroactive constructed memory since both my brother and I saw many war movies of the Pacific War in the 1950s, *Sands of Iwo Jima, The Battle of Tarawa*, etc. The mind is of course capable of making up "memories", but scent is more reliable. The scent of gunny sack never fails to bring back the memories. Even now, I can feel the texture of the sacks and recall the peculiar pungent scent of hessian. The memories are real. In my memory of that fateful day, I felt no anxiety. I was too young to know what fear was. Instead, I remember the cosy feel of family warmth in the velvety gloom of the air raid shelter. I also remember the clacking sound of milk being made in an enamel mug as the spoon struck the sides rapidly. There was only condensed milk in those days. I still like the taste. These are my earliest memories.

My mother says that the family was on good terms with our downstair neighbours. I remember a green painted steel door at the ground floor landing that connected the two flats on agreement between the two families. Today, such a design is unthinkable. Imagine the legal and social consequences, not to mention the building regulations and culturally fixated ideas about privacy, etc. What a wonderful potential for neighbourly relations then! And so it was that both families were able to share the safest place in their houses during those anxious days.

The next earliest memory I have is the journey by train up Malaya to the Cameron Highlands. It was stuffy, hot and crowded. I remember skinny, dark Indian men sleeping on the netted shelves above the seats and even under the benches. We huddled together between the benches, surrounded by our luggage. Then there is the mental picture of the floor tiles in the train's toilet. I remember them to be large, chamfered, yellow ochre tiles. Years later, I made it a point to have a good look and was astonished that they were no larger than mosaic tiles. Indeed, the tiles were chamfered and yellow ochre in colour as I saw them in my mind's eye. But of course, I was much closer to the floor then!

My father made a wise decision to evacuate the whole family to Cameron Highlands. It was possible because he had gotten a special travel permit from the Japanese. Before the war, he had volunteered as an air raid warden for the Serangoon Road area where the family flat was. His group was based in Kandang Kerbau Police Station, where the present Tekka Market now stands. When the Japanese arrived, the group disbanded but the chief of his unit was drafted by the Japanese to keep the peace along Serangoon Road. This was the stretch from Tekka Market to the now demolished Rumah Miskin Police Station at the junction of Serangoon, Balestier Road and Lavender Street. The former chief, now a big shot at the police station, gave my father the permit. It was stamped on my father's white shirt sleeve that he was certified a "not undesirable" person and could therefore travel about. My father said that he didn't take off that shirt for weeks! Thus, he was able to evacuate the whole family, including some relatives, to Cameron Highlands, and he had learnt from friends who had gone there earlier that food was plentiful and the situation quite peaceful. It proved a very wise move, and the family thrived in the cool and tranquil atmosphere save for a few terrifying incidents.

Before moving, my father set up a small pharmaceutical business during the first year of the Japanese Occupation. This business was consolidated and enlarged to become the Central Medical Hall at the junction of Bras Basah Road and Victoria Street. It is where the administration block of the Singapore Management University (SMU) now stands. My father had earlier got my mother's brother a placement as a pharmacist's assistant at the "Red House", which was the Federal Dispensary in town, at Battery Road. This qualified my uncle for the two-year pharmacy course in Raffles College. The two of them worked out the chemical ingredients of Gripe's Baby Water and they began a lucrative business making and marketing their import-substituted version, Johnson's Baby Water. It sold wildly. Why did he not call it Ah Hock's Baby Water? Obviously, "Johnson" sounded more authoritative to colonised ears! Little has changed! Some fifty years after independence and nation-building, Western authorisation still matters in Singapore! Our radio and television announcers still strive to speak with marbles in their mouth! My mother washed the bottles, filled and labelled them in our upstairs flat at Serangoon Road. I do not remember the operations, but I remember seeing the dusty wooden shelves when we returned to the flat after the war. The stock was stacked on these shelves. Business boomed as families bought the bottles to sooth their fretful babies in those stressful times. My father told me years later that they put in a little codeine, an opiate, to make the babies sleep happy!

A New World in the Making

The business boomed and my father got ambitious. He cornered the black market for "693", which was what the antibacterial medication produced by May & Baker was then known as. It was the highly demanded mighty cure-all for most tropical bacterial infections. The stocks were probably looted from hospitals and British army stores and then sold on the black market. My father bought them all up with the profits from the "Baby Water" business and began his own distribution network. His talent was always in establishing, motivating and maintaining his sales agency network. He was so successful that the Kempeitai began investigating his activities and he was advised by his informants to get out of Singapore as soon as possible. He did so hurriedly. After checking out the Cameron Highlands and renting a house there, the family moved soon afterwards.

We arrived in Cameron Highlands with only a little wad of "Banana" notes. While my father had big-money profits from the business then, he did not take it along but stashed $5,000 of British Malaya currency in the bedroom cupboard at the Serangoon Road flat. Amazingly, the cash was intact when the family returned home after the war. Only $500 was used by my father's sister who looked after the flat all through the war. She used it to start a small business in the nearby New World Amusement Park during the Occupation. Despite the general chaos, life for the little people went on seemingly as usual. At Cameron Highlands, we all lived in Ringlet, a small distribution town on the fringe of the Boh Tea Estate. My father quickly established a business but also received monthly dividends from his partners who continued to run Central Medical Hall in Singapore throughout the Occupation. He supported the family with the dividends and also traded vegetables for fertiliser with the farmers. He did well. I remember going to Ringlet monthly, perched on his bicycle handlebar, when he went to square the accounts. Sometimes, my brother went along too, one of us in front, and the other behind on the carrier.

Cameron Highlands was a child's dreamland: flowers everywhere, misty mountains, and vegetables growing in the garden. We could wander in the fields and woods around the house and wade in a clear, cool stream nearby. At an elevation of over 900 metres, it was a respite from the heat of the lowlands. There was plenty of good food and friends and cousins to play with. The war was a distant reality we children knew nothing of. There was plenty of space for the family around the bungalow and life was quite secure. We were self-sufficient with a vegetable garden in front of the home. The house was symmetrical and small, but it was huge to my child's eyes. There was a front porch on the central axis of the house plan. Behind were four rooms, two on each side flanking a central passageway that led to the covered rear porch where we had our meals. Behind the porch was a narrow air well where I remember the womenfolk settling starch flour in vats of water. The flour was made by squeezing grated tapioca strained through cloth filters. Separated by the air well from the main house was the smoky kitchen and utility room. Next to that, was an oxidation pond outside into which the excrement went. This included that from the family and from two pigs my mother reared. Over time, they became her pets and she shed copious tears when slaughter time came!

The Language/Class Divide

At Ringlet, my maternal grandparents, eldest uncle and second auntie lived with their spouses and children in a nearby house which my father got for them. Not knowing the owner, and desperate to secure it for his in-laws, he was in a weak negotiating position with the main tenant who levied an exorbitant rent — "tea money". This was a sore point between him and my mother's siblings who had never liked him in the first place. I remember them as rather emotionally remote from us. Now I know why. They were Chinese educated and there remains a gulf between them and the English educated of that time. It not only affected relations in families but shaped politics all through the independence movement in Singapore and thereafter. In those days, families were large. Many Chinese families sent some of their children to Chinese-language schools and others to English-language schools. They wanted to preserve their link to their Chinese-ness but were also hedging their bets. And so, the practical thing was to send some children to English-language schools to increase their advantage in job and business prospects within the British colonial environment. My maternal auntie, the eldest, as well as the second, third and youngest uncles went to English-language schools. Thus, there was a cultural and educational split between them and their eldest brother and second sister who went to Chinese-language schools. Although my third uncle was educated in the English-language ACS, he was decidedly anti-British. He denounced them publicly to such an extent that he was taken to be a communist, picked up by the British Special Branch, given a severe beating and then banished to China. He eventually died in Guangzhou as vociferous as ever, so said my mother. The cousins I played with had parents who went to Chinese-language schools and spoke Teochew together. I later learnt that one of these cousins was banished by the British and decamped to China. He rose in the Chinese Ministry of Foreign Affairs, but we lost contact.

The language/class divide persists. The Chinese who did not know Mandarin were regarded as betrayers of their heritage. Even today, there is still the notion that to be Chinese, one has to speak Mandarin. The government's Speak Mandarin campaign tapped into this deep vein and so it worked. It also left the uneducated Chinese feeling that to only speak a Chinese dialect was somehow to own up to a low status in social class. Speaking Mandarin somehow elevated oneself. I never felt that way. Thus, my youngest uncle decided in his adulthood to take on a Chinese identity. Although English-educated and running a toy business dealing with American and European business partners, he often spoke Mandarin with a habitual stutter because he was not fluent in it. He had some basic tuition in the language and improvised. He also changed his surname from the Teochew "Pang" to the Mandarin "Fong". My second uncle, clearly English-educated, only felt drawn towards Chinese culture and history in his later years. He showed such an enthusiasm I was hard put to offer critical comments of mainstream Chinese culture. But he was the only uncle I could talk at length with as he was also more Malayan than the others. And it gelled with my own Malayan-ness. I define myself culturally as "Malayan" rather than "Chinese" and this means being "locationally modern" and ethnically Hokkien and Teochew. At any rate, certainly not Han but decidedly Southern Chinese. Finally, I also see myself as Southeast Asian, identifying with the geographical locale, its cultures, richness and complexities. My eldest maternal auntie and uncle were decidedly China-oriented even though they were English-educated. In those days, that meant also to be somehow communist-oriented even though not actually communist. Then, the wobbly definition of identity could not draw a distinction between nationality and statehood. There was no way to differentiate political affiliation from one's nationality. And so, youngest uncle, who did not feel any communist orientation, solved the dilemma by looking towards Taiwan rather than China for the psychological sources of his Chinese-ness. It was therefore perfectly natural for him to marry a Taiwanese woman, to enjoy Taiwanese movies and to visit Taiwan often.

I was acutely aware that my youngest uncle's wife was somehow different from all the other aunts but could not pin it down then. Their children also took on the same outlook with a decidedly American slant. Somehow, Taiwan's American orientation rubbed off. When China opened to the world after 1978, many Singaporeans were indeed surprised that their concept of Chinese-ness was different from what they encountered there. All these were unknown to us in Cameron Highlands then. For the children, dialect bridged the gap that the adults might have felt.

Life in Cameron Highlands

Not too far away from home, the Japanese encamped a garrison up on a small knoll. They had commandeered a solid, grey concrete industrial building as their headquarters. Behind it, they constructed a wood-fired vegetable drying factory and everyone in the district had to send a person to work there. We sent an aunt and the maid who took turns. The work was light though tedious. Every farmer also had to "donate" a quota of vegetables, preferably cabbages, every month. After the war, we learnt that these supplies were sent back to Japan to feed the hungry cities. My memories of days in Cameron Highland were entirely happy ones. The mornings were cold, and I remember blowing out frosty breath. Once, hailstones as big as chicken eggs fell. They dented the zinc roof! Sadly, Cameron Highlands has now become warmer due to over-development. Only on rare occasions is it cold enough for one's breath to condense. My paternal grandmother, who died at age 104, used to recall laughingly how my tiny skinny legs could not hold me up due to the cold mornings and I would fall over. I remember falling off the chair on the porch. We shivered so much, losing control of our limbs because of the cold!

There are also wonderful memories of roaming the fields, collecting flowers and returning to tell my mother the things I saw. I remember seeing huge logs, cut by the woodcutters, rolling down the hill. I was a little over two years old when we arrived in Cameron Highlands and stayed till I was nearly five. My parents were unusually liberal and raised us not to fear being unchaperoned. Every morning, my mother would collect a cache of fish caught in an Orang Asli bamboo fish trap which she set aside the previous night in the stream beside the house. I remember the beautiful sinuous shape of the trap. Large at one end and small at the other, with lines that defined a beautiful tilting curve from one end to the other. A conical array of sharp spikes formed the entry funnel, through which the fish could not back out once they had entered. The trap was weighed down by heavy iron leaf springs from a lorry and secured to a nearby tree by a rattan halter. I remember the shallow but swift flowing crystal-clear water over the sandy bottom of the stream. I remember the shapes and colours of the fishes. I now know they were *ikan kawan* (Malay for "friend fish"), and *ikan daun* (Malay for "leaf fish"), as told to me by an Orang Asli many years later. When I went back to visit the Cameron Highlands in 1995, the house was still standing. The stream was still there, but totally polluted by chemical fertilizer run-off from watercress farming activities upstream. The water looked and smelt bad. It was dark brown and low in oxygen content. Nothing could live in it. It was a sad sight. A past sullied!

When the family was in Cameron Highlands, there were two army officers that we came in contact with. One was "Ah Tan" and the other "Ah Ang". Both were Taiwanese drafted into the Imperial Japanese Army. There was a belief that the Taiwanese in the Japanese army were especially brutal. Ah Tan was a fearsome fellow, crew cut, grim-faced and had a bad temper. He lived up to the image of a General Tojo. Ah Ang was different. He used to come to the house and give us children Japanese sweets; square bars of toffee wrapped in rice paper. It was a luxury. He was always smiling while the other was always scowling. One day, our neighbours and us were summoned to the parade ground in front of the garrison to witness the public beating of a thief. He was an emaciated Tamil youth who had stolen some geese. These were displayed ostentatiously as evidence of his guilt. It was to be an object lesson for the community. All of us were terrified to witness the hammering the poor man would receive, and we all stood in fear in a circle on the parade ground. Of course, Ah Tan was the one to do it. Before delivering the walloping, he swaggered about, striking the ground with his wooden samurai sword to emphasise the seriousness of the crime committed, and how bad it was to steal. And then, without much ado, he turned upon the man and delivered the first blow to his back, which resonated with a horrible, hollow boom. We shut our eyes and ears as the blows came fast and furious. The man huddled on the ground and called for his mother piteously. It was too awful to watch. To this day, I can hear his terror-stricken cries in my mind. No one was in any doubt that the Japanese meant business. And no one believed that the Greater

East Asia Co-Prosperity Sphere they promised for "liberating" us from the British was going to be any kind of paradise. "Pax Japonica" was no picnic. We were to be kicked and slapped into the Japanese paradise!

Another grim memory was a picture of my father striding determinedly to the garrison to complain about unjust treatment he received from Ah Tan. Neighbours had complained about my father's pet dog digging up their vegetables and Ah Tan had slapped my father. Maltreatment at the hands of Ah Tan was legendary. The whole family waited in fear and trembling of what might happen since my father was defiant and unrepentant. Wouldn't that invite even more severe treatment? That episode inspired in me a sense of righteous indignation ever since. Seething with resentment afterwards at the indignity, my father plotted revenge as the war drew to a close and rumours floated about that the Japanese were losing. The very ones who had earlier complained about my father to the Japanese were among the plotters too. Such is human nature, where proximate irritations cloud perception of bigger injustices. At the moment of Japanese surrender, the plotters egged each other on to deliver Ah Tan's comeuppances. But it was all big talk, ventilation of grievances and bravado. When it came to killing Ah Tan, the wisdom of the womenfolk prevailed and they all backed off, busying themselves with arrangements to restart life where they had left off. My father was busy preparing to hire a lorry for the long and tiring trek back to Singapore. I remember the journey, wrapped in a thick brown tartan blanket with frilly edges, cradled in my grandmother's arms as we slowly wound our way through Tapah, Ipoh, Kuala Lumpur and finally down the peninsular to Singapore.

Return to Serangoon Road

The scene of arriving back in Singapore is seared into my memory. The city seemed dim and deserted. I can clearly recall the drive down dark Bukit Timah Road and arriving at Serangoon Road late at night. There were lorries parked in the middle of Serangoon Road and no streetlamps were lit. Whatever light there was came from the few yellow lighted windows of the shophouses along the road. We too parked our lorry in the middle of the road and got off. There was no traffic at all. The sense of emptiness was surreal in the warm, dark night. It was like returning to a ghost town. Walking up the staircase, I had the feeling of entering a deserted house. It was dark, dusty and deathly still. At the top of the stairs, I remember seeing the dusty wooden shelves against the wall. Each room had a dark wooden slatted ceiling ventilator that looked ominous. To my young mind, they were mysterious openings into a dark mysterious space above, perhaps inhabited by unspeakable horrors. I imagined menacing beings lurking, looking down at us.

The flat was the upstairs of a two-storey row house along Serangoon Road, between the New World Amusement Park at the junction of Kitchener Road and Lavender Street. It was part of a row of red brick terrace houses with clay tile roofs and wooden shutter windows. The flat had two bedrooms. One in front was accessed from the staircase landing and the master bedroom was to the rear. It opened off from a short corridor that led to the back kitchen and bathrooms. The master bedroom's window opened onto the indented rear air well through which we could see the comings and goings of the neighbours downstairs and the wasteland behind the row houses. Privacy was not an issue. No one minded. Such was neighbourliness those days. On one side of the air well was the little kitchen which had a cooking plinth for charcoal stoves venting into a large, galvanized iron hood which let smoke out through a chimney. Behind this was a bathroom and a bucket type toilet compartment. It smelled of Jeyes cleaning fluid. Behind this was the rear open roof terrace, save for a projecting structure that sheltered the staircase which led to the back lane and scrub land behind. On this open terrace, my father grew orchids on raised benches. The entire terrace was meshed-in with rusty expanded metal for security. It was my favourite play space for doing Tarzan stunts from the projecting roof ledge. I would swing from this to land on the ground and climb the enclosing mesh.

Each morning, the "night soil" carrier was let in from the back lane and he came up the rear staircase to take the bucket of waste away from the toilet. He had a carrying stick slung across his muscular shoulders from which hung empty lidded buckets which he exchanged for the full ones. I used to watch these strong, barefoot characters. There was never any eye contact. They went about their work, oblivious to us; it was their way to distance themselves from normal society so that their lowly social status, too painful to bear, could be endured with some dignity. I felt sorry for them, yet I was in awe of these tough men in their blue denim long sleeve tunics, unbuttoned at the chest, with their strong legs emerging from black shorts. They exuded an aura of purposeful power, yet they seemed to be in a different world, one they were assigned to and resigned to.

One of my most vivid mental pictures of the end of the war was the sight of shiny American B-29 Superfortress bombers flying high over the jungle. Parachutes blossomed from the bellies of these flying liberators. It never occurred to us to wonder what American planes were doing over British Malaya. It was only years later that I became aware of the global effort to re-establish old colonial mandates. The Japanese were not wrong in attempting to break Western imperialism, but it was only to substitute it with their own. At that time, the return of British law and order was gladly welcomed. Only the Malayan Communist Party (MCP) and their sympathisers knew anything of imperialism. The rest of the population were blissfully unaware. They gladly flew British flags and welcomed back the colonialists and the re-establishment of the "British Sky" over Malaya and Singapore. Whereas people flew Japanese flags earlier out of fear, they now flew British ones. Freedom, independence and self-determination were concepts that were to come later in the political mobilisation by the MCP and other nationalist parties in Malaya and Singapore. The independence of India and Indonesia also served as models of what would come. I learnt later from Tan Chong Tee's autobiography *Force 136* and Spencer Chapman's *The Jungle is Neutral* that the Allies were air-dropping supplies and men to prepare for the British re-occupation in collaboration with the armed wing of the MCP, the Malayan People's Anti-Japanese Army (MPAJA) and patriots from the British intelligence organisation Force 136. But as official accounts would have it, this was the "liberation" of Malaya. One imperialism for another! Through Tim Harper's *The End of Empire and the Making of Malaya*, I became aware of British plans behind-the-scenes in choosing who should take over from them. The battle for independence was less of a battle than a selection process of eliminating undesirable political elements. It involved a protracted war against insurgents in the jungles of Malaya and the labour unions of Singapore, a conflict that served as the backdrop of my professional adult life. What became increasingly clear to me was the contestation between the repressive institutions of state and my own urge towards creativity and consciousness. That became the story of my creative struggle.

Becoming

*Me showing Dr Toh Chin Chye
(right) my thesis project, a fine
arts centre for the University of
Singapore's Bukit Timah Campus.*

03

Off to School

My parents decided to send us to Anglo-Chinese School (ACS) Primary in Coleman Street because my mother's second brother went there. They also thought it the best school then. We went to school daily by trishaw from our Serangoon Road home, a half hour ride away. Later, my father sent and picked us up in his brand new flashy Chevrolet—much to our embarrassment! The chapel was the centrepiece of the Methodist school. It stood splendidly, dominating the classroom blocks arrayed around it, fronting Coleman Street. The interior of the chapel was plain with rows of wooden benches surrounded by plaster walls painted with yellow distemper and punctuated by classical arches framing tall, wooden louvred windows that were painted brown. At the top of the wall was an eye-catching surrounding entablature where the authoritative texts, "Trust In The Lord With All Thine Heart; And Lean Not Unto Thine Own Understanding, In All Thy Ways Acknowledge Him, and He Shall Direct Thy Paths" (Proverbs 3:5–6), were painted in bold, black Roman lettering. Though it held little meaning for us children then, the words remained in our minds when we understood better later.

Our family was not Christian, but there were enough Christian ethics built into our own values to feel comfortable at school. As a result, we felt no compulsion to convert. When the distinction between religious ethics and religious faith is not made, it leads to many problems between people of different faiths. We had no such problem. In ACS, the church led by example and did not proselytise. And I still believe that should be so for all schools in a secular society. In any case, I am always put off by proselytising, whatever the faith. School chapel service was simply part of school life. It was held every Friday morning. Even Muslim children went, though they were not compelled to do so. In later years, some stayed away, and that was also not frowned upon. The sermons, though often based on a biblical passage or concept, were brought into everyday context as a moral lesson more often than not. The Rev. Goh Hood Keng, Dr Thio Chan Bee and the Rev. Michael Robert Doraisamy made deep impressions through their sincerity and good sense. Christian ethics was thus infused into the students without much ado. No histrionics, brimstone or fire. The urging to be kind, humble, loving and forgiving was eminently sensible. The teachers were the most impressive. They were very dedicated. I remember Ms Morton and Ms Smith in particular. Ms Morton was kindly and patient in explaining things. Ms Smith was hot tempered and exacting, and we feared but respected her. I also remember a Mr Woon who taught us science. He introduced sexual reproduction by drawing the rear-end view of a dog to show us the difference between the male and female anatomy and taught us what the different organs were for in a humorous way. We giggled as we had seen the neighbourhood dogs go at it, and it all made sense now. He also drew our attention to the way dogs trotted, whereby the front legs were not in line with the back legs, and so the body of the dog was actually angled to the direction of its travel. Wow! We never noticed that! What we learnt in the classroom was echoed in real life. This was a lesson I never forgot. I continue to believe that in the teaching of planning and architecture, the environments should be rich in information and experience, and include the contradictions and conundrums in life. Design has to be information-rich, not just look good.

Adventures in Braddell Heights

In 1949, my family moved to Braddell Heights where I spent the best years of my youth with a bunch of neighbourhood boys of similar age and interests. It was then the Korean War boom, as commodity prices shot up due to the American war effort to stem the tide of Communism threatening to sweep domino-style down into Southeast Asia and Japan. The prices of rubber and tin, the principal products of Malaya coursing through Singapore, shot up. As a result, there was plenty of money sloshing through the Singapore economy. Combined with a huge middle-class housing shortage after the war, it fueled the first post-war building boom. Braddell Heights was the first suburban housing estate in Singapore.

Soon after moving in, I came to know some boys of my age in the neighbourhood. Their middle-class families had also moved from the congested town to Braddell Heights. We formed a sort of neighbourhood gang and roamed the vegetable and fruit farms around the estate, initially on foot but later on bicycle. We found grass tunnels formed by the farm pigs burrowing through the lallang patches, and we crawled through them to get at the tapioca fields without being seen by the farmers. We relieved them of their tapioca and cooked them over open fires near the house. Before cooking the tubers, we knew to strip off the skins, which contained a poisonous substance. There was also a deep mining pond and a cliff next to the nearby Hock Ann Brickworks. Its deep turquoise water beckoned to us. On the cliffs overlooking the pond, we staged war games using congealed clay lumps as "hand grenades" to attack the "enemy". Braddell Heights was surrounded by farms and waste land. When we moved in, construction was still going on into the later phases of the development. There were a lot of scrap building materials and natural materials for the taking. We availed ourselves of them. I built an underground tunnel house by turning piles of sand belonging to the contractors into exercises in shoring and tunnel-building. Later, I built a kayak out of wooden battens from my father's orchid house and "saltwater"-stained khaki cloth, which I "smuggled" from my schoolmate's father's shop for a pittance. I stretched the cloth over the frames, and it became waterproof once painted over. The kayak was tested in the pond and worked like a dream. It was a great sense of fulfilment. It saw service in the ponds of Potong Pasir, near St. Andrew's School, before it met its demise there.

Aeronautics was learnt hands-on too. I tied several umbrellas together and jumped off the roof of the house. And I survived! My brother and I built what would have been the first hang-glider in Singapore, using brown paper and bamboo cut from the nearby wasteland. We had no technology to attach the frames to the spars and improvised with lashings. It proved inadequate and the craft buckled. Luckily, it did not fly. Otherwise, one of us would have perished as there was no harness to hold the pilot. Aeromodelling was another passion. My brother and I built kit model planes through the night. We found that once you started, there was no stopping till it was completed! Many nights were spent like this. We could not afford the fancy glow plug motors that the Japanese were making but a rich neighbourhood boy, Herbert, had a ready-made stunt plane his contractor father had bought but he did not dare to fly it. Another neighbourhood friend, Jim, convinced him that he knew how. So, we all went to the Shell Sports Club at Paya Lebar in tense anticipation. The engine started after some coaxing. Jim went to the centre of the field and all of us stood at a safe distance. At a signal from Jim, the plane was released, and it swept round an arc at the end of the two control cables linked to his control grip. Herbert looked on in apprehension as the craft rose sharply, did a spectacular wing-over manoeuvre, and promptly crashed on the other side. An anguished cry emerged from all our lips and that was that. End of flying! The beautiful red stunt plane lay on the ground in bits, its engine buried in the soft soil and the propeller broken. We all moved away from the scene feeling bad. The poor Herbert was left sobbing in the field...

Adolescence, Power and Purpose

Growing up is a chancy business. Despite all my middle-class advantages, plus the rich experiences and opportunities I enjoyed, my emotional development was slow. I do not know why. Perhaps I grew up in an all-boys environment and had no sisters. All my best friends had no sisters too. Perhaps I never learnt that girls were human in the way we were but with some differences. What these were, I was to learn the hard way. Then there was the natural process of forming and trying out identities. The adventure of life provided all the distractions, and I went from one experience to another. I was seriously into athletics. It was part of defining myself and my identity. I was always third or second in every event, seldom first. Shot put, high jump, pole vault, the sprints, triple jump, long jump, discus, javelin—I did them all. No one else had the span of abilities I had. What interested me was the total use and development of all my capacities in whatever I did. After finishing lunch and my homework every afternoon, I bicycled back to the school field an hour away just to train.

Riding solo as a teenager was a time to think. I remember some of my musings about life as I pedalled quietly along. I thought to myself what a boring life I live. I have everything. Health, a happy family and enough money to spend. I felt physically powerful as I looked down at my legs pumping at the bicycle paddles. They were perfect. I was extremely fit and muscular. Admittedly, it was narcissistic self-admiration. The curve of my highly articulated thigh muscles stretched against my well-formed bone structure, the deep tan and the flawless skin. They all made me feel primed and ready to go but I somehow held back. Why? I did not know. I was 14 when I passed puberty. The pimples had cleared up, my shoulders broadened to manly width. The veins on my hands and wrist indicated the status of a young adult. I was no longer a skinny kid. The power in me was raring to go. But where and to do what? Then, my brother's classmates organised a picnic at the Pasir Panjang beach house of Ng Keng Siang, one of only two qualified Chinese architects in Singapore then. (The other was Ho Kwong Yew.) My brother seldom invited me to join his outings. For some reason, he did this time and the group had also invited some girls from our sister school, Methodist Girls' School. I was the youngest there. A pretty young lady caught my eye. I could not help admiring the way she carried herself, rather quiet but mysteriously beautiful. I wanted to know her better. Suddenly all the questioning of self vanished. I thought I knew what life was all about!

Scouting Days

I don't remember why my brother and I joined the Wolf Cubs, now called Cub Scouts. My mother recalls that we were impressed by their uniforms and asked to join. The meetings were held every Wednesday afternoon at the laterite playground on the upper terraces of ACS Primary. We wore a green cap trimmed by radial yellow seams, a khaki tunic and our blue school shorts. Our feet were shod in khaki canvas shoes with no socks. Finally, we had a blue and yellow scarf whose ends were tied together by a reef knot to signify we obeyed the Cub Promise. Meetings began with the Cubmaster leading the Cubs on a merry chase around the grounds crying out, "Pack! Pack! Pack!" Coming to a suitable spot, and suitably roused, we formed a circle around the Cubmaster and declared, "Akela, on our honour we will do our best!" What did we know of doing our best? But we yelled the words lustily, nonetheless! We were grouped in separate teams of six and led by our own "sixer", an older boy, and we bonded in our own little bands. Scouting emphasised self-leadership and teamwork from the youngest age. As we matured, we moved up to be a "sixer". The youngest was at the tail end of the band.

Every scout meeting was filled with activities. We would do knots on some occasions or play a memory game, called "Kim's Game", derived from Rudyard Kipling's *Kim*, or learn campfire songs or practice simple first aid skills. Everything was done with gusto. We roughhoused sometimes. My favourite was "Chung Kuda", which was a horse race. One boy carried his rider across a distance to see who was fastest. Cock fight was another favourite. Holding onto one foot behind, we jostled each other till our opponent lost balance. It built cheerful competitiveness. Much hilarity accompanied all our activities. By the end of each session, usually at 5 p.m., we were all covered in sweat and dust, but happy. From Cubs at primary school, I continued scouting in secondary school at ACS (Barker Road). I joined the Junior Scouts, then the Senior Scouts. Having climbed the Scout Badge ladder all the way, I attempted the Queen's Scout Badge which is the highest attainment in scouting. The prerequisite was to obtain a whole series of other key badges, which I had. The last badge was the Venturer's Badge. It was a rigorous trek. The test was to take a new Scout member, known as a tenderfoot, safely on a two-day hike. We had to log the entire trek with sketch maps and observations, and cook all our meals, including bringing a piece of fresh meat along the way. No sweat! I had done so many treks before.

We started from Tanah Merah on the eastern tip of Singapore. My plan was to trek across to the Scout Camp in Jurong on the western end of the island. My route brought me to Paya Lebar, Kampong Batak, Jalan Eunos, through to Bukit Timah, along the railway track to Kranji, fording the Kranji River, and from there, to camp on the western bank of the river. The next day, we would stroll down to the Scout Camp at Boon Lay Road, in what was then known as Jurong Park. Carrying a heavy canvas backpack, an ex-British army gear with stiff straps that cut into the shoulders, we made it to Kranji River by 6 p.m., just as the sun was setting. We found a boatman to take us across for a pittance as he took pity on these two bedraggled scouts, thoroughly soaked in sweat. It was a memorable experience. The entire still river surface was golden as it merged with the sunset. We were floating in a paradise of light despite our tiredness. As it was still light, we decided to press on. I was blasé about the test. Instead of camping as we had planned, we completed the trek in one day instead of two. We arrived at the Boon Lay Road police station accordingly and got the Officer-in-Charge's signature as proof of arrival. We then took a bus home. I could have faked it and gone back the next day to get the signature but did not. Honesty did not pay in this case. Bad mistake! Failed the test! Goodbye Queen's Scout Badge! But it was enough for me having completed all the tests. I was satisfied that I had completed my scouting career as far as I was concerned. There were much more interesting things than scouting by then. Life beckoned and into life I plunged! But scouting and all its life lessons never left me. The scout's badge system and the patrol system taught me a lot. It instilled in me the habit of skill attainment based on initiative and interest. The patrol system taught me leadership and camaraderie. Scouting opened capacities in myself and I remember more of scouting experiences than all the tedious lessons in school.

The 12 School Boy "Apostles"

Taking initiative, developing conscience, learning organisational skills and a sense of social duty — the experience of the church community was an important part of growing up. When asked why I eventually left the church, I say, without being glib that I "graduated". I am grateful for the ethical development. I can separate Christian ethics from the element of faith. Ethics is valuable socially whereas faith is an individual's concern; faith should never be mobilised. The politicisation of faith can lead to disastrous consequences as current world events testify.

The natural leader in our neighbourhood gang that I had started, the Braddell Heights Boys' Club, was Jim Teoh. He and his two younger brothers also went to my school, ACS (Barker Road). He was a big-hearted soul, very enthusiastic and full of energy. Jim first tried starting a socialist club in middle-class conservative ACS. He had gotten hold of a copy of *The Communist Manifesto*, which he read and then was passed on amongst us. Its stirring message of revolution and social justice was intoxicating stuff to young minds. "Workers of the world unite!" A world of comradeship and cooperation beckoned us! "To each according to his need!" Wow! That would be a wonderful world. The club had hardly started getting active when then principal of the school, Thio Chan Bee, called him up to disband the club or get the sack! He promptly did so. God aside, communism and Christian ethics did not seem so different to us after all! Ideas such as the Samaritan spirit, altruism and the idea of nobility and chivalry from scouting all coursed through our veins and filled our imaginations. And so, the Braddell Heights Boys' Club got together to start worship services instead. There were all together 12 of us, including Jim, his brothers Sonny and Bobby and my brother and me. We first started meeting on Sundays from 1956 in Oldham Hall, a rickety old building behind ACS (Barker Road). Later, we met at ACS's school hall, the Lee Kuo Chuan Auditorium. We invited Rev. Peter Lim, a teacher in the school, to be the pastor. Little did he know that at the next Easter Sunday service, the stage would be festooned with flowers that Bobby and I had "liberated" from the houses along Chancery Lane at 5:30 a.m. "The Lord hath need of it!" we said to ourselves. It was indeed a beautiful Easter! Our hearts swelled with pride!

The church grew, and more members came. Finally, it got recognition from the Board of the Methodist Church. Barker Road Methodist Church was granted a narrow piece of land to build a church next to the Missionary House on the top of the hill, overlooking the ACS (Baker Road) sports field. The site was next to a beautiful Chinese-style building for the pastor designed by British architect Frank Brewer. It had typical huge overhanging eaves and upturned corners that gave it an oriental look, similar to the school building that he designed for the Methodist mission at Cairnhill. Its walls were rendered with fish scales plasterwork just like those that Brewer had designed for St. Andrew's School, where we used to play. Many church missions had retired to Southeast Asia from China due to persecution by radical Chinese Nationalists who were anxious to rid China of foreign influences, hot on the heels of the May Fourth Movement in 1919. The name "Anglo-Chinese School" stems from this vintage. In the early days of the Barker Road Methodist Church, the house served as the residence of Rev. Robert Foster and his wife Joyce. The parsonage was the meeting place of many intellectual discussions. Foster was a pacifist, socialist and humanist. His quiet, kindly and principled manner influenced us all greatly. For his refusal to be drafted into combat role in the Second World War, he had a scar on his eye; testimony to the brutal treatment he received from the British Army. We respected him greatly. He was assisted by Elmer Hall, a theology student and an intellectual who led many of the discussions that opened our minds to the joys and rigours of intellectual debate.

The church that we 12 schoolboys built was a raw timber and concrete block structure with full height wooden louvre-doors, cement block infill walls and was naturally ventilated. It had an asymmetrical roof. The social hall could be joined to the sanctuary by opening the folding-sliding doors in between. The unpretentious and straightforward design expressed our unconventional taste. There was an honesty about the building that also appealed to our socialist-realist sense. We had by then all "graduated" from Wesley Methodist Church in town, which we disdained as a rich man's social club! I was studying to be an architect in Singapore Polytechnic when I drew up the first design of the proposed new church building. I was 20 years old then. We raised S$65,000 through various means and appointed my lecturer Lim Chong Keat to do the final design, which was the one finally built. His partner in Malayan Architects Co-Partnership (MAC), William Lim Siew Wai, was assigned to undertake the project. The design was modest and honest, characteristic of MAC's philosophy. The only thing that I was disappointed with was that my original idea of a glass altar-wall viewing into a garden, inspired by the Garden of Gethsemane where Jesus was betrayed after the Last Supper, was replaced with a blank end wall. Lim did it on grounds that it would not be glaring. I was too young and inexperienced then to counter the argument, especially as it was made by a partner of my lecturer! To this day, I regret not standing firm on this point. One day, I would want to build a religious place of supreme contemplation overlooking a serene garden. What better way is there to be at one with the beauty of nature and the cosmos than to be immersed in the beauty of nature in contemplation? Are middle-class values the fruit of development? Does the verve and freshness of ideals have no place in the developed world?

The wood and concrete block building stood for many years until it proved too small and was rebuilt. By then, I had long left the church. The redevelopment was a double tragedy. The old Brewer house next to the church was demolished, and the new church design bore no trace of the idealism in the old one. What was put up in place of both reflects the much more middle-class pragmatic values that prevail in Singapore today. Its large, air-conditioned interior is normal and cosy in a middle-class sort of way. The honesty and the rawness of the original building that signified the pioneering spirit of the old days was replaced by the kitschy-ness of today. Though I am no longer a churchgoer, I regret that the church was rebuilt in this way. The spirit of the pioneering sentiments has been lost. Many will say that's progress. I say we have lost our way!

The Spiritual Experience

Our young religious biases were toward social conscience rather than spiritual edification. This was the spirit among the original founders of the Barker Road Methodist Church. Although we went through the motions of worship and bible study, our sympathies were really towards the downtrodden and the dispossessed. As the result of this attitude, I remember my own antipathy towards the simplistic proselytising zeal of some Christian friends, especially from the evangelistic churches and Christian youth groups. We tried to live our lives in a spirit of honesty, free from dogma of any kind. As we matured, there was a parting of ways. Many eventually became evangelical or mainstream Christians and a few of us carried our ideals into life in different ways. But the Spirit moves in mysterious ways, and we did not question it.

I now understand the underlying psychology of people who surrender reason to something beyond, as the means to console the disquiet they feel. They need to be embraced by something larger than themselves. This need stems from the existential anxiety they feel. If the Spirit so moves one towards the ethereal, so be it, I would say. But a sceptical attitude, I believe, is necessary to maintain a creative stance. Remember, it was doubting Thomas who brought the Christian message furthest east to Madras. Faith must never be forced, induced or mobilised.

I chose to confront the disquiet in myself through seeking solace and experience in confirming and expanding my knowledge of nature. Like Odysseus, I too "follow knowledge like a sinking star" and "drink Life to the lees". I seek to merge with the universe in body and mind. Soul? I always doubted its existence. But some of the original 12, including my brother, later went the way of "charismatic" literalism. They really put me off! I could not bring myself to be literal in anyway. And so, I sought harmony in total immersion in nature, adventure and life.

My great passion then was snorkelling, skin-diving, as it was then known. Spearfishing became my consuming passion for two decades after the church. I understood the "moment of truth" when all time stands still, holding one's breath, sensitive to every move of the fish, completely unaware of my own suspended state of mind, and at the precise moment when everything lines up, I squeeze the trigger and the hunt is over. Time unfreezes and the mundane ticks away. It is hard for others to understand this feeling that has nothing to do with killing or being macho or anything people care to call it. It is an experience that becomes an obsession, like a prayer. How strange to call it that!

Sonny, the second of the Teoh brothers who became a psychiatrist, later wrote a paper on the power-dimension of religiosity. It was entitled, if I remember correctly, "Power and the Black Robe", in which he described the psychology of priesthood; the deliberate mystification which distances oneself from others through donning the black robe. It is actually and figuratively the means of awing would-be believers. The relationship is two-sided. The priest has his reasons but the believers too. Each has his needs and between them their religion is cemented. It lasts for ages. It is not because I do not believe in the possibility of the sublime, it is just that I cannot believe in any sort of personification of the sublime. If anything, the sublime is a verb. It is certainly not a noun. Not a thing. Indeed, I seek the verb all the time through experience, in design, in nature, in experiencing ambience. I cannot believe in any ready-made prescriptions, institutions and organisations set up to propagate such beliefs. There is a spiritual dimension by which I mean, the experience of the ineffable that resonates from within, not something that is external. I have had such "spiritual" experiences, but not of the "prescribed" or "alluded-to" kinds. For example, I was traveling by train through the south of England. It was an improbable place for a "spiritual" experience, and I was totally taken by surprise. It was late afternoon; the sun was low and the light cast slanting shadows across the stubble of freshly cut wheat fields making them stand out in sharp relief. I gazed from my seat in the train, lulled by the rhythmic sounds of the track and vibrations caused by the movement of the train. The texture of the wheat fields drifting past suddenly struck me as particularly articulate and I had an abrupt sensation. I literally felt a sudden thump upon my chest. The experience surprised and shook me. I was astounded and the feeling and memory of it has never left me. It was such a deep experience, it resonated through my whole being. It is of such importance to me and yet it is entirely private. I felt an indescribable joy after the initial jolt. How could such an experience mean anything to anyone else? Can or should a religion be made from these experiences? Ethical ideas can of

A New World in the Making

course be systematised, but with the ineffable, I feel that these should remain very private. And so, for me, and only me, it really matters. Such experience serves for me as a benchmark of excellence. Something to measure quality by. It is the quality of total integrity of something that matters. One is privileged if one can experience such a benchmark feeling to serve as a measure of wholeness that is of utter coherence. Measuring quality by any other man-made means, especially those prescribed by authorities, just do not have any power of conviction. I feel that to accept second-hand values is so inferior once one has experienced the primary. Deep experiences of this kind are devoid of all "meaning". The experience was a "spiritual/aesthetic" experience and only someone who has experienced such a thing can recognise it. Yet, such an experience will seem totally trivial to someone else. But it serves as a touchstone for me. There is then a deep doubt about religion. Religion is thus, I believe, a construction of such experiences made into a plausible narrative and is conveyed as a set of beliefs and rituals. I prefer the raw form of it. This is the difference between the spi(ritual) and the ritual. And so when I visited the new, homely feel of Barker Road Methodist Church, I could not but be disappointed. It is now a plasterboard painted over with baby pink and cosy cream, veneered wood, suffused with processed air and calming mood lighting — totally practical and devoid of any sense of the real. But then, this is just what is wanted today. It is the normality of middle-class Singapore, and the congregation does not know anything else. Almost every condominium and private home is just like this; smoothed-over reality! The success according to the materialist model is, it seems, middle-class kitsch! What else can it be after all the rough edges have been rubbed off? Religion is, after all, also not immune to the forces of such history.

Through the turmoil of adolescence, there was a pattern emerging. It only became clear much later in life. After many experiences and constant introspection, I can see that the process of growing up is the process of integrating the head, the mind, the heart, the senses and the hand. With the integration comes power and insight and therefore confidence. This sort of confidence is not vain nor defensive. It is a confidence that successful living brings. In different circumstances, it may be gained by the successful hunter or gatherer or seer. For middle-class people growing up in an industrialising economy, a profession is a vehicle for integrating the self.

Pursuing Architecture

While in my final year in ACS (Barker Road), I was reading books on building construction and architecture history under the desk. Three possible careers appealed to me: agriculture, aeronautics and architecture. I was told that I had green fingers. I had planted small vegetable and flower patches around the house and they thrived. I also turned the ground beneath a leaking water pipe into a small pond which I constantly refreshed and reared fish in. Building model airplanes was also a preoccupation of mine for many years. As the scope for the preceding two was next to nothing in Singapore, I enrolled in architecture school.

When the family moved to Braddell Heights, I had the chance to build a small hut in the garden out of scrap cement sheets left behind by the builders. I drove in twin wooden battens to form the support for the walls and the roof. Between the narrow slot of the stakes, I placed the sheets one on top of the other to form the walls. By overlapping the same cement sheets, which were about 4-by-1 feet wide, I made a simple sloping roof. A window was made with a shelf and a flower helped the house come alive. The flower somehow signalled the inhabitation of the space, which was a mere construction prior to its presence. It was a tight squeeze in the tiny hut. But I had the wonderful experience of enduring a rainsquall in a structure I had built all by myself. It leaked! Years later, my experience was vivified in *The Poetics of Space* by Gaston Bachelard, who gave me the words to understand that there is "no sense of shelter greater than that provided by a leaking roof!" How right! But no other words can sufficiently convey the feeling of satisfaction, accomplishment and fulfilment produced by making a building all by yourself. I have often wondered what the real appeal was. I have concluded that it is my primary drive for me. Designing and constructing a building is to get into a deeply sensual and erotic experience! The sense of the total enclosure, to be wrapped up in the tissues of the building, is deeply satisfying.

My family could not afford to send me abroad and I knew that instinctively. They could only afford to send my brother. He was the top scholar for the secondary school cohort in 1957, and for the pre-university cohort in 1959. It was therefore expected that he would be awarded the State Scholarship, but this was not to be. In 1959, there was a changeover from the Queen's Scholarship to the State Scholarship when Singapore got limited self-government from the British. Due to the delay, he could not wait and applied to universities in the United Kingdom and received offers to several. My father believed, to his dying day, that the then Minister of Education, Yong Nyuk Lin, formerly an insurance man and a business rival, deliberately delayed the processing. Thus, when the scholarship was finally announced, my brother was disqualified on the grounds that he had already committed himself and accepted an offer to go to an overseas university. And so, that was that. I stayed in Singapore, and my brother went to England. I have no resentment as I plunged into architectural studies eagerly. I even planned a work-study program for myself. After secondary school, I enrolled in a correspondence course on architecture while working as an apprentice draftsman in Ang Kheng Leng's office. His was a prime architectural practice in those days because Mr Ang, as I used to call him, was one of the few fully qualified local Chinese architects and therefore got most of the local jobs. So, when I joined the firm, there was plenty of scope for me to indulge in design. This I did with alacrity!

When I heard that there was to be an architecture course at the Singapore Polytechnic, I was overjoyed. But I also worried that I would not get a place. I knew that the assessors would want to see my drawings. All I had were drawings of flowers and landscapes that I did in school. So, I hurriedly did a series of pencil drawings of the main buildings around the Padang to show my ability. I went to see the new school's head of department, Mr D. J. Vickery, with my drawings and the designs I did in Mr Ang's office. He declared that I would have no problem getting in! I was walking on clouds! I was really going to become an architect! There was never any doubt in my mind that I would be one. It was only a question of how and when. I rose fast in Mr Ang's office and was soon doing three designs a week. This was amazing given that I was only 18 years old. Designs then were really simple, and clients did not have high expectations. If a design was practical and cheap to build, that was enough. In those days, contractors would build from a 1/8-inch scale drawing without any detail drawings. I remember attending an early meeting of the Society of Malayan Architects (SMA), the precursor of the Singapore

Institute of Architects (SIA). The architects present were swapping stories and Mr Ang bragged that his contractor was so diligent that he actually built the North Point shown in the drawing! To top this, another said that he got two houses for the price of one because the contractor built on the wrong site the first time!

When it was time to leave for the Polytechnic, Mr Ang said he would increase my pay by $100 each year when I came back to work for him during my vacation. My starting pay was $50 a month which could not even pay for lunch, and my father subsidised the difference. Mr Ang soon doubled the amount. Nonetheless, it was a good working experience. I eventually broke with Mr Ang on a bitter note. This is the story: My last project was to design a house in Siglap for a client of his. Prior to that, I was creating really derivative and indulgent designs. But I made a breakthrough in the project after meeting a "real" architect, a Mr Ho Pak Toe who had just returned from Melbourne University. He joined Mr Ang for a short while and did the initial drawings for the 1959 Singapore Constitution Exposition which was held at the former Kallang Airport. Anxious to have Pak Toe's opinion, I asked him to look at my design drawings. He passed a cryptic remark, "Form follows function", indicating that my forms did not! I was quite taken aback. It was my first and most important design lesson! Mr Ang was too busy on the business side of his practice to give me any design tips. And so, when it came to designing the house in Siglap, organising the rooms was easy enough, but I wanted something special. The house was very exposed to public view as it fronted the road. So, I asked myself what sort of windows I should design. I concluded that instead of a wall with windows, the entire wall of the living room facing the road should be made of wire mesh and grown over with creepers instead. This would keep the place cool and keep out prying eyes. Wow! It was a breakthrough. I quickly drew it up and got Mr Ang's approval. I even made him promise me that he would not change the design while I left for the Polytechnic. Months later, I happened to be in Siglap and saw that the house I designed was totally different. I was furious and stormed into Mr Ang's office to confront him. He was apologetic but said one had to be pragmatic to practice architecture. We must first earn our bread and butter, then we can go for the jam. This young upstart replied disdainfully to an architect twice his age that if you live on a diet of bread and butter, you will never change. On this note, I left the firm and never saw him

Early Design Exercises

My interest in the tropics and tradition started as an architecture student in Singapore Polytechnic (below). In my first year, I designed a tourist information bureau (right and across top). During my second year in school, I designed a modern kampong house (across below) that was realised decades later as the Kwan House (1994) in Singapore and the Kim Hao House (2005) in Saigon.

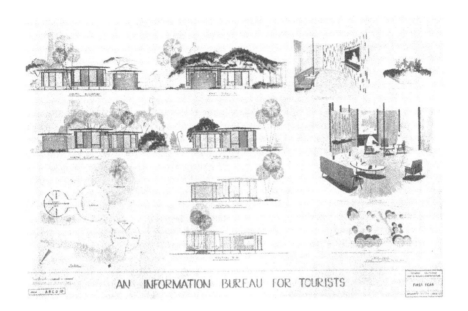

AN INFORMATION BUREAU FOR TOURISTS

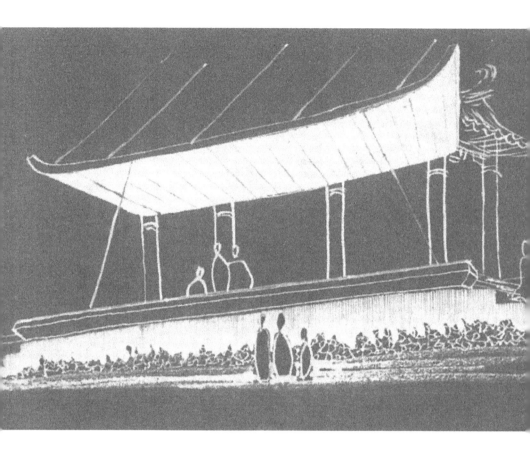

1960: Nanyang University Convocation Stage

In March 1960, I was invited by my classmate, Wee Chwee Heng, to help his friend design a sheltered stage for a convocation at Nanyang University. It was to be erected on the steps of the University Library, which was designed in the classical Imperial Chinese style. It was a work by Ang Kheng Leng when he was working for Ng Keng Siang, as a young returnee architect from Manitoba, Canada. Chwee Heng and I stayed a few nights in Nanyang University to design and supervise the building of the canopy and stage in situ. It was a daring structure made of a huge cantilever canopy with upturned corners in the Chinese manner, which was created by hanging timber joists using steel cables slung from the structural columns above. Everything was eyeballed, and we relied entirely on our guts and intuition. There were no engineering calculations! Having erected tents and built

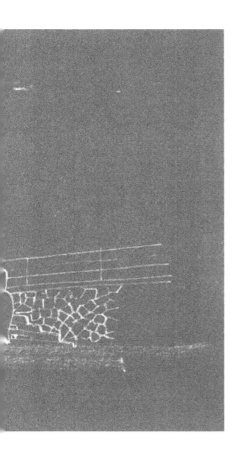

numerous rope bridges as a scout, I instinctively strung cables exactly along the lines of force and tensioned each joist until they were aligned. The horizontal members were nailed on, and waterproof building paper was tacked on the whole assemblage from above. We used very lightweight expanded polystyrene sheets for the ceiling and the whole canopy came together elegantly in double quick time. The platform was easy too.

It was a matter of lofting supports from the steps to form a level deck. We worked with a small-time contractor who later became one of the captains of industry in the 1970s. Everything was completed in two days!

While our experience at the Polytechnic was no different from secondary school, campus life at Nanyang University was a new experience for us. We envied the nightlife on the university campus, strolling around its pond, dining in the canteen, visiting friends in their dorm rooms and chatting into the night. There was a difference in culture too. The Chinese-educated students were much more disciplined. There was no yelling and the rough language we were used to. Everyone went about their business in the campus peaceably. We left the campus with pleasant memories. Later, we learnt that some of our friends who were involved in student politics in opposition to the government self-exiled to Canada where there continues to be a strong Nantah contingent today. We have lost touch with them, and it is regretful that cross cultural discourse was divided by a political gulf.

1960: The National Theatre Competition

When the National Theatre competition was announced, we were disappointed that it was restricted to five selected architects. As students, we watched the local architecture scene like hawks as we were going into the profession. Firstly, we did not like the selected site at the foot of Fort Canning opposite Tank Road, which we felt lacked dignity and was too exposed to traffic noise. As nationalists, we suggested in a letter to the press that a better site would be in the Istana grounds as there was a natural desire to do away with the colonial edifice and give the site to the people. In the end, we ran a design competition in Singapore Polytechnic and invited local architects to view our works, including mine (across and above).

1961: Low-Cost Furniture Exhibition

Another competition we eagerly participated in as part of the Singapore Polytechnic Architectural Society (left) was organised by the Housing & Development Board (HDB) to furnish a typical two-room rental HDB flat at MacPherson. It was part of the HDB's overall effort to popularise high-rise living, as many were still living in squatters, attap huts and cubicles inside shophouses of Chinatown. High-rise living was something new to the population. We came up with two designs to address the important aspect of space constraints in the flats. One was furnished with standard, bulky furniture to show how it would normally have been done. The other

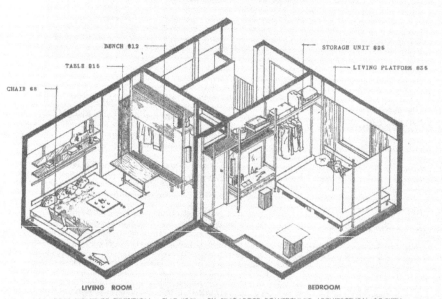

LOW-COST FURNITURE EXHIBITION — FLAT "56" — BY SINGAPORE POLYTECHNIC ARCHITECTURAL SOCIETY (across below) was decked out with lightweight furniture, built-in storage frames, and platforms for living and sleeping with below deck storage bins. This second design (right and below) eventually won and there was an outcry from the local furniture manufacturers. They were incensed at the indignity of being beaten by a bunch of students. HDB architect Alan Choe, who was the competition organiser, called for a meeting with us. In the interest of peace, we agreed to accept a special students' prize. Many of the participating furniture firms remained friends with us well into the days when we joined the ranks of the profession, and they undertook interior work for us. Nonetheless, a lesson was learnt about face and friendship.

1963: Barker Road Methodist Church

While studying in architecture school, I designed a new building for the church I co-founded. My lecturer Lim Chong Keat was eventually appointed to design the building and he assigned it to his partner in Malayan Architects Co-Partnership, William Lim. While the building was modest and honest, I was disappointed that my original idea of a glass altar-wall viewing into a garden was rejected and replaced with a blank wall (across below) instead.

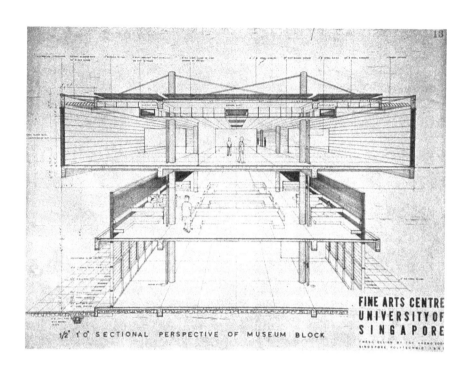

1/2" 1'0" SECTIONAL PERSPECTIVE OF MUSEUM BLOCK

FINE ARTS CENTRE
UNIVERSITY OF
SINGAPORE

BIRD'S EYE VIEW PERSPECTIVE

FINE ARTS CENTRE
UNIVERSITY OF
SINGAPORE

Fine Arts Centre

For my thesis in architecture school, I proposed a fine arts centre for the University of Singapore's Bukit Timah Campus (across). It would accommodate the activities of the school of architecture and the department of extra-mural studies.

Trip to Java

A highlight of our 1960 study trip to Indonesia was a visit to the Bandung Institute of Technology where we met Professor Vincent Van Romondt and his students (this page).

again. I lost contact with him for 35 years. It was after the completion of my Kandang Kerbau Hospital project that we reconnected in 1995. He asked his wife to call me to convey his appreciation of the design and say how proud he was of me. I regret that I did not go to see him, and I later learnt that he moved to Canada and did poorly.

Taking Charge of One's Own Learning

The Singapore Polytechnic building was in town, at Prince Edward Road, which was at the end of Shenton Way. The Polytechnic was one of the important institutions planned by the British as part of the handover. It was officially opened by the Duke of Edinburgh even though by then the People's Action Party government had taken over Singapore in 1959. As young students of an independent state, we felt it rather incongruous that a British dignitary should do the honours. So, we threw firecrackers from the upper floor as the motorcade came in. It was an ambiguous act, which could be interpreted as celebratory, but it sent the security people scrambling. We fled from the scene.

The Polytechnic had full-time and part-time architecture courses. The part-timers were much older than most of us in the full-time course, and they worked in government and private offices. There were 40-odd students in the full-time course, and I had an advantage having worked for almost a year in Mr Ang's office. The first day of school was in a classroom laid out with drafting tables and high stools. Expectedly, at the front, was the blackboard. Vickery, who was from Brighton Polytechnic, briefed us on the course. There would be a balance between workshop practice and design studio work. There would also be a remedial English course as well as lectures in building construction, history and building science. Later, a tall, crew-cut, handsome young man strode in. With a flourish, he wrote his name on the blackboard... "Lim Chong Keat". He pronounced "Keat" as "Kiat" in case we got it mixed up with John Keats, the English poet! There was an air about him that we had never encountered before. He was decidedly different. There was a precision in his words, a decisiveness of his manner and movements. His dress was also somehow different. He wore starched white short-sleeve shirts and beige cotton long pants without pleats—this was very American. He had just returned from the Massachusetts Institute of Technology and certainly made an impression on us. We were even more impressed when we later learnt that he was taught by Walter Gropius, László Moholy-Nagy, György Kepes and Marcel Breuer. They were associated with the foremost design school in Europe, the Bauhaus of Weimar Germany. This was the radical design school from which most modern designs can ultimately be traced. At last, we in the backwater of Singapore were to be introduced to the mainstream of European design and philosophy by someone who knew those great architectural designers personally. And so, the course started on a high note. Chong Keat stressed the mastery of practical construction knowledge as a basis for creative design. Our first task was to make our own drawing boards and T-squares. We did this in the ultramodern workshop under a Mr Wearnes and a Mr Rowlands. We were introduced to the radial saw, the table planer and the four cutter. We were also taught how to use hand tools, sharpen the cutting blades, etc. The drawing boards had a hardwood edge on the right, which the T-square locked against and slid on. Thus, horizontal lines were drawn by moving the T-square up and down the board. I was amused that many fellow students put the board the other way around. We were that green!

Within six months, the class dwindled to twenty something as many students felt unsuited and transferred to accountancy, engineering and the building courses. I learnt later from Chong Keat that it was his policy to weed out the unsuitable. It was a case of being cruel to be kind. Those who moved to other courses were all ever grateful for the opportunity for alternative careers. In the end, they became outstanding builders, engineers and accountants. Chong Keat was the intellectual, and Vickery was the practical organiser. The two made a splendid team. Vickery said that architects must be able to drink, and so promptly took us to the Tanjong Pagar Railway Station bar for beer. Mr Wearnes and Mr Rowlands were ever helpful with tools and machines. We had easy access to the workshops with a minimum of administrative fuss. They took risks to allow us to use the machines. We might have lost fingers or wrecked the machines. Though they kept a watchful eye, they allowed us to get on with what we wanted to do. And so, we did welding and woodworking to make our own self-initiated projects beyond the assignments we were required to do. I made a huge metal sculpture to hang in the studio.

We spent many hours each day at the coffee stall under the trees that lined Prince Edward Road, adjacent to the field on which the former Singapore Conference Hall and Trade Union House now stands. We debated all manner of issues that bothered us, from religion to philosophy, existentialism, Marxism, aesthetics, history, Singapore society, etc. Many evenings were spent working on design assignments in the studio. Occasionally, we slept in the dorms of the nearby Asian Seamen's Club. It was a handsome building and it charged only $2 a night in dorms of eight. One night, the seaman next to me was moaning and groaning so loudly that I could not sleep. He was shivering and had a high fever, so I brought him to the General Hospital, and he was warded for malaria. Getting a taxi and hauling the sick man out of bed to the hospital was a major logistical exercise. My classmate Wee Chwee Heng helped. Not knowing what was ailing the man was also harrowing. What if he was suffering from some terrible infectious disease? Putting our fears aside, we just did the necessary. The dim nightlights, the scent of disinfectants at the hospital and the ghastly pallor of the nurses under fluorescent light added to the grim business. We left the hospital drained and returned to have coffee in the canteen as the sun rose. It was an eventful night we chalked up to life's experiences.

Architecture school was really, in those days, much like school. The Polytechnic was buffered from the city by a stretch of open ground opposite the campus. Our only neighbour was the Norwegian Seamen's Mission building where the former AXA Tower stood. For security reasons, we were not allowed to stay overnight. The watchmen employed by the Polytechnic were told to ensure we all left by 8 p.m. This was impossible because of our studio assignments and us goofing around during the day. So, we stayed late many a night to the ire of the jagas, as the watchmen were called. One particularly obnoxious character was especially nasty, bugging and harassing us, and we decided to teach him a lesson. The school was deathly quiet at night. Donning sheets and making weird sounds from different directions, we scared him out of his wits. He had previously complained about us staying late to Vickery, who ticked us off with a twinkle in his eye. He admonished us and recited the rules— he was duty-bound to do so of course—but the message was clear, carry on! This endeared us to him evermore. It was with a heavy heart that we finally bid him farewell as he sailed back to England. A new polytechnic board chaired by Dr Toh Chin Chye had taken over. In those fevered nationalistic days, the colonial master had to be axed and Vickery must have felt the vibes. We did not know this then, but there were frictions between the expatriate administration of the Polytechnic and its board, which consisted of political appointees. The upshot is that Vickery resigned, as did many of the excellent expatriate teachers in the workshop from whom we learnt a lot. They were not only technically knowledgeable but took a serious interest in us. They were not "colonial" in any way. Vickery's departure was sorely felt. He was an avuncular figure to us all and his departure left a vacuum. In the four years at the Polytechnic, we changed three heads and there was a lot of staff movement. We were all rather unsettled, but the intellectual and aesthetic boost given by Chong Keat was enough to propel us onwards. The wealthier ones left for London to finish their studies. How we envied them!

In 1960, Chong Keat brought a few of us on a motoring trip to Penang with a break in Melaka. It was then onwards to Seremban, Kuala Lumpur and Ipoh. This was a never-to-be-forgotten trip that broadened our minds. In Melaka, we studied kampongs, especially the characteristic Melaka Malay kampong houses. That raised an interest in the whole question of house-form and culture. How did the distinctive Melaka house evolve its distinctiveness? Were there antecedents or did the form evolve in situ? How did Chinese-looking details in the house get incorporated? What was the relationship between the Chinese and the Malays in Melaka? As we drove up Malaysia, it became obvious that the Malay house styles were different across the states. Why is that so? Why did the roof ridge of the Seremban houses have a distinctive curve? Though of Minangkabau origin, why was it different from its antecedents? Why were they not as sweeping as those in Sumatra? There were the ubiquitous Chinese shophouses that also differed, in slight detail, from place to place. Why did a shophouse stand all by itself sometimes and not as part of a row? Are house-form ideas independent of location and context? Do human beings carry with them fixed notions of normality despite changed circumstances and place?

Chong Keat was the first true-blue artistic intellectual that we knew. I personally got from him the notion of aesthetic and intellectual integrity. He often spoke of integrity but at that time I only understood it as professional integrity, that is something about not taking money from contractors and suppliers. But he meant more. He meant the notion of wholeness, integrity as integral-ness. Later, when we met his mentor, Buckminster Fuller, the idea of integrity was further enlarged to the concept of "comprehensivity". This was much harder to understand as it is more a sense and an integration of complex knowledge. Something beyond intellect, something one felt, and through which one valued a thing. Having a sense of wholeness, one could therefore sense imperfection, falsity and lack of moral completeness. Yes, there is an ethical dimension to sense. It is also a recognition of the moral character of a thing as though morals could be applied to a design. Yet, it is possible not as a thought but as a sense. He taught this by word and example.

The other great teacher we had the privilege of having was Lee Kip Lin, a humorous and kindly person. Kip, as we fondly called him, came from practice. He was one of the early graduates from the Bartlett School of Architecture in London where he was during the mid-fifties. When Kip joined the Polytechnic, he said he heard about the "monsters", namely some of us irascible students who would "terrorise" the teachers. So, he came in "prepared". He offered us stylish Du Maurier cigarettes, in the way one does with natives of the countryside to strike up a conversation and as a gesture of friendship. Well, he succeeded, and we learnt smoking from him! Kip had style though in a low-key sort of way. He taught "humanity" to us savages and that walking quietly through life meant being sensitive to beauty, culture and history. Kip introduced us to genteel and cultivated home life. He lived in a beautiful house he designed along the seafront at Amber Road in Katong. His wife created wonderful meals and we chatted with his conversationalist little son. On one occasion, we all quit the design studio of one Terazaki, whom we nicknamed "Terrorzaki". He was a well-intentioned engineer and architect from Japan who was extremely disciplined and an obsessive methodologist. He treated us like children, just as he was treated in Tokyo University, I suppose. Learning by rote and obeying your teacher absolutely was his way. We adjourned to Kip's house to pour out our woes. Kip was sympathetic though in no way conspiratorial to our escapade. He lent us his speed boat and we sped away into the eastern horizon, riding the waves to and from Changi Point, burning off steam and petrol! Returning totally soaked and with all our frustrations and anger fully dissipated, we were ready to return to Terazaki's studio to do the impossible tasks he assigned. We had to design a huge conference centre at Shenton Way, and none of us had any conception of what was involved.

Some of the important design exercises that made a deep impact on me in Polytechnic were the not big ones. In fact, they were the small ones. The memorable design exercises—a fisherman's shelter, a modern kampong house, a minimal dwelling, the graphic rendition of a piece of music by Solomon, a study of colours of dead leaves, a composition of lines, permutations of a square, studies of warped surfaces, the geometry of hyperbolic paraboloids—were the ones through which our design sensibilities and planning skills were honed.

Trip to Java

My classmate Chwee Heng and I, formed the Singapore Polytechnic Architectural Society in 1959. Chwee Heng designed the beautiful logo: four gear-like black bars and the society's name surrounding a vermillion square. It was inspired by the logo of our hero then, American architect Frank Lloyd Wright. I organised many visits for the society's members to architects' offices as well as building materials factories and suppliers' offices, such as Sime Darby and Guthrie's. Once, we went unintroduced to see the Managing Director of Sime Darby, a Mr Desmond King. He was thrilled by the novelty of our student initiative and entertained our requests generously. Our gumption was a refreshing difference from the cowering and obsequious Asians these "white" managers were used to. We got along well and received their full support when the time came to raise funds and solicit donations of building materials for our projects. On one such occasion, we organised a dinner and dance in 1960 to raise funds for a trip to Java. The ground floor lobby and hall of the Polytechnic was decked with luminous painted murals and other decorations for the occasion. Supporters like Desmond all came and had a jolly good time as beer flowed and music filled the space. We raised a princely sum from supporters and the dream trip became a reality.

I had read a book on the historical relics of Java and desperately wanted to see them. Names like "Borobudur", "Prambanan" and the "Dieng Plateau" sounded magical to me. Jogjakarta, Bandung, Tangkuban Perahu, Besakih, Tandjung Sari, Ubud were places that beckoned my imaginations. The five of us sailed on the Kimanis, a small freighter belonging to Kie Hock Shipping, a local shipping company that plied between Indonesian ports and Singapore. We were treated royally onboard and given the

A New World in the Making

captain's quarters! The cook exceeded himself and feted us with five sumptuous meals a day. All this for free! What we did not know then was that this was all part of a larger Indonesian plan to impress us with the idea of "Indonesia Raya". It was then-President Sukarno's grand vision of a united Malay world, with Indonesia playing the role of big brother. Later, the idea was called "Maphilindo", a union of Malaya, Philippines and Indonesia. The imagination of a socialist Indonesian republic was layered over with a decidedly Malay overtone. The whole saga exploded in 1963 in the form of "Konfrontasi", when Sukarno publicly denounced the formation of Malaysia as an imperialist plot. War broke out. Indonesian commandos penetrated Johore. The 1st Battalion, Singapore Infantry Regiment saw action in the steamy swamps of South Johore. We knew little of this then. Indonesian marines were later sent to plant bombs in Singapore. MacDonald House along Orchard Road was partly damaged by such a bomb and the saboteurs were later caught and executed. It was only years later, after then-Singapore prime minister Lee Kuan Yew laid a wreath at the military cemetery in Jakarta as a gesture of reconciliation for the execution, that the relationship between the two countries returned to normal.

The Indonesian ambassador was instructed to make the arrangements for us to tour Java and Bali. Everywhere we went, we were treated like ambassadors of our country. At the Universitas Indonesia (UI), we had an audience with the entire upper echelons of the university and were greeted as part of the regional fraternity. We only had a vague knowledge of regional politics and found the attention to be a bit over the top. That us striplings were accorded such deference was indeed a new experience. Soon, the Indonesian foreign affairs ministry assigned a young man to accompany and guide us on our journey. He stayed with us and became our guide, friend and confidante. His name was Bambang, a very likeable fellow who was slightly older than us. He had seen action as a young activist in the Indonesian revolution. Next to him, we felt like such a sheltered bunch. He told us stories of how they used sharpened bamboo to fight the Dutch and recalled one incident where he climbed a flag post to bring down a Dutch flag at some risk to himself. He could have been shot dead! It was an eye-opener for us cosy middle-class youths, who were too young to have experienced the political and social upheavals that he spoke about. We stayed in the student's hostel at the UI. I remember the dimness of the Jakarta city in its efforts to conserve fuel. At every street corner was a vendor selling air! A bicycle pump and an oil lamp signalled their presence. There were few people about. Jakarta gave the distinct impression of a laidback town that had seen better days. Our meals at the student canteen were another eye-opener. Nasi *rawon* was served on plates with heaps of rice. It was a few strips of long beans, a small cube of beef and lots of *rawon* sauce. Everyone ate the same food. Nothing to complain about. It was tasty, but we remained famished. We were taken on a bus to Bandung where we stopped over in Bogor and saw the Botanical Gardens set up by Sir Stamford Raffles. It was beautiful. There was the ever-present scent of *kretek* (a type of Indonesian cigarette) everywhere. After driving up the winding road, we finally arrived at the beautiful old hill town of Bandung where the old Dutch hotels impressed. I only learnt recently that the Grand Hotel Preanger was designed by Wolff Schoemaker, a Dutch architect who had worked briefly for Wright. It was a thrill to see an Art Nouveau building that had the flavour of Wright in the flesh. It was indeed something we did not expect. We stayed in a little bungalow nestled in the suburbs of Bandung. The morning air was clear and crisp, flowers were everywhere and the children sang as they walked to school. Such an idyllic sight. This was Indonesia in the 1960s, poor but seemingly at peace with itself. Here was tropical montane climate at its best, something that reminded me of the Cameron Highlands of my childhood. In the distance was a high mountain range, the famous Tangkuban Perahu. Bambang arranged for us to climb it and we were escorted up the steep slopes by an armed platoon of tough-looking crew-cut commando-types who were festooned with weapons. It seemed that there were bandits about. The rim of the crater was dramatic, heat on one side and a cool breeze on the other. There were clumps of yellow sulphur. The steam jets spouted from the crater floor. It was a spectacular sight. We were on the edge of the "ring of fire". This was something new to us. In Singapore, there is no geographical vista and drama of this sort. But the clear impression was that Indonesia's "guided democracy" had a distinct militaristic feel. It was not the sort of impression that would go down well with us potential citizens of "Indonesia Raya".

After the jaunt, we went to the Bandung Institute of Technology (ITB) and met architecture professor Vincent Van Romondt, and some of his students. We were shown measured drawings of Indonesian buildings, monuments and humble village huts. These were reams and reams of beautiful drawings done in ink and colour pencil. Van Romondt had a documentation program running for some years. Every student was assigned to measure and draw up a specific building. We were very impressed at the sheer scope of the work and the richness of the built heritage of Indonesia. Since then, I have often wondered what happened to these drawings. Are they lost or in the Netherlands? The ITB campus was designed and built by the Dutch. It was designed by a Henri Maclaine Pont, a Dutch architect born in Java. He had a deep interest in traditional Indonesian architecture and had researched catenary structures as a means of implementing large span Minangkabau roofs. The campus design demonstrated a very sensitive use of materials and forms clearly inspired by Indonesian tradition and heritage. The steep thatched roofs were *belian* (iron wood) shingles, supported on large timber rafters and held up by huge concrete columns. Round river pebbles on these rafters made up the language of the design. Attached to the columns were wooden trellises festooned with colourful climbers. All the buildings and covered passages were set in lovely, manicured lawns. The architecture and setting must have left a deep impression on me as the language of tropical design surfaced in my later thinking and work. Our next destination was Jogjakarta, the royal capital of Java, where we met the top brass of Universitas Gadjah Mada. We were ushered into the great conference hall to meet the greats of the university, as if we were dignitaries from a foreign land. We tried our best to act the part and I do not know if we did our country proud. There was a sense of dignified vacancy about the place: dim lights, old paint, spartan furnishings and scruffy landscapes. Next, a visit to The Kraton with its cropped trees and the town's symmetrical axes introduced us to the richness of Javanese greatness in the past. Enveloped in the velvety darkness and witnessing the slow movements of the dancers' controlled elegance to the sombre sounds of Jogjakarta gamelan was an invitation to imagine the gravitas of a time long past. From Jogjakarta, the bus took us on a high road on the southern plateau to Banyuwangi on the east of Java. A ferry took us across to Bali. When we arrived at Denpasar at nightfall, it was lit by flickering coconut lamps and scent of *kretek*. The sense of heightened expectation was intense. I had read the books on Bali and my first impressions were as magical as I had expected. We stayed in a cheap *losmen*, one of many local travellers' inns.

Morning lit up the magical colours of Bali. We visited the home of Adrien-Jean Le Mayeur, a Belgian painter who married the famous legong dancer Ni Pollok, at Sanur beach. He had passed away, but Ni Pollok was there. I was struck by her serene, dignified beauty. She gracefully showed us the house and the paintings. Here was a Gauguin-esque abode of supreme enchantment. It was the European dream of an earthly tropical paradise, the original garden of Eden. Everywhere were pools of water, Hindu god statutes with hibiscus stuck in their ears, frangipani, incense in ritual offerings and pools of lotus and water lily. Here was fine scale. Every little thing is tweaked for the last ounce of effect, all adding up to a tapestry of charm and delight that modern living can only contrive—our "boutique" restaurants and hotels are artificially coaxed into existence by "design". There was no "design" at Le Mayeur's home but a guiding spirit and a quiet sensitivity that wanders lovingly over every nook and cranny, surface, the curve of a path, and the weep of a tree branch arched over a window, framing a view. Here is the celebration of contemplation and a love of life. Whenever life gets too hectic and demands too onerous, my mind returns to Le Mayeur and Ni Pollok's house in Sanur, and I am at peace again. Why can't we have such places in Singapore? It is not the lack of resources or space. I can think of many such potential places. But they lack love. The lack of libido. There is no one that will lovingly tend to the place and make magic out of it. It is something that cannot be administered, tendered out to the highest bidder, fast-tracked to be designed, built and contracted out. When we are going fast, we see only the outlines. Only when the pace slows down do we appreciate the detail. I decided that if I were to design, I must slow down and be at peace in a tranquil place. This is so hard in fast-paced Singapore: with the phone constantly ringing, the client screaming and government submissions aggravating! In the years of living and practicing architecture, scouting, the outdoors life, and later, the sense of Bali, never left me. Especially the interplay between landscape and building, and of passion and place. The feeling of burgeoning natural tropical growth was in me from young. What is architecture, or for that matter, life, if all was calculation and logic but little feeling? And so, I understood early on that learning is not just through the mind but through the skin too.

Being

*I was a biker from my teens.
This 1970s photo of me was
taken at Ponggol Marina
where I kept a boat for spear
fishing in the waters along
the Johore Straits.*

04

Malayan Architects Co-Partnership

I joined Malayan Architects Co-Partnership (MAC) after graduating from the Singapore Polytechnic with a Diploma in Architecture. In my mind, the firm was the most progressive architectural practice in Singapore at that time. Moreover, it was formed by my teacher, Lim Chong Keat and two other British-trained young Malayan architects, Chen Voon Fee and William Lim Siew Wai. MAC was set up along the lines of The Architects Co-Laborative of London and the Boston-based firm, The Architects Collaborative, which was led by the modernist pioneer Walter Gropius. Such studio names encapsulated what their founders believed in: collective group practice and teamwork within a democratic structure. At MAC, designs were collective efforts, and everything was discussed in the studio. The axiomatic aspects of design were subject to rigorous rationalisation and "systems analysis". "Design methods" were the rage then. "Group dynamics" were also popular as companies in non-communist countries sought to evolve new ways of working that were participatory and cooperative instead of replicating the hierarchical top-down methods stemming from both extremes of the political and ideological spectrum. These ideas suited the mood of the times. William (or Willy) told me recently that the name for MAC submitted to the Registrar of Companies included "Collaborative". However, this was turned down as it was reserved for the trade unions! It would have more accurately described the firm's intentions in its working, but so "Malayan Architects Co-Partnership" it was.

When MAC came about in 1960, the spirit of creating a fresh new society was in the air. Malaya had already obtained independence in 1957, while Singapore had elected a new government in 1959 under the People's Action Party (PAP) with autonomy on all other matters but internal security and defence, which the British retained control over. The concept of a democratic architectural practice was particularly appropriate to the young, newly qualified architects, many of who considered the old-style autocratic practice to be passé. This was especially so for those who trained in England and had imbibed democratic socialist ideas there, such as MAC's partners. The trio knew each other while studying in England and first met at the Tropical Architecture Conference of 1954. They became good friends and decided they would practice together when they came back to Malaya. Both Willy and Voon Fee graduated from the Architectural Association in London. Willy then did graduate studies in urban planning at Harvard University, while Voon Fee travelled overland back from England. Chong Keat was schooled in Manchester University before heading to the Massachusetts Institute of Technology (MIT) for his masters. These experiences made a deep impression on all of them. They gained some local experience with other architects in Singapore before setting up MAC. While teaching at the Polytechnic, Chong Keat did a few projects in association with Eugene Seow, an established Singapore architect practicing at that time. One notable example was the Nanyang University Students' Union House. Willy worked for James Ferrie, an expatriate architect who chose to stay in Singapore after the British left and was responsible for the Fitzpatrick Supermarket extension building opposite the former Ngee Ann Building along Orchard Road. The huge structure in the style of Le Corbusier's *Unité d'Habitation* made an impact on me. Voon Fee was the main stay of the partnership while the other two were working to support the idea of the firm. I vaguely remember that the partnership won a competition for a commercial centre in Voon Fee's hometown, Ipoh, during this very early period. The steep roof of the design was to be clad in the indigenous material of pewter, and I was struck by the innovative idea and how their "nationalism" extended even into the use of materials.

The project that launched MAC was when they won the 1961 competition for the Singapore Conference Hall and Trade Union House. It was designed for large meetings as well as concerts and musical performances to promote culture among workers, as part of the vision to produce the cultured worker similar to the ideals of the British Trade Union Congress. One of the principal movers of this project was the left wing intellectual and political activist, Sydney Woodhull, whom Willy knew as he had a socialist bent and was very interested in seeking out the leading local intellectuals of the day. The trade union house was also one of the first new buildings conceived and put up by the new local government to signal a new beginning in Singapore. Another was the National Theatre which became a venue for the making of a new culture. Both buildings were put up for design competitions too. While the National Theatre was limited to five chosen architects, the trade union house was the first open architectural competition in Singapore and drew a huge response. It was also the first time that local Singaporean architects were on the panel of assessors, including Tio Seng Chin from the Public Works Department (PWD). MAC won the competition against the more established practices. Their design was a fresh breeze through a profession then dominated by Australian-trained practices and the remaining British practices. The MAC submission also most inspired us students. The spatial organization was volumetric rather than plan extrusions. It had an openness about it that was totally new. Terraces cantilevered from the core spaces formed spill-out spaces. Vertical and horizontal spaces flowed from one to another through the main circulation spaces of the building, linking foyers and gathering spaces. Five vertical stair and elevator shafts—reminiscent of Louis Kahn's medical research laboratories for the University of Pennsylvania—were striking as they provided the visual unity necessary to the composition. This was all topped by a huge butterfly roof, seemingly disavowing the vernacularism of traditional pitch roofed architecture. It was a time of heroic gestures towards being modern. How far we have drifted from this since! The trade union house still serves as a marker and a benchmark of local architectural endeavour. The design drawings were printed on ammonia sepia paper, with delicate pencil shading and sensitively drawn-in trees, cars and people. It left a deep impression on everyone, not least on us. We watched the building materialise from our studio windows at the Singapore Polytechnic at Prince Edward Road. It was 1963, our final year at the Polytechnic, and the building heralded a new age which we were excited to be graduating into.

Chong Keat versus Willy

I joined MAC after graduating at the end of 1963 and winning the Palmer and Turner Prize for being one of the top students of the cohort. There was no class barrier in the democratic atmosphere of the office. Competence and dedication to the work was the ethic. As young architects, we learnt a lot from the senior draftsmen. Some key personnel who played important roles in the office included Wong Fook Kay and Sannie Abdul, two very capable and experienced draftsmen. Sannie was also a good designer and pitched in on many projects design-wise. He later received a scholarship to study in the Illinois Institute of Technology and qualified as an architect. On his return to Singapore, he joined the government's Design Centre. The partners had their own rooms whereas we worked four to a room. There was easy access to the partners. We were constantly hopping in and out of their rooms to discuss things. Every Monday morning, there were project reviews. The partners and everyone reported on the jobs, raised issues and got advice in an open collegial atmosphere. Minutes were taken and required actions assigned to be reported on at the next meeting. There was a culture of discussion and communication and Willy and Chong Keat both hosted intellectual parties in their flats too. We were privileged to meet interesting people through them. Chong Keat leaned more towards the arts, and Willy more towards ideas and intellectual matters, including politics. Both continue this tradition up till this day. In a book for Willy's 70th birthday, I penned a tribute to him as "the great convener" for his role in putting people together.

But both Chong Keat and Willy had very different work styles. Willy did not draw his ideas; he articulated them. Chong Keat was verbally articulate, and he could also develop design ideas very well through beautiful drawings. There were other divergent trends among the two principal partners that led to antipathy between them. Willy was very sociable and developed his intellectual and social interests, including publishing important magazines such as *Monsoon*, and later *Temasek* to give a voice to the new social democratic, literary and political ideas fomenting at that time. Chong Keat was getting increasingly irritated by Willy's socialising, which he saw was at the expense of the work in the office. Chong Keat was developing his interest in the arts too and had started Alpha Gallery as a venue for the emerging young artists of the day. He was also cultivating government contacts. Howe Yoon Chong, Permanent

Secretary of the Ministry of National Development and chairman of the Housing & Development Board (HDB), was a good friend. During his days in the Polytechnic, Chong Keat also befriended its chairman, Dr Toh Chin Chye, who was also Singapore's Deputy Prime Minister and chairman of its leading political party, the PAP.

While Chong Keat got appointed to the HDB board, Willy was held at arm's length by the PAP government. It must have rankled him. Much later, Yoon Chong told me that the Government would not touch Willy with a "ten-foot pole". I did not know then that the sins of the father were visited upon the sons. Willy's father, Richard Lim Chuan Hoe, was a prominent member of the Labour Front party that opposed the fledgling PAP in the early 1950s. I was aghast by Yoon Chong's statement. There must have been undercurrents given the small place that Singapore is; attitudes percolate through the elite. And all this must have played on the relationship between Chong Keat and Willy too. However, the personal tendencies of the two were divergent fundamentally and as their relationship deteriorated, it affected the atmosphere in MAC's office and the work too. The office was soon split into two: Chong Keat went upstairs to a studio in his own apartment at Ngee Ann Building. Willy occupied a studio downstairs. I was assigned to Willy's studio. In some ways I preferred to work with Willy because I had the freedom to exercise my own initiatives in design, although I consulted him often. My relationship with Chong Keat also became a little strained. While handling the Holland Court apartments project, I had told him not to undermine my authority with the contractor by giving instructions directly on site. I was only 23 years old then. I told him that he could tell me anything in the privacy of the office but not at the site that I oversaw. Chong Keat agreed but the relationship was strained after this incident. He chose Koh Seow Chuan to work with him upstairs. Ever diplomatic and diligent, Seow Chuan was the administrative architect Chong Keat valued to carry out his instructions and designs. Seow Chuan was trained in the architecture school at the University of Melbourne and joined MAC soon after I did. He had impressed us students during a visit to the Polytechnic while on vacation when he showed us his design drawings. He could very eloquently explain what we thought to be very mundane designs! We were so envious that he was able to spout philosophical ideas he acquired at the University of Melbourne. At the Polytechnic, we longed for such

A New World in the Making

intellectual nourishment. But there was none to be had. We made up for this deficiency with our own reading and by inviting foreign-trained architects to the Polytechnic. Being the first architecture students in this country, we always wanted to gauge ourselves against them because we had no idea where we stood. Another student architect who visited us was Kenneth Chia, who later formed SAA Architects. He too showed the same sort of "nothing designs", nondescript and mundane works which truly perplexed us because we believed that design was everything in an architect's capability. It was only years later that we realised that it was not design that would get us anywhere in Singapore, but the ability to communicate and influence people. So much for meritocracy!

The antipathy between the two partners was further strained by the deteriorating political relationship between Malaysia and Singapore. There was a tussle between the Malay "ultras" in Malaysia's ruling party, UMNO, and Singapore's PAP led by Lee Kuan Yew. The tensions had parallel repercussions in MAC as well. The partners debated whether MAC's head office should be in Kuala Lumpur, Malaysia, while Singapore became a branch. This idea was espoused by Chong Keat. It was interpreted by Willy as a tactical move to sideline him and the Singapore office. He argued that there should be two offices, and neither would be subordinate to the other. The issue came to a head over the designing of the Bank Rakyat Building in Penang. Voon Fee, based in Kuala Lumpur, was assigned to lead the project design team. It had always been difficult for him to be between the other two partners. I think it was why he chose to play the technical role in projects rather than get involved in the generating of design ideas. I thought he was very capable technically and thorough in the design development phases of a project. He was the one who did the working drawings for the trade union house. Much to Chong Keat's embarrassment, Voon Fee was at a loss in the design generation phase for the Penang project. It seemed to me that it vindicated Willy's view that it was not really viable to have Kuala Lumpur as the centre of MAC. Anyhow, I was sent to Kuala Lumpur, ostensibly to work with Voon Fee. This was a sort of triumph for Willy's two-office thesis, and Chong Keat was not relishing it. He deliberately stayed out of the design process but hovered around uncomfortably. In my usual rapid-fire way, I quickly brought the design to a conclusion while Voon Fee played the technical resource person to me. It worked well for the both of us. I was inspired by the Boston City Hall design just published in *Progressive Architecture* magazine. I thought the visually busy, projecting upper storeys contrasted well with the formality of the palisade of the lower supporting columns. This gave an almost classical coherence to the design that I felt was suitable for the Bank Rakyat building.

The Rise of Local Firms

As young architects in the office, the rivalry between Willy and Chong Keat seemed personal and quite inconsequential as long as good work was being done. Both offices had a surfeit of work as there were so few talented local firms then. In contrast, the old British practices, such as Palmer and Turner, Swan & Maclaren, James Cubitt & Partners, Iversen Van Sitterren & Partners and Raglan Squire & Partners, all saw dwindling work as their old boys' network dried up. New work from local businesses and the government were going to local firms through direct appointments and competitions. The old draftsman-based local practices were no match for the bright and talented young British- and Australian-trained local architects coming on stream. The British-trained ones came from upper middle-class families with lots of family connections from whom job recommendations flowed in the heady days of new building in the first flush of independence. The Australian-trained ones, returning in the early 1960s, were from poorer families and went to Australia because it was cheaper. Many were also on Colombo Plan scholarships and had to serve a bond with the government on their return. Most joined the HDB and PWD. After an initial period of camaraderie, a deep-seated rivalry emerged between the two groups, fuelled by resentment over the disparity of opportunities, advantage and earning power.

Within my first year at MAC, I designed and built a coffee processing factory in Tanglin Halt. It was exciting to be working with production engineers to accommodate the machinery, and to find the appropriate architectural expression for the process. The result was a tall pyramidal tower in the middle, which housed the elevators and silos. This was flanked by two wings of conveyor belts for hundreds of workers to sort and grade the beans that cascaded down from the silos above. Natural ventilation was crucial to ensure comfort in the working environment. I made sure of this by having the external walls made entirely of metal louvers. There were also perimeter slots in the floor plate to facilitate vertical airflow. This building unfortunately only functioned shortly for its intended purpose as world coffee prices fell. The son of the owner, who had just returned from abroad as an electrical engineer, had a rescue plan. He turned it into a factory for assembling Setron television sets for the domestic and Indonesian markets. Such was the volatility of the market conditions then. The rapidly changing conditions led to equally quick responses too. The government successfully courted the first-tier Indonesian entrepreneurs to bring capital and markets with them to Singapore. The economy changed from commodity processing and entrepot trade to electronics and manufacturing in a matter of a few months. Incentives provided by the government such as pioneer industry status and tax exemption for approved industries yielded the desired effects. Local entrepreneurs also began to venture into real estate development. In my first project at MAC, I got to design and build Holland Court, a high-rise apartment block. The client was part of the Sim Lim Group, an important local trading house that competed with the established British ones such as Sime Darby and Guthrie's. Sim Lim was one of the first local firms to bring in Onoda Cement from Japan in a time when the industry was dominated by Western building products. British companies exercised a monopoly on Portland cement, which was specified and recommended by the PWD's British architects and engineers. Another major supplier was Hume Industries, a privately-owned British company specialising in pre-cast concrete pipes and lampposts. They were also assigned by PWD to do cement testing too, and the potential conflict of interests was overlooked. I was told by retired Sim Lim directors that they had great difficulties getting test approval certificates and succeeded only after many attempts. It was one example of the struggles local firms experienced bringing in building materials, which we have taken for granted today. Sim Lim prospered and became one of MAC's major clients. Another sector that underwent rapid change under the new government was banking, as local companies expanded and whittled away at the dominance of the British banks. A major MAC client was United Overseas Bank (UOB), then known as United Chinese Bank and headed by the young and dynamic Wee Cho Yaw. I handled the bank's rapid expansion program where a new bank branch was designed and built over two weeks. I dealt directly with Mr Wee, who came down to the job sites personally on numerous occasions. Chong Keat enjoyed a special relationship with him and was able to influence him to support the arts. Accordingly, UOB established a program to collect paintings and probably has the largest single integrated collection of Singapore and Malaysian art in the region today.

Awakening the Malayan

I remember very distinctly that as the radio announced Singapore's separation from Malaysia in 1965, Chong Keat stormed into the office, black-faced and muttering an expletive loudly. He does not recall this. But I remember this very well because it awakened the unconscious Malayan sentiments in me from that day onwards. Like most ordinary people, I saw Singapore's battle for a merger with Malaysia as one between the PAP and the Left. The Left saw the formation of Malaysia as a post-colonial plot whereas the PAP saw it as vitally necessary for Singapore to have a share of the common market and the larger hinterland. As a result, the issue of Singapore and Malaysia is still unfortunately seen purely in political terms. Its implications, however, linger and continue to dog Singapore's cultural and intellectual development. The sentiment of the people to the poetics of place that gives identity and engenders love of locale got shunted aside. My own cultural sentiments were awakened by the Separation, and I refused at the emotional level to accept it. I am still pained at how the cultural and sentimental aspects of my "Malaya" were obliterated from memory and emotion by subsequent events and media treatment. I am pained to read references to those "Malayan" days as "Malaysian" even though "Malaya" is the accurate historical term to use. The term Malaya still lingers in obscure company names such as Malayan Motors, Malayan Banking .... Malayan Architect's Co-Partnership was one such name. It embedded both the firm's "Malayan" identity and its democratic working methods as represented by "Co-Partnership". I felt somewhat truncated by the Separation. My childhood growing up in Cameron Highlands, the many forays into Malayan forests, reefs and remote places cemented in me a love of place that transcends politics. The two are never the same for me. Whereas I used to travel freely to Malaya, I now had to go through the tedium of passports and forms. It was only much later that I realised that my aesthetics were very much "Malayan aesthetics". It is hard to pin this down. And because of my inherent "Malayan-ism", I am quite at home anywhere in Malaya, now Malaysia. I have a special liking for

A New World in the Making

Malay culture. I find the language and manners beautiful and likeable in a way that I find the sound of Mandarin guttural and unattractive. I find mainstream Chinese aesthetics lacking in sense value, being almost totally constructed out of symbolic contents. It is an aggregation of virtues assembled arithmetically and so to me it is literally a non-sense!

This is a subject I come back to again and again throughout my life. Only after reading the Chinese aesthetician and historian Li Zehou did I finally understand my antipathy. He showed how mainstream Chinese culture marginalised the intrinsic schools of thought and culture to an extent that the sensual and emotional directness of Chinese sensibilities were so utterly displaced. Almost everything in the mainstream is codified and stylised. This is what I battle with every day of my design life. It is a subject I have pondered over endlessly. In Malay culture, I sense that there is a natural grasp of the intrinsic and this is the part of Malayan-ism that I cling to. This is what I mean when I say I am a Malayan. I once said in a public interview that I was not Singaporean but a Malayan, which disappointed George Yeo, who was then-Minister of the Information, Culture and the Arts. I found it impossible in an off-the-cuff discussion to explain how political realities do not correspond to aesthetic rootedness. While I accept political separation, I cannot separate my feeling of the unity of people and place just because a line was drawn. Malaya and Singapore cannot for us be cut into two just like that. I could not also say that the kind of pragmatism Singapore espouses is exactly the kind of deadening of the senses I struggle against. Being Malayan juxtaposes the poetic against the pragmatic.

In 1966, I left MAC for a year-long architectural pilgrimage around the world. Both Chong Keat and Willy very generously wrote ahead to their friends to expect me and gave me valuable contacts. During the trip, I carried on a continuous correspondence with Willy as I was much closer to him at this time than with Chong Keat. Trouble was brewing in MAC. The two of them were down to not talking but communicating by notes! I wrote back suggesting the setting up of a federated studio system under the umbrella of MAC, which had by then become a very well-known and respected firm. Rather than dissolve, MAC could benefit from its diversity of talents and views. But this was not to be. When I returned in February of 1967, both Willy and Chong Keat told me that dissolution was imminent. Lawyers were drafting the separation agreement. I went to see Chong

Keat in his studio upstairs. He was friendly and received me back warmly. Willy then took me out for lunch and asked me to join him when the firm broke up. On our return from lunch, we bumped into Chong Keat as he was leaving, and he must have sensed my alliance with Willy. I shall never forget the daggers in his eyes as we passed each other in the lift lobby. He did not speak to me again, until the early 1980s at an architectural conference in Kuala Lumpur. Chong Keat was walking towards me along the narrow corridor. We were both heading for the coffee table. He could not avoid me, and I was determined to break the ice. We greeted each other. As we stood by the coffee table, he nudged me to pour him a coffee. I said jokingly that he could pour it himself! The old pecking order was at last broken; we were uneasy equals from then on! The old friendship returned. He shall always be my great teacher and I shall always be his star student as he is often fond of saying.

Singapore Planning and Urban Research Group

The Singapore Planning and Urban Research Group (SPUR) was formed in 1965, during a Singapore Institute of Architects (SIA) publication committee meeting that failed to have a quorum. The meeting was held in Willy's flat. Besides him, those present were Ho Pak Toe, Tan Jake Hooi, Wee Chwee Heng and Charles Ho. All were architects, except for Jake Hooi who was the chief planner of Singapore. Back then, relations between government officials and private architects were natural and collegial. There was easy exchange of ideas and communication was simple and direct. Jake Hooi was quite prepared to discuss ideas and to explore possibilities. He was always objective as he discussed ideas at the level of principle. Pak Toe was a senior architect in the PWD and became Chief Building Surveyor when Ong Eng Guan was the Mayor of the City Council between 1957 and 1959. Pak Toe was trained in Melbourne and was a member of the Socialist Club together with Teh Cheang Wan, who headed the HDB and later became the Minister for National Development. They were part of a coterie of socialist-inclined students in Australia and maintained those ties when they came back to Singapore. They played a significant part in shaping the politics of the profession, its character and its alignments. The group ended up chatting about issues of development and housing. It suddenly occurred to all present that it would be a good idea to set up a discussion and research group dedicated to the urban planning and study of the environment in Singapore. And so, the group was spontaneously formed. Willy was naturally the first chairman. He was somewhat socialist and had done planning studies in Harvard. In Singapore, he consorted with left wing intellectuals in the PAP as well as those in the opposition parties. He was well-connected and knew the ropes, so to speak.

The choice of name was interesting. "SPORE" was a possibility as it captured the idea of small ideas germinating and was also short for Singapore. But it was difficult to construct as an acronym. It was dropped in favour of "SPUR" which was very suitable as an acronym and stood for "Singapore Planning and Urban Research". It lacked a "G" for "Group", so the name "SPUR Group" came about. We met weekly in the first year to review the findings each of us was assigned to study on topics such as housing, transport, industry, schools, community facilities, etc. I reported on transport. After a year, the group felt ready to make public comment. The opportunity came when the government announced plans to widen Collyer Quay from a four-lane road to a 12-lane highway. I wrote to the press objecting to this, arguing that this would cut the city off from the waterfront and called for a public discussion. This raised a furore and received a sarcastic reply from the Permanent Secretary of the Ministry of National Development. He advised SPUR to focus on drains and refuse collection rather than interfering in the serious business of remaking the city. Little did we know that the state was shaping a political culture to empower it to monopolise all ideas and decisions, to discipline Singapore towards industrialisation and economic development. All values were to be shaped in this direction: unquestioning obedience, totally focused diligence; technical skills, pragmatic compartmentalisation of views and duties; acceptance of hierarchical authority. This all stood in opposition to the freedom of expression, broad vision, initiative, creativity and critical thinking that most of us schooled in modern thinking were much more attuned to. We expected that one could agree to disagree yet remain friends. That synergies can be found in seemingly contradicting propositions. That economies of scope could be as important as economies of scale. That diversity was a virtue. We were so wrong. In the state's drive to industrialise the economy, we had to have "hard digits" to be of value. There was no place or patience for "fluffy thinking".

In retrospect, those of us from the middle classes did not see the new political imperatives espoused by the new government and their administration. Realising the growing animosity towards critical voices that SPUR represented, especially since we were seen as a group of architects clamouring for professional entry into government jobs, the group's composition began to change. Jake Hooi and Pak Toe resigned. Their participation in SPUR became untenable for them as civil servants even in their private capacities. Private views would no longer be tolerated. The line was being drawn between the sheep and the goats. The sheep were government architects. All the others were interlopers who benefited from the state, but who ungratefully bit the hand that fed them. This atmosphere poisoned the relationship between government planners and architects and those of us in the private sector.

Meeting Lee Kuan Yew

In 1968, I wrote a paper, "Housing, Identity and Nation-building". It impressed George Thompson, an advisor to Prime Minister Lee Kuan Yew, who sent a copy to him. Out of the blue, I got a call from the Mr Lee's office to arrange for a date to see him at City Hall. I remember going up the wide central stairway and was impressed by a massive painting by Raden Basoeki Abdullah on the staircase wall. It was an epic piece on heroic nation-building themes. How it got there and who chose it is still unknown to me. I entered the reception area on the second level and was greeted by the prime minister's personal secretary, a Mr Sankaran. I was shown to a little waiting area beyond his desk at the door. There were a couple of simple lounge chairs, which were backed to the window overlooking the Padang across the street below, a rectangular coffee table and an aquarium across from me. Mr Sankaran said that the prime minister would appreciate if I did not smoke in his presence. I nodded. I soon noticed there was an ashtray on the table with a cigarette butt in it, but I didn't think anything of it. A little later, Mr Sankaran came in and saw the cigarette butt and said in an irritated tone that he thought he had told me not to smoke. I replied that I did not, and he should have his ash trays cleaned regularly. He gave me a scowl and took the ashtray away.

After some time, Mr Sankaran came in again and asked me to proceed through the door on my right where the prime minister was expecting me. When I entered, Mr Lee rose from his chair behind his large tidy teak

Singapore Planning and Urban Research Group (SPUR)

I was part of this independent group formed in 1965 to study the urban planning of this new nation. One of our major achievements was drawing attention to the noise pollution to residents arising from the government's plans to expand the existing Paya Lebar airport (right). Instead, we proposed moving the airport to Changi. Our proposals and ideas were published in two volumes, starting with 65-7 SPUR.

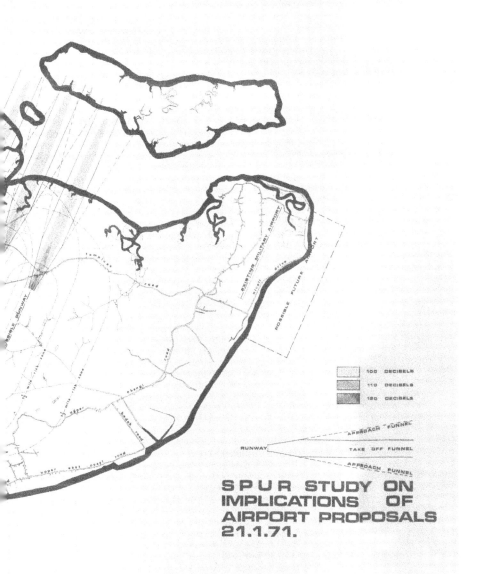

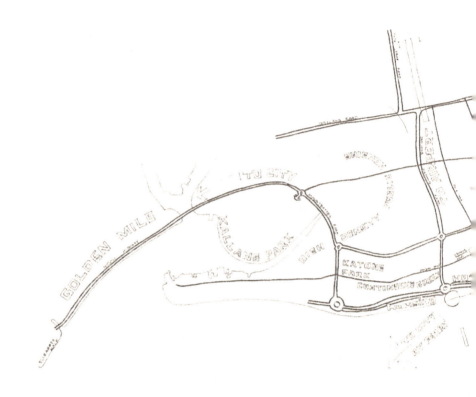

Sketch of locality of reclaimed area indicating positions of proposed lagoons and the land use of the surroundings.

Imagining Future Singapore

In 1968, SPUR also proposed reclaiming a South Sea Lagoon and a long island (above) to replace the beaches lost from reclaiming Singapore's east coast. The same year we also held an exhibition on the past, present and future of Singapore's environment at Elizabeth Walk (across). While it was praised by Prime Minister Lee Kuan Yew, an exhibit comparing public housing to chicken coops drew the ire of Member of Parliament Rahim Ishak and I had to block it out!

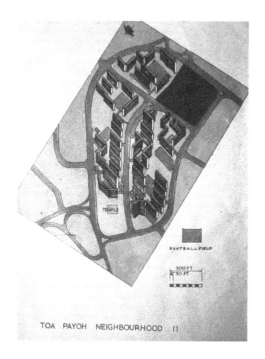

TOA PAYOH NEIGHBOURHOOD II

Low-Rise Housing in Toa Payoh

In 1975, I proposed an alternative to the government's plans to build 10-storey high-rise flats in Toa Payoh (above). As the density of the plot ratio was relatively low (1.75:1), a low-rise solution based on "perimeter" building forms could work. By linking all the housing in one perimeter block along the plot (across top), it created a 13-storey development but enclosed an open space that was equivalent to almost 50 football fields! Breaking the development down to more perimeter blocks increased the length of each but lowered their height further (right and across). This proposal earned me official hatred from the authorities!

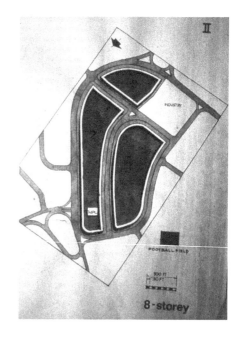

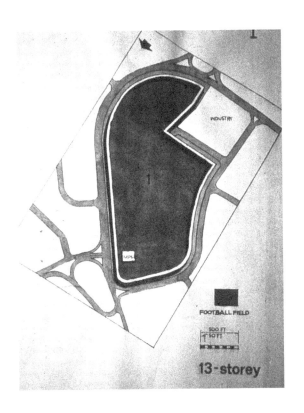

13-storey

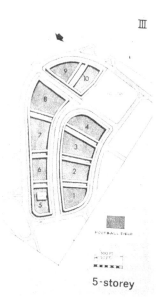

5-storey

Cheras Housing Project

My vision for a high-density, low-rise housing project was finally realised in 1976 in Cheras, Kuala Lumpur. Every house in this project has a small garden (top left) and sits back-to-back in clusters of four (below). They are organised around a 2.5 metre breezeway that also serves as pedestrian passages and naturally shaded public spaces for gatherings (across bottom). The homes were positively received by residents (left) and recommended as a housing solution by the Malaysian government.

table and extended his hand towards me. I was struck by his height and ruddy complexion. I thought he had been in the sun. He had on a well-starched short-sleeve shirt and white slacks. The window was on his left, I supposed so that the light would not cast a shadow when writing. He shared that George had shown him my paper which he found interesting. I reiterated what I said in the piece that I thought housing was the tangible connection between the people and the State. I added that there could be more participation and neighbourliness among HDB residents to develop a sense of community, which was missing in housing when people were uprooted into new surroundings. Along these lines, the Malay kampongs were an important heritage of this *gotong royong* spirit and I suggested they should be kept so that the genius for community could grow from there. I was being idealistic. Mr Lee disagreed as he felt that the backwardness of the Malays was holding back the community, and this should change. I had the distinct feeling that it was not the content of discussion that was important. The man was sizing me up. Clearly, he saw that I could stand up to him. On my part, I felt that there was no use disagreeing with him as he held firm to his views on things even though he enjoyed the contest of ideas. With his intellect and skills as a lawyer, he knew he would win every discussion. But beyond argument, I also felt the weight of his overbearing presence. It was palpable. You could not prevail against this colossus of a man. After a while, Mr Lee abruptly stood up and said that he had another appointment. Extending his hand again, he bid me goodbye, and I left the room the way I came in.

A few days later, George asked to see me. He inquired as to the meeting and then looking at me earnestly through his beetled brows, asked if I would consider standing as a candidate on a PAP ticket in the upcoming elections. I was rather taken aback. I said I had to think about it and added that I was not even a PAP member, my feeble attempt to fob off the question. To this, George blithely said that it was not a problem. All I had to do was to go the PAP headquarters at Tanglin Road and pay seven dollars and become a member. It was as simple as that! I thought it very strange. Anyway, I gave the matter some serious thought. It was during the time that many SPUR members were resigning. Several alluded to pressure being applied on them. The academic members were told in no uncertain terms that they would be denied access to data they needed for their research, which was especially important to the social scientists among us. Many architects also left because of fears that they were being discriminated against by the authorities on which they depended for planning approvals and building permits. The pressure on SPUR members rankled. I eventually replied to Mr Lee directly that I regretted that I would decline the invitation to be a PAP candidate. I also said that I was disappointed that the party had added some dubious characters to its ranks. As a 28-year-old hot-head, I said what I felt, adding that he did not need people like me. I was no "Yes man".

Sometime later, the first new wave of PAP's self-renewal was in progress. My brother was inducted into the party and so was the architect Ong Teng Cheong. Another was Augustine Tan, a Singapore University Economics lecturer who was associated with SPUR activities. I liked him as he was very incisive and clear-headed. I later asked him what Mr Lee thought about my refusal. He said that the "old man" was annoyed by my letter. George had also earlier shared that the man "thought less of me" after my reply. That was that, I thought. My life was never the same from then on. It was an uphill battle.

To Kuala Lumpur and Back

In 1967, Willy, Seow Chuan and myself started Design Partnership. Chong Keat started a new firm named Architect's Team 3. I was eventually expelled from Design Partnership in 1974 because I participated in organising a demonstration against the US bombing of Vietnam. Willy was told by the Commissioner of Police, Tan Teck Khim, to get rid of me or suffer the consequences. The threat was that the firm will be closed. We did not doubt that this would happen given the arsenal of weapons at the government's disposal. My partners asked me to resign to save the firm, but I refused. Instead, they shut down the firm and reconstituted it without me to form DP Architects. I felt no rancour. Afterwards, I decided to stop practicing architecture and to become a photojournalist producing educational material instead. My architecture practice restarted in Kuala Lumpur after a chance meeting with Low Keng Huat. He was a contractor of the People's Park Complex development and also a shareholder with Ho Kok Cheong. When Keng Huat saw my research on cluster link houses, which I had pursued right up to my expulsion from Design Partnership, he immediately recognised how it addressed the challenge of building low-cost houses that Malaysia's Prime Minister Tun Razak had put to the

A New World in the Making

country's Housing Developers Association (HDA) in 1975. The HDA chairman, Tan Chin Nam, had assembled a large team but could not achieve that target of RM5,000 per dwelling. Keng Huat did a quick calculation and said he could do it with my designs. He eventually subcontracted the project for RM3,500 each!

It was thus through Keng Huat that I met Chin Nam. I was impressed with Chin Nam's intelligence and quick thinking. He saw my design and immediately arranged for me to meet with the mayor of Kuala Lumpur, Datuk Yaacob Latiff, who also agreed with the design. Thus, I was able to realise my vision of high-density, low-rise housing in what became known as the Cheras Housing project. It made me well known among developers, especially because of the favourable opinion the upper ranks of the Kuala Lumpur administration had of me. I had the opportunity to work on many extraordinary design projects. Although most were never built, they allowed me to pioneer many new ideas. One example was an unbuilt shopping complex in Surabaya for which I researched the effect of using solar heating to induce the stack effect to accelerate air flow through a naturally ventilated building. While working in Kuala Lumpur, I also maintained a small office in Singapore with some former staff from Design Partnership. Some of my loyal clients in Singapore stuck with me against advice that I was a marked man! I did a mixed development in Lorong Chuan, but the client's land was unfortunately acquired by the government! Another submission for a condominium and marina at Ponggol was also denied planning permission many times before the land was subsequently acquired. Meanwhile, my Kuala Lumpur office was very busy. We eventually completed Ampang City, a huge mixed-use development. We also completed 10,000 low-cost houses based on the high-density low-rise housing research model I had developed earlier.

My breakthrough in Singapore began in 1982 with the completion of Ming Arcade. It was on an impossibly small and narrow site along Cuscaden Road, behind Ming Court Hotel. The design had to pack in many small shops and offices and stack many storeys efficiently. I knew from my experience in Tokyo that height did not matter if escalators served every level. This reassured my client and Ming Arcade turned out to be profitable in the end. That this project obtained planning approval broke the seeming evil spell I was under. I began scoring several significant commissions such as Corona Ville, which was based on the Cheras houses in plan form but dressed in a Mediterranean style. It was a great success that sold like hot cakes. My client was very pleased. The major breakthrough project in Singapore was Dairy Farm condominium. It was commissioned by Leo Properties, a subsidiary owned by one of the richest men in Asia, Robert Kuok. It was a terrifying experience because of the many challenges. I was trying to make my high-density, low-rise housing design appeal to the middle-class market in Singapore. While I was grappling with this design challenge, the planning approval for the project kept getting rejected for often spurious reasons! I suspected political bias and was terrified that my failure to obtain planning approval from the Ministry of National Development (MND) would seal my fate once again. Then Minister of National Development, Teh Cheang Wan, hated me for my criticisms of the HDB's high-rise concept. Back then, the plot ratios at only 1.5 were low enough to not require high-rise design solutions. I reached out to my friend Pathmanaban Selvadurai, who was then a member of the Ministry of National Development's Parliament Review Committee, about my predicament and he was sympathetic. He made discreet inquiries on my behalf with the Minister to get to the crux of the problem. Teh was evidently aggrieved by my criticism, and I was told to rescind my views about the HDB to obtain planning approval! Having no choice, I did so in a carefully crafted letter which Teh mistakenly took as my "confession". My career was saved, and it allowed my practice to grow in both Singapore and Malaysia.

I was never good at marketing myself. My critical and public comments set me apart from the usual crowd. I did not hobnob with the rich and powerful. I did not play golf or fraternise in social clubs. Instead, I taught at the School of Architecture, and I was active in the Singapore Institute of Architects (SIA). In the SIA, I served as editor of the newsletter and then instituted the Professional Development Committee, organised design discourses and participated in international conferences on design and environment. In 1986, the then-Minister Teh, who regarded me as his enemy, committed suicide after being charged for corruption. Mr S. Dhanabalan was appointed as the new Minister of National Development. He was a very straight-laced and honest person, and took the opportunity to clean house and introduce many new ideas. Around the same time, I became President of the SIA, having worked for nearly a decade to become a senior member in its council. I was able to gather a caucus of younger members who, unlike the conservative in-group that cosied up to Teh, were hungry for change. In 1990, I was elected to office with a record number of votes. Unlike the incumbent, who was regarded by the younger members as a stooge of the old order, I was the candidate for change. As SIA President, I was able to engage the new Minister in a series of dialogues. These resulted in major changes in the scope of practice and participation in public housing in the form of the Design and Build Scheme (DBS). The DBS generated many new innovations and introduced many new urban planning ideas about integrated tropical urbanism and waterfront designs into the realm of public housing. I also initiated dialogues with the Ministry of Finance on fee structure and design selection innovations. These are long standing issues that continue to bedevil the profession, but the basis for conversation and engagement was laid down during my presidency. My practice also continued to get important projects through winning anonymous design competitions. The Kandang Kerbau Hospital project was the defining moment of this period in my professional practice. I won the design tender, but the PWD stole the project from me after the site was changed. I fought back. In this, Minister Dhanabalan righted this injustice in my favour. He listened as I explained that having won the design competition, I should be appointed as the architect for the project. He agreed to look into this and informed me a week later that he could only get me the design part. The rest of the project was to be managed by PWD director-general Tan Swan Beng and his team of architects. They were very resentful. I was eventually disbarred from visiting the site while the building was under construction. They blamed my "bad" design for rising costs arising from changes to the original design brief. One example was the need for structural beams that had to be erected to incorporate an air raid shelter in the basement carpark. It is just one of many trials and tribulations a critical person like me faces in Singapore in a monopolistic bureaucratic system.

Being

My Expulsion from Design Partnership

18 December 1975

Dear friends,

I am writing you this personal letter to explain the situation I am facing.

As you know over the years, I have been rather outspokenly critical of the environment I live in. I felt the need to draw attention to the sociological and psychological problems of Housing & Development Board (HDB) housing and the general deterioration of the environment. In 1967, together with Singapore Planning & Urban Research Group (SPUR) I organised a public exhibition on Singapore's physical environment, *Singapore: Past, Present & Future*, which drew attention to the increasing pollution, physical decay and regimentation of housing. In 1968, I was invited by the ruling party to stand in the by-election to be a Member of Parliament. After considerable pondering, I declined as I felt that I would not be able to discuss fundamental issues in Parliament and felt that in my role as a free and independent person, I was freer to examine and express my views about my society better. I was, in February 1971, also involved with the SPUR Group to press for the removal of the Paya Lebar Airport expansion scheme to Changi so as to minimise the noise pollution to a large community of people living in the Katong, Geylang and Geylang Serai areas. In my discussion in 1974 on transportation problems in Singapore, I drew attention to the conflicts of interest in the bureaucracy and the lack of public voice in the bargaining process for a cheap and efficient public transport system. In the four years of tutoring at the School of Architecture in the University of Singapore, I emphasised a more scientific approach towards physical design and concentrated on the thinking process involved, stressing the need to be clear about the assumed value premises in the process of reasoning a problem through and also the need to go down to the real situation in order to learn and feel for it. In helping to organise the Anti-US bombing of Vietnam demonstration at the US Embassy in Singapore in December 1972, I felt a great need to express outrage at blatant aggression and also to create an opportunity for people in Singapore to express their indignation and their humanity as we have so little opportunity to do so. In 1971, when the government moved against the *Singapore Herald*, a slightly independent English language newspaper, I with a small group of citizens concerned over the need to have a good community newspaper tried to organise a cooperative of Singaporeans to buy over the paper from the Official Receiver on the basis of the government's statement that if the paper was exclusively owned by Singaporeans, a licence to publish would be granted. We applied for a licence. The licence was not granted, and the cooperative was not registered, and as you know the paper could not be resuscitated.

Whilst teaching and tutoring at the School of Architecture, I emphasised that in designing public housing, architects must live in HDB flats in order to experience first-hand the housing environment. Towards this end, the students who were tutored by me were invited to live free of any charge in my housing board flat. The HDB was most displeased with this and have tried through constant harassment over a period of three to four years to recover the flat from me even though I had full legal right to own it and to invite guests to stay with me. At the time of my purchase of the flat, I was fully qualified to do so, so there was no ground to evict me either. Various harassments to the occupants of the flat and to myself took place in an effort to stampede me into relinquishing the flat. These efforts included raids by immigration and narcotics agents and threatening legal letters. The HDB-created problem of my ownership was finally resolved with the passing of an amendment to the Housing & Development Act in 1975 made retrospectively so that any owner of an HDB flat who subsequently owned other property is obliged under law to relinquish it. The acquisition of my flat by HDB is now in the final stages, bringing to a close a period of harassment now that it has been made legal.

Recently, I was invited by the University of Singapore Students' Union to participate in a forum during the Freshmen Orientation Week on "Cultural Subversion". In my talk, I discussed the emergence of two cultures: one, the culture of control and obedience and the other the culture of freedom and liberation. I explained that because of our greater knowledge and more liberal pattern of family relationships and also due to greater individuality, there has emerged more distinctly a feeling amongst people of their own right as well as a sense of freedom, I explained that each one in his own existence in this society has to contend with these two directly opposed cultures and at some point a decision has to be made which culture one wishes to promote as no decision is a decision to go along with the dominant culture of control and obedience.

Political and bureaucratic pressures on me and my firm increased over the years. But this pressure cannot be pinpointed or specifically proved as it was so skilfully applied and there was always some room for ambiguity. Though we somehow managed to survive as a firm until now, the build-up of pressure is such that the partnership now feels that the survival of our practice is in serious jeopardy. The other four partners have consequently decided to dissolve Design Partnership as on 31 October 1975 and to resume practice under a new firm called DP Architects (Pte) excluding me. This in itself is evidence of political harassment against me as my partners and I have no professional, financial or personality differences which necessitate such a step. These are the mechanics chosen by my four partners and it is tantamount to my expulsion from our partnership in the face of mounting pressure. As to my future professional plans, I have decided not to set up an architectural practice at least in the foreseeable future. This also helps in the transition of jobs now commissioned to Design Partnership to be transferred to DP Architects (Pte) with the minimum of problems, I have also with the other partners jointly recommended to our clients to re-appoint the new firm to carry on the jobs as the reason for my expulsion has nothing to do with professional, financial or personality differences but are due entirely to pressures experienced by the partners of Design Partnership as a firm.

Personally, I will continue to examine my environment in a spirit of concern and to develop a greater empathy with those who are suffering in my society.

Signed:
Tay Kheng Soon

05

A Tribute to the Malayan Generation

This essay is a tribute to the "Malayan". It is about that cosmopolitan and expansive character of persons of Chinese, Indian, Malay, Eurasian and European descent, who inhabited British Malaya from the early 20th century onwards. They have a distinct set of values. This is their story.

The Malayan cluster of values, ideals and sentiments grew from seeds planted by Sir Stamford Raffles and other forward-looking British administrators. Teachers and clergy of both European and Asian extraction were role models who inspired them with their values and sentiments. When Malaysians and Singaporeans of the Malayan generations meet, they find much in common. That is the extent to which Malayan values still exist. Malayans are united by their English education background and their lingua franca. They possess an affinity and affection for the place. Their education gave them a modern outlook. Malayan self-determination was thus the natural product of Malayan sentiment and enlightenment. The independence movement was launched after the war. Malaya became independent in 1957. Singapore attained self-government in 1959. It merged with Malaya, Sabah and Sarawak to form Malaysia in 1963. On 9 August 1965, Singapore separated from Malaysia and became an independent nation.

Malayan Values

The modern, moderate and humane attitudes which characterise Malayan values, were embedded in the structures of everyday life in the upper reaches of society and to a certain extent in the street mass culture. The Malayan as a distinct group ranged from the upper to lower middle

A New World in the Making

classes of every race. They place an emphasis on modernisation and the importance of secular institutions associated with economic growth despite their different political complexions. They possess systematic administration and modern institutions. This is testimony to the same set of values they share. Though a minority, the Malayan is a moderate moderniser who imagined a future we now recognise as the present. However, there was by no means an unanimity in vision, for the future spanned the whole spectrum of political ideologies from extreme left to extreme right. The views even encompassed different geo-political configurations not confined to the Malayan peninsula and the island of Singapore. There were dreams of a pan-Malayan entity. Some harboured thoughts of a new Chinese hegemony, with Malaya as part of it.

To debate the prospect of independence, Singaporean and Malayan students in London formed the Malayan Forum in 1946. Some of the key personalities of today's political leadership were active in it. It was formed to discuss political ideas and to shape ideas for the future. This generation should therefore be called the "freedom fighters" of the immediate post-war period. Despite their political and ideological differences, they all shared a collective desire for modernity, human dignity and self-determination. In the ensuing struggle for primacy of ideas, a democratic modernism based on constitutionalism, with concessions made to ethnic and linguistic realities, emerged victorious. Despite the necessary compromise, the emerging political culture was premised on social tolerance, acceptance of ethnic diversity and it placed priority on a better material quality of life for all.

The transformations leading to the present were not inevitable or automatic. They were compromises derived from the complex social forces that existed. The minority English-educated Malayans led the constitutional direction. Once the rural and urban masses, mobilised by the Chinese and Malay vernacular-educated elite, entered the political fray, their combined motive power became a major factor in politics. Malayan ideals, as an English-educated phenomenon, had to strike a workable compromise before independence could be secured without bloodshed. This succeeded. The reality today is the result of the continuing evolution of that original compromise. The compromise was between English-inspired liberal, democratic ideals and the vernacular demand for an equal share of the pie. The workings of this compromise dictated the trajectory of change. In including and accommodating the vernacular masses in this march towards progress, Malayan values began to erode.

The Vernacular Dilemma

It is vital that we establish a proper perspective on the vernacular question. This concerns the marginalised status of the Malayan Chinese-educated intelligentsia and the Malayan Malay intellectual class under British colonial rule. A proper perspective is that the problems of economic backwardness facing the Chinese in Malaya were identical to those faced by the rural Malays. Both were marginalised by the British but for different reasons. For the Chinese, it was because they were a potential threat to British imperialist interests in the East as they had been in China. Chinese manners and values were also unattractive to British sensibilities. On the whole, the British found the Chinese difficult to mould to their designs. They were suspicious of them. The rural Malay was the victim of a British policy that denied modernisation to the Malays in the belief that rice production would suffer. They therefore kept the rural Malay in a benign state of backwardness. By fiat, they were denied English education.

The tragedy for the Chinese was and still is the fact that their budding sensibilities of place were short-lived. The Chinese intelligentsia's growing affection for the people and place was cut short by events beyond their control. Having lived in Malaya for a long time, they earned a livelihood and acquired a modicum of security that enabled their intelligence and talent to emerge in a creative form. From this group, a nascent but large body of Malayan Chinese art and literature emerged. Over time, this could have matured and transformed growing affinity into affection. It could have made a tremendous difference to life in Malaya, the Malays and triggered the evolution towards a more broad-based Malayan culture. But this was not to be. Post-independence events were not conducive. The growth and expression of Malayan Chinese affection for the place through the growth of sensibilities rooted in Malayan soil is thus still tentative. The nation-building process has long neglected this important and unfinished business. It is hoped that through directly addressing this issue as Malaya's tragedy that it will be recognised. The prospect of the evolution of a vibrant new Malayan consciousness depends on this in Singapore and

Malaysia. As it is, a tentativeness continues to retard the blossoming of a truly modern, tropical, Southeast Asian identity.

Malayan Nationalism

The growing affinity and affection for both people and place, together with a modern outlook, produced Malayan nationalism. Goaded by the real and perceived injustice of colonial rule, Malayan independence drew its fervour from these factors. Despite a colonial education system aimed at producing low-level clerical staff and the like, the English schools and the church broadened the Malayan mind. The latter, through its broad social and educational mission, gave a sense of justice, morality and to one's fellow man. Higher education heightened a sense of dignity and purposefulness later. The defeat of the British by the Japanese destroyed ideas of British invincibility. It gave courage to the notion of self-rule. In all their experiences, the English-educated Malayan tended to be moderate in their outlook—a product of British liberalism and Enlightenment ideas, acquired in schools and through the work of the church missions in hospitals, schools and the social services. It was this sense of moderation that finally prevailed in the struggle for independence. Thus, the Malayan contributed pivotally to shaping contemporary life in Singapore and Malaysia. These humanistic roots of Malayan history need to be properly acknowledged. Malayan-ism as a distinct outlook began with the establishment of law and order by the British. It accelerated with the opening of English-medium schools and peaked when higher education was established in 1926. Its steady decline occurred during the process of nation-building. With a strong emphasis on the sciences, the humanities were displaced in the education system. Bilingualism eroded the Malayan sensibilities, humour and understatement that are grounded in English. These developments irretrievably eroded the basis of Malayan-ism.

The Malayan Personality

The Malayan is tuned to the Malayan landscape, peoples, and the flora and fauna of Malesia. He or she possesses a broadness of vision and a decency in dealing that was acquired from the best of the British. The Malayan make-up is founded on a special fondness for the land, its smells, places and past times; indeed, its poetry. The Malayan is mostly English educated. The sound of the Malayan voice is unmistakable. His or hers is not an English voice. The Malayan speaks two kinds of English; one with a characteristic diction with turns of phrase and intonation unique and unmistakable, and the other which employs Malay and Hokkien colloquialisms with diminutives and concessionary gestures to soften the impact in case the utterances come across too hard. Through gesture, the Malayan communicates inclusiveness and candour. The Malayan possesses a broadness of interests beyond his or her field of specialisation. He or she has a love for quiet wit and studied understatement and a love of unpretentious beauty. He or she is simple in dress and unpretentious in choice of building style. He or she takes pride in being able to get along with different strata of society and possesses a Samaritan-like kindness. He or she believes in fair play, at work and at play. The Malayan has tidy personal habits at the table and is considerate towards others in public places. These were all learnt from the best of the British, encountered in their roles as teacher, pastor and friend, as distinct from their other role as ruler and enforcer. As such, the hallmark of the Malayan character is open and generous.

And thus, despite the political separation in 1965 of Singapore from Malaysia, the Malayan on both sides of the Causeway still retains, at an emotional level, a love of the undivided land, even though he or she now accepts the new political reality of separation. Malayan sentiments, though never really conscious, underpinned Malayan nationalism. In the events post-World War II, these sentiments shaped Malayan politics. It is not the task of this essay to enter a discussion of Malayan politics, but the intention is to draw out the deep-seated sentiments and affinities which gave and continue to give meaning to the shaping of the Malayan landscape though in much diminished ways today.

The Malayan Landscape and Pastimes

The Malayan landscape had a distinct character, a certain natural gracefulness in the mix of British, Malay, Chinese and Indian buildings and whole quarters set in a sea of tropical lushness. The effect is not Dutch colonial, not French colonial, but unmistakably British Malayan colonial. How does this character come across? The character of the Malayan landscape was created by British administrators, engineers and architects. They imbued it with a taste for the simple, the natural and the poetic in most of what they did and constructed in Malaya. The Malayan, being English-educated and therefore higher in the pecking order of the colonised society, constituted the old middle-class. They were the ones who imbibed the most British values. Their means and confidence allowed them more leisure to experiment, and to indulge in a broad spectrum of interests. They continued to set the tone and taste of the place until the emergence of a new middle-class years later. Tastes and manners then changed beyond recognition.

In the old quarters of the cities and town of Singapore and Malaysia, modest embellishment and refined proportions of utilitarian or grand structures built by the British and local builders are juxtaposed against the native huts set among coconut palms, flame trees, and *dusun*. This natural landscape quality can be seen in the old law courts and administrative buildings, the civic centres of the main Malayan towns, hospital buildings, rest houses, hill stations, military cantonments, mosques and schools designed by the Public Works Department. In the countryside, the effect is evident, with verdant unmanicured growth occasionally disrupted by the pointed tips of Malay huts and mosques. There is a non-striving sort of accommodation between power, piety, people and place that somehow lingers on in the mind of the Malayan.

These are the settings which all Malayans remember: Strolling along the waterfront, the natural beauty of the reservoirs, satay by the beach, family outings to the museum, the diminutive scale of civic buildings, *sarabat* stalls beneath old trees, gathering places in kampongs, coconut groves and lallang patches, tenements, street-side stalls, European bungalows on spacious lawns, the exclusivity of the European institutions, Cold Storage supermarkets, swimming clubs and golf courses, double-breasted shark-skin suits and white-spat shoes, ladies in *cheongsam* or *sam-fu*, *baju kurong, sarong kebaya*, P. Ramlee movies and Cathay Keris films, taxi dancing at the cabarets, dedicated teachers with broad interests, switching between perfect English diction and the local patois, Malay/Hokkien interspersed speech, lurking Chinese idealism, Indian lawyers and beer at railway bars, bullying clerks and brawling British sailors. Malaya was all these and more. But the regrettable decline of Malayan-ness as a casualty of progress and forgetfulness is the result of a new-found consciousness.

Being

For it is a truism that one is seldom aware of ones' culture until one is about to lose it. Thus, in this event, a consciousness of what it means to be a Malayan becomes clearer suddenly. This is a moment that must not be lost. Malayans want to remember.

Affinity, Affiliation and Allegiance

The Malayan was, however, never fully conscious of their identity. They could not step away from their colonised mental status to consciously affirm their own identity. What constituted their affinity, their affiliations and their allegiance therefore remained largely unclear. Their identity vacillated between these—a Westernised oriental person of Malay, Chinese or Indian descent and that of a modern but localised Malayan. They had to contend with their multi-layered identities as they switched back and forth between them as situations and sentiments warranted. In the period just before and after independence, the Malayan harboured to the greatest extent such mixed identities. This period also harboured a social dynamic in which rejecting British imperialism meant rejecting all things British. The necessary involvement of the Malayan masses in this transition played a significant part in the erosion of the Malayan identity through its rejection of British values and the British contribution. Thus, the Malayan character was and still is under assault. This is the abiding Malayan dilemma. Political rhetoric does not resolve an essentially emotional issue. The inexorable rise of a new middle class predicated on materialism and devoid of all consciousness of their Malayan-ness condemned the Malayan identity to its inevitable extinction. Pragmatics and economics dominated the human imagination. The external conditions of life were being reshaped for a new age of material consumption. All emotional matters were put on hold. We thus have a nationalism with little sentiment. Malayan affinities and sensibilities await favourable conditions to re-root. And if the Malayan mind-space is not the basis for a re-rooting, what is possibly there that is authentic to the Malayan experience?

The Malayan Identity

One cannot discuss Malayan identity without discussing the situation of the Chinese intelligentsia and that of the masses. Chinese-educated Malayans could not and did not have the opportunity to articulate their

A New World in the Making

Malayan emotions clearly enough to be able to relocate their sentiments from China to Malaya during the period of British rule. They were focused on the problems of Chinese backwardness and foreign domination and exploitation. In this sense, the Chinese-educated class already saw through the British ploy of oriental enlightenment merely as part of British imperialism. Their antipathy towards English-educated Malayans can be seen in this light. They regarded them with reservation. The feeling was mutual. It is also a sad fact that under the British, they had nothing to gain and actually suffered negative discrimination from the imposed social and economic order. The British were naturally suspicious of the Chinese. The Chinese were thus marginalised in the colonial scheme of things. Of course, in the circumstances, the Chinese intellectual developed no affinity whatsoever for British manners and ways. They were thus not in tune with the kind of Malaya being imagined and fashioned. Chinese passion for liberation as an act of resistance was later to find expression in the united front tactics of political mobilisation towards independence and nation-building thereafter. In the meanwhile, China absorbed all their emotional and intellectual energies. Despite this, it must be said, Chinese writers and painters did express their natural artistic responses in a not insignificant body of work that reflected budding Chinese Malayan sensibilities. Such budding sensibilities were, however, interrupted by events beyond. The Chinese-educated Malayan thus remained in cultural limbo as far as the notion of Malaya was concerned. In the period of post-independence nation-building and with a resurgent new China, the problems of realising the "Malayan Project", an authentic identity and culture rooted in Malayan sensibilities, remains unfulfilled. Is it to remain unfulfillable?

In the meanwhile, unburdened by intellectual considerations, the Chinese, Indian and Malay masses who were not formally educated were actively localising their lives through adopting and adapting diverse Malayan cultures in their everyday lives in the cities, towns and villages of Malaya. Through the mere fact of living, an affinity with the place was inexorably being formed. This is localisation, the first step towards rootedness. The results of the process can clearly be seen in the street culture. In the evolution of street food, street language, street humour and street theatre, the adaptive and creative process was taking place with vigour. The process of adaptation, integration and creative invention of the social and cultural milieu was taking place in a totally unconscious and uninhibited manner. A Malayan culture was being formed. Here was the affinity of people and place being enacted daily.

But throughout the Malayan period, all Malayans experienced mixed sentiments towards the British. This was a love-hate relationship which continued well into the post-independence period. In the case of the English-educated Chinese, Indian and Malays, especially of the generations prior to independence, the amplitude in this vacillation increased greatly as independence drew nearer. This fuelled the extremism in political ideologies which swung from extreme left to extreme right. In all cases, however, they were uniform in their affinity, affiliation and allegiance towards Malaya which had been awakened as their obligations and enforced allegiance to Britain weakened after its defeat at the hands of the Japanese in World War II. This added confidence to the drive produced by emotional compulsion, propelling the independence movement forward. The Malayan came to the fore, but the cultural ambivalence remained through the period of nation-building. When will the time come to address unfinished emotional business?

Essays

In 1975 my essay on the challenges faced in Singapore's public transport planning was published in a booklet titled "Transport dilemma in Singapore". This was one of the illustrations.

06

Essays

THE CULTURAL ROLE OF SINGAPORE CITY
1 June 1966

An essay written a few months after the separation of Singapore from Malaysia. It was published in the Singapore Institute of Architects' journal, Rumah.

In the context of a newly independent Singapore, while it is vital to give economic development top priority, the problems of cultural and social integration are equally important in the process of nation building and the evolution of a national identity. Industrialisation has broken down racial barriers by creating job opportunities which are not dependent on traditional ethnic and family backgrounds but on individual and educational merits instead. In our housing and educational programmes, we should also cope with the problems of integrating the various ethnic groups. The city core can also play an important role in the social and cultural integration by having points of convergence for the people to participate in common activities of work and recreation. It is through this close contact of people that all the diverse talents, trends and forces meet, react, blend and develop, and hence there is a hope for a genuine integrated culture to emerge.

Culture as we define it, is the total effort of a people in organising and expressing their corporate life. Culture is therefore not only the revival of tradition and the veneration thereof, but the sum of all the activities that enrich the life of a people. Thus painting, sculpture, architecture, literature, drama, films, sports and all the other media of mass communication contribute to culture. As such, it forms an integral part of everyday living. The city of Singapore as a seaport, dependent on entrepot trade, is young in existence and had attracted people of various ethnic backgrounds. This migrant population under colonial rule was impeded and discouraged towards the development of nationalism. Consequently, Singapore like Kuala Lumpur and Penang have developed with a governmental, administrative, commercial and recreational centre for the colonialists, surrounded by settlements of concentrated ethnic groups with their own centres.

This form of our city is anachronistic in the new era of independence. Fifty percent of our population is under 21 years old and are local born. Unlike their parents, they have no yearning to return to their ancestral lands. As many parts of our city need to be redeveloped, we should take the opportunity to plan our city with a core for an integrated population and make it play a more vital role in its cultural development.

The prime importance in the planning of such a core is to make it conducive to attract people of different races and at all levels to participate in the activities offered. Therefore, it should not be only commercial, but should have other functions incorporated into it, such as cultural, social, recreational and residential. These functions by their very nature complement one another. It is only through the intense multi-usage of land that the city can be transformed into a hive of activities both by day and by night. The problem of traffic in the core should not be overlooked. There must be pedestrian and traffic segregation to give pedestrian safety and ease of traffic movement, and at the same time the pedestrians and city dwellers will be comparatively free from the fumes and roar of traffic.

Just imagine in our city where there are pedestrian precincts, with offices, shops, restaurants, art galleries, museums, concert halls, cinemas, community centres and they are all easily accessible to the people from their high-rise flats as well as from their multi-racial residential areas. The shops, restaurants, and cafes with their brightly lit displays will be opened day and night to cater for all types of crowds, such as those in the Ginza of Tokyo, Piccadilly of London and Champs Elysees of Paris. People can shop and walk in comfort and safety. These will contribute to the image of the city in its cultural role and be identified by the local people and visitors as representing the nation. Raffles Place and its immediate vicinity can be transformed into such a precinct. As at the moment, it is mainly commercial. The area can be vitalised both day and night by the injection of entertainment, night shopping and eating facilities. Another example is Chinatown, which has, however, developed in spite of lack of conscious planning. The cinemas, shops, People's Park eating stalls and high-density cubicle dwellings have created this stretch of New Bridge Road into a vital centre of activities day and night. This phenomenon is largely unplanned and has therefore many attendant unsavoury features such as an inherent traffic problem in which vehicles and people intermix to the peril of both. The high-density cubicle dwellings while giving life to the place is at the same time extremely unhealthy and insanitary. The challenge in our new urban redevelopment programmes is: can we recreate areas of such activities and integrate the different ethnic groups while maintaining good planning and health standards?

The building of a core in Singapore, which is more than a commercial and administrative centre entails vast expenditure, but it must be argued that this expenditure is as necessary as expenditure on economic development. At the present moment, vast amounts of money are being spent on urban development and renewal projects, multi-storey carparks, and road improvement schemes, public monuments and civic buildings to name but some of them. The question is one of objective. Is the objective of these projects far reaching or are they ad-hoc in nature? Does the sum total of the effect of these projects contribute to the creation of a city which can perform its cultural function so vital in the creation of national identity? Therefore, there is necessity to re-evaluate the impact of these projects in a broader context. We must also account for rapid changes in the social order in our time when obsolescence may threaten our new developments soon after they are completed. It is therefore a challenge to the people and to the capacity for vision and ingenuity of our political leaders and planners in establishing policies upon which our cultural city of tomorrow will emerge.

THE FUTURE OF ASIAN CITIES
May 1966

This article for the Singapore Planning and Urban Research Group (SPUR) expounded on new urban redevelopment and was published in the Hong Kong-based Asia Magazine.

Imagine a city where we have dwellings that stretch upwards towards the sky, and beneath them people humming with activity in the business houses, governmental offices, educational centres, theatres, open spaces and recreational centres. Imagine a city where the various centres of activity are linked up by an efficient rapid transport system, where traffic hazards are eliminated by the well-conceived siting of pedestrian precincts and traffic ways and where these are no peak hour traffic jams and car parking problems. Imagine a city where people make their living by day where people live by night. Centres of entertainment and culture in the heart of the city that light up in the evening when the tempo of our business houses subsides. Schools right beneath where you live, where problems of transport and safety for your children are eliminated. Open spaces that serve as resting places for the weary shopper in the day, playgrounds for the children in the afternoon, and open grounds for the aged or the weary worker in the evenings. Spaces where people can sit and enjoy the sessions of storytelling, hear the occasional performance of their local band, or watch the gaiety and grace of their local dancers. Imagine clean parks and roads free from scores of hawkers and street vendors, and open drains unlittered. This is our "Asian City of Tomorrow".

The world-wide problem of this age is: too many people. Conflict ranging from minor skirmishes to war results from the inability to cope with the population expansion. Population excess has led Japan into the Second World War and now we hear of expansionist inclinations amongst the more hard-pressed Asian nations. The population of the world at the turn of the century was 1.5 billion; it was doubled by 1960. By the end of this century, it will be doubled again to six billion (6,000,000,000). And Asia is burdened with the greater proportion of this population blight. Half of the world lives in Asia and thus by the year 2000, the population will be three billion. Apropos with the Asian population explosion every one of us must inevitably ask what will happen to human settlements in our portion of this planet in years to come. We must expect radical transformations, not only in the concept of urban society as we know it now, but also in the urban form. The question is: How? It must be defined now.

In emergent countries, many of the cities began as trading centres under colonial influence. With independence, the role of these cities has changed; some into capital cities, others, to keep pace with growth and the urbanisation of population, require drastic overhaul. With independence has also come new and greater expectations; expectations that can only be allayed with tangible improvements in living standards and conditions. Where colonial governments could ignore substandard living conditions, a nationalist government cannot. Yet many nationalist governments have hardly begun to direct the shift of resources to the production of and investment in capital equipment. Capital accumulation is a necessary condition for any societies' survival and progress. National monuments, temples, pyramids, mansions, jewellery, and not least, warfare, are ill afforded means of squandering current saving.

The by-word of today is industrialisation. To industrialise, large amounts of both capital and human labour are required to develop roads, railways, dams, power stations, factory buildings, and the machines for them. It has been found true in the past that in a free enterprise economy, the transition of an agricultural society into an industrialised one is accompanied first by the presence of flourishing trade. The industrialist is inevitably from the ranks of the mercantile sector. This is particularly evident in the case of Britain where in the 17th and 18th century the sudden expansion of the mercantile sector brought about the emergence of the first Industrial Revolution. The preconditions for rapid industrialisation means that we can no longer forestall the development of efficient cities; cities that enhance trading facilities at the same time conserve the limited resources for capital accumulation.

Sixty per cent of Indians, that is 240 million people, subsist on an income of less than M$45 per month, and half of these have an income of less than M$36 per month. Malaysia and Singapore are fortunate to be able to enjoy the highest per capita income in Southeast Asia— the income being M$800 and around M$1,300 respectively.

The previous average for Malaysia as a whole of M$860 was twice the per capita income level of Thailand or the Philippines. Whilst this might appear to be satisfactory in the Asian context, this level of

A New World in the Making

income is perhaps seven to eight times behind the average developed Western countries.

Having dealt with the scale of incomes, let us examine the human scale within Asian cities. In common with present day societies, there exists a trend of migration from the countryside to the towns. The cause of this "rural-urban drift" lies in the attraction of the cities with the possibilities of more profitable employment, better standards of living, fuller range of social services and other amenities. But this common problem that cities face is different in Asia because the scale is magnified and the resources available to deal with the situation are limited.

Britain in the 1970s will witness a surge to the cities to the extent that 65 per cent of British citizens will be living in these areas. The Russians estimate the size of their problem as this: 33 per cent of their people are city dwellers now, thirty years hence it will have increased to 50 per cent. If we take it that Asia's share in the growth of world population at the end of this century to be three billion, and we assume, conservatively, that one-sixth of this increase is to be allotted to the cities, the nett result is a further 500 million people more than the total population of Western Europe. The question that will arise is: Will Asians then have approached anywhere near the affluence of Western Europe today? No answer is needed.

Are there any limits to the size of a city? Calcutta has a population of seven million and Tokyo, 10 million. Can these cities really cope? In Calcutta, the problem of securing basic necessities such as a good water supply is unsurmountable. Only 22 per cent of the city of Tokyo is served by a modern sewage system. In the remaining areas, sewage flows into unsanitary ditches. Tokyo also suffers from a shortage of water and the suspension of water supply occurs at many places during the summer. But even assuming that there is adequate supply, there is still the problem of filling the gap between the supply lines that have been installed before the war and the additional population which make use of them now. The disparity of these and other amenities such as power supply, roads, educational facilities, etc., will have no opportunity to catch up with demand unless the population is stabilised. All indications are that cities must be limited in size.

What then are the positive steps that can be taken to deal with the over-concentration in large cities? The two most widely propagated theories are the construction of satellite towns and urban renewal. Whilst the intention of satellite or new towns is to relieve the population pressure in the mother cities by the creation of job opportunities and living accommodation some distance away, but by the very nature of the proximity and dependence on the mother city, they often fail in the purpose and assume the role of dormitory towns or huge commuter housing schemes. On the other hand, the relevance of urban renewal schemes is undoubtedly necessary for many parts of our outmoded cities. Yet, in view of the limited resources, extreme care must be exercised in the selection of areas to be renewed. The destruction of any part of the city for rebuilding is destruction of national assets. It must always be borne in mind that urban renewal is costly and brings with it higher rents, often to the very areas which can least afford it. The Singapore Housing & Development Board found that despite the Board's moderate rentals of between M$20 to M$60 it was still beyond the rent paying ability of 30 to 40 per cent of the population in the central area. It is clear that neither satellite towns nor urban renewal is likely to relieve the pressure over much or stem the tide of the drift to the city.

A radical economic policy aimed at securing a balanced development to the country as a whole must be pursued. A policy that reaches beyond rural development projects and their aims to increase agricultural output; but further to implant and expand social amenities in the form of education, public health, shopping facilities, entertainments and other community services to rural centres. Wherever possible, industries which are insensitive to location should be moved out to provide employment for the seasonal unemployed. In other words, to initiate a more equitable distribution of wealth between the rural and city folk. Unless this is done effectively within the context of a democratic form of government, then the likelihood of an authoritarian take-over is inevitable as exemplified by the restriction of population movement practiced in China.

What of the urban form itself? Not quite the phoenix from the ashes. In Asian cities tomorrow, the new will grow side by side with the old. We have pointed out the danger of indiscriminate urban renewal. Cities are the results of evolution. We would want local character and local identity to be preserved, but on the other hand we must not make the mistake of identifying the requirements of modern living and the process of industrialisation with de-Orientalisation.

A New World in the Making

Anyone with any appreciation for the sense of a city will agree that a true city is a congested city, congestion not of cars but of people drawn close together by a multitude of related activities. We must reject outdated planning principles that seek to segregate man's activities into arbitrary zones, no matter how attractive it may look in ordered squares on a land use map. We must reject arbitrary standards laid down that limit the intensive use of land. Rather there should be in cities many areas that are of multiple land use where all the advantages of city living—shops, schools, recreation and even work, if not for the main breadwinner, for those who seek a supplementary income—is never far away.

Two-dimensional planning on the horizontal should give way to planning in four dimensions: introducing the element of the vertical (buildings in height) and the element of time (in transportation and programming of areas for building).

High buildings will be the norm rather than the exception. The technology of high buildings today in the development of reinforced concrete and of lifts makes it feasible as an effective planning tool. With high buildings it IS possible to achieve densities of more than 1,000 persons to an acre without entirely banishing nature from the city. With high buildings, there is hope of restoring or maintaining (as the case may be) a semblance of balance to a man's working day where ideally a third of it should be spent on sleep, work and leisure; instead of the situation where commuters spend as much as three to four hours on travelling. High buildings synonymous with high concentration of population makes a mass rapid transit system viable, or better still, eliminate travelling by living above one's place of work. High buildings mean a saving in services: roads, water, sewerage, gas, electricity mains. Five hundred dwellings in a single building require three miles of services placed vertically and only 500 yards of road. Five hundred dwellings in individual houses require a total of 35 miles of services and 3.5 miles of roads, quite apart from the savings of 500 individual systems of foundations and individual roofs, both costly items.

For reasons of economy, it would seem inevitable that we shall live in higher concentration and only by a more intensive use of land and by checking urban sprawl can we hope to accommodate the geometrically-accelerating population growth. To some people, there is a real need for a bit of outdoor space as an extension to the house especially for young children. And some planners in Western countries will even say that there can be no family life at densities much above 70 persons per acre. Yet what glamour is there in the many low-density housing estates? What intimate dialogue between man and nature is there attached to a house standing on a piece of ground 24-by-100 feet with his neighbours in identical houses surrounding his? Cultural obsolescence! These so-called park developments and garden estates. If we look into our Asian cities, you will find that Asians have been conditioned to live in a highly concentrated manner. What we want is to find the right living pattern for our present needs and the right symbols to satisfy our present cultural aspirations.

Cities were built in a radial pattern around a harbour, mouth of river, railway terminus; or were situated so as to incorporate a number of these and other natural advantages—suitability for defence, protection of a rich agricultural plain, etc. The factors to which they owe their origin then is no longer valid now. Our industrial working-class cities have been freed from these considerations with the progress of modern technology—road transport, piped water supply. Further, the growing complexity of cities makes it imperative that we strive for a more organic city form. The radial plan has given rise to problems of "ribbon development", choking our main traffic arteries; of areas known as "twilight zones" in planning circles, where the concentric expansion of the city has passed over these once fashionable areas, which are now in the shadow of the prosperous city and are now slums; of sporadic and isolated development resulting in the necessity of constantly relaying all the services as witnessed by the common sight of roads being dug up. As a result of intuitive radial planning, millions have been spent on ring roads linking perimeter communities without alleviation of traffic jams. A traffic survey would have shown that the main "desire lines" contradicted this assumption.

The idea of a lineal city is coming into favour. It is free of the traffic confusion of a radial city, which by extension and improvement of roads bring more confusion to the centre. Because the lineal city can be controlled along certain lines of growth, it would permit frictionless expansion and renewal when the cycle of regeneration occurs. As mentioned earlier, it is important to program areas for building so that the public services provided are fully utilised. It is just as foolish to under build as to over build.

Land, like the water we drink, like the air we breathe, is a commodity that is the right of all men. In cities where it is apparent that there is a

A New World in the Making

crisis in population growth and therefore a desperate need to apportion the use of land in a planned fashion, can laissez faire ownership of land continue? Whilst we are not suggesting that a section of the community should be penalised for the public good (indeed, it is not necessary), it has been found practicable to initial agrarian reform in the country. Is it not timely to introduce urban land reform as the kind of planning executed is directly limited by political policy and the legal powers taken on by a government to ensure its implementation?

With the pressure of population, the continual rural-urban drift to seek employment, and the demands of industrialisation, we are all pressing hard upon the city. The oversized city in an underdeveloped country will become a squalid hot bed of disease and human degradation. In the attempt to catch up with the rest of the world, faced with limited resources being in the main primary producing countries, Asian planners must exercise ingenuity, imagination and foresight in planning their cities. But no amount of ingenuity can make up for a lack of political leadership for any planning action must be accompanied by a political decision.

Essays

COLLYER QUAY'S 12-LANE COASTAL SUPERHIGHWAY
5 July 1967

This letter for the Singapore Planning & Urban Research (SPUR) Group was sent to The Straits Times *and* Nanyang Siang Pau *and sparked an exchange with the Housing & Development Board.*

Dear Sir,

While we applaud the Government's concern in regenerating decayed parts of our city by its urban renewal programme, we would like to raise some queries on the proposed 12-lane coastal superhighway linking Collyer Quay to the Bedok reclamation area. Your readers may not be generally aware of this proposal since the recent publicity has been highlighting the 14 proposed urban renewal sites, but this proposed superhighway and related extensive reclamation of the Singapore seafront are illustrated in the S$50 brochure released by the Urban Renewal Department of the Housing & Development Board.

It has been generally known for some time that a new coastal road was to be constructed in conjunction with the Bedok reclamation but the full implications of this proposal were not seen until plans showing this superhighway were revealed two weeks ago via the brochure publicising the 14 urban renewal sites. It is regrettable that such a major undertaking which will have serious visual and environmental impact on our city and on the lives of its citizens should not be given more publicity to kindle greater public interest. While on the one hand, the public is urged to exercise greater social discipline with respect to public property, as the Prime Minister and other government officials have been stressing, it is just as necessary for the public to be brought into greater participation in civic developments which affect their lives.

It is only by publicising civic projects and inviting views and criticisms from the public at large that it is possible to promote greater civic pride and responsibility. In evolving from a transient society of the past into a new society determined to stay, civic pride and civic values do not come naturally, and continued lack of opportunity for public participation only serves to create more disinterest in civic affairs.

This proposal of a superhighway and related reclamation areas is a fit subject for public scrutiny and comment as it has such a major effect on environment. The superhighway as illustrated, however, has insufficient

129

information to mount an objective evaluation but the subject is of such great importance that we have to pose certain queries based on what has been revealed although this may be preliminary. The section showing Collyer Quay seems, however, very firm and we would like to begin our queries here.

Collyer Quay

As the plans only show the new superhighway continuing from Bedok at Tanjong Rhu and running up to Collyer Quay on the reclaimed part outside Elizabeth Walk, we would like to ask if it is the intention to terminate this superhighway at Collyer Quay or to continue it through the central business district to connect the west coast of Singapore. If it is the intention to terminate at Collyer Quay, then the whole theory of bringing vast numbers of vehicles into the heart of the city is questionable. Would it not be more reasonable to terminate this highway somewhere outside the central business district at large capacity multi-storey carparks and allowing people to come into the city by means of public transport.

If, however, it is the intention to extend this superhighway to connect with the west coast and Jurong, we wish to question the validity of allowing East/West traffic to cut through the central business district, and heavy trucking traffic at that. Even if recent traffic origin and destination surveys show that there is little desire for traffic to go from East to West, what is to guarantee that this superhighway will not create the desire for this movement once it is built. This superhighway, whether it terminates in the city or cuts through it, is costly in environmental terms for a 12-lane superhighway is an effective visual and physical barrier.

Collyer Quay is extremely strategic in economic and planning terms and is Singapore's more prestigious site as well. If properly developed, it could be what Times Square is to New York, the Champ Elysees is to Paris and the Ginza is to Tokyo, all of which have one common denominator: being pedestrian orientated and not vehicle orientated. The possibility of an intensely active, gay, and thronging sea fronting place, full of people on foot, would be lost if it were isolated by cars, mechanical noise and fumes. Singapore city as a man-made entity would have lost its opportunity to express its uniqueness as a city grown from the sea.

Essays

The highway, reclaimed land and recreational areas

The problem of the superhighway's effect on environment is a universal one and careful thought has to be paid to minimise its undesirable aspects. A narrow strip of land left over is just not good enough especially when it is flanked by a roaring 12-lane superhighway. With the increasing demand for land for development commensurate with a fast-growing population, the coasts are extremely valuable recreational areas to be preserved. The proposal as shown needs to consider its effect on the coast and recreational environment. Again, we would request for public viewing of details of this scheme. Many countries have learnt too late that their motorways, autobahns and turnpikes testify to their thoughtless carving up of their cities and countryside. We can afford few mistakes in such a small country as ours.

It has been announced that from Collyer Quay, it would be possible "through landscaped settings" to walk all the way to Kallang Park via Elizabeth Walk. (*The Straits Times,* 24 Jun 1967.) We wish to point out firstly, that the whole object of Elizabeth Walk as a seaside promenade would have been altered by the proposed reclamation which stretches out from it seaward by 3,000 yards. We feel that the citizens of Singapore should have a say about this and be presented with full details showing the proposals and the alternative promenades, if any, being provided. However, for pedestrians to get from Collyer Quay to Elizabeth Walk, it would be necessary to cross the new superhighway, we would like to know how this is to be effected. Is it by elevating the highway to allow free access below or is a tunnel or an overhead footbridge intended? Detailed plans should be exhibited for public viewing and comments.

The point we wish to emphasise is civic development is for the people. The people, ought to be consulted. The railing along Nicoll Highway which obliterates the view, and bus shelters and multi-coloured concrete slabs at Pasir Ris spoiling a natural beauty spot are examples of "civic improvements" which could have been avoided if these schemes were put to the public before they were implemented. We realise that this would mean allowing more time for projects, but such is the process of awakening civic and environmental consciousness in our people. Admonitions are futile if not backed up by opportunities for creative contribution in an atmosphere of nation building.

We write as members of the Singapore Planning and Urban Research Group, a private voluntary body consisting of planners, architects, surveyors and people from related fields in planning and most important, as citizens of Singapore, intimately concerned with the future of our environment. We hope that this letter will stimulate greater dialogue between all persons genuinely concerned with the future of our island city state as a pleasant place to live, to work and to play in. A place we can all be proud of.

Yours etc,
SPUR Group.

Essays

DEVELOPMENT AND ITS IMPACT ON CHANGING VALUES
June 1970

An essay written for Singapore Undergrad, *a magazine published by the then University of Singapore Students' Union.*

We are living in a period of rapid change. The industrial revolution and its concomitant process of modernisation as observed in Western Europe and the United States has evolved over a period of approximately 200 years. These societies', since the invention and the application of the steam engine to industrial purposes, have been transformed from a feudalistic society to a modern one with modern values necessary at each stage of the industrialisation process.

We have crossed the threshold of our industrialisation programme and it is likely that we will achieve a stage of affluence within 20 years instead of 200. This is assuming there are no major political upheavals in the region or elsewhere, which will retard the rate of progress. We are late comers in industrialisation and are therefore able to skip steps and take advantage of the latest technological and management skills, which are the basis for our accelerated development. As a consequence of this rapid change, we can expect considerable social, cultural and moral stresses to develop, notwithstanding the relatively youthful population who will be able to adapt faster to the change. The change affects the social, cultural and moral spheres as well as the physical environment which is undergoing rapid transformation.

The whole urban and rural landscape is undergoing rapid change as the result of land demands due to industrialisation, urbanisation and economic growth in all sectors. It is necessary and vital to consider the impact of this change in all these sectors since their impact will be felt in the immediate future and in the long run will pre-determine the quality of life which we are striving for. We should not make the mistakes of other industrialised countries who are now facing the impact of their negligence in the forms of social unrest and moral bankruptcy. We witness in these countries also the alienation of the younger generation, the decay of city centres, the spoliation of the countryside. The lack of recreational facilities, poor living and working environments due to congestion and pollution. In general, whilst these industrialised countries

A New World in the Making

have created affluence, they have not created the quality of life nor the living environment which should come with it. Moreover, the distribution of affluence itself leaves much to be desired and it is the poorer and less affluent who have to endure without relief the unwholesome by-products of the economic machine which produced that wealth. The wealthy too cannot escape from the pollution, the chaos and the moral decay. They however have the means and do increasingly use it to escape by travel and by other forms of psychological escape.

The most significant social and cultural impact of the relentless drive for industrialisation and economic development within a materialistic culture is the submergence of human sensitivities and the increasing alienation of individuals from society. This results from a centralisation of decision making at all levels which makes individuals more and more remote, resulting in a feeling of hopelessness. Different age groups feel the urgency of the alienation problem to different degrees. It is the younger generation who feel it most acutely and this whole area has popularly come to be called the "generation gap"! The older generation are more accepting of the feeling of alienation, and it results in their greater acquiescence and general apathetic attitude towards their total environment. The feeling of apathy in the younger generation is expressed in many forms modified by the prevailing social and cultural structures. It is often expressed in militant and extreme behaviour but more often it turns inwards and the individual "drops out of society" and goes into his private world. Drug taking is one of the results of the individual's withdrawal from society.

In our society, there is a more dangerous manifestation of social apathy: a sort of non-reaction, uninvolved attitude and this is something which can do great harm. Yet, this attitude can be understood when viewed in relation to the existing situation. Migrant values, cultural reflexes, plus the non-involvement conditioning during colonial days has created a situation where the individual is concerned only for his own personal survival and considers public and community matters as too remote to concern him. This attitude is further enforced by the lack of choice in a small community. Economic and other social pressures weigh heavily upon any individual who does not conform. In the face of such a situation, any intolerance displayed by any authority against non-conforming behaviour has multiple effects not only to the individual but upon like-thinking colleagues and the public at large, who, very often at the end, exercise the final censure on non-conforming behaviour. This kind of public reaction can be utilised to control the population in a totalitarian system. Therefore, we can see that there are strong motives for individuals to conform.

Yet, it is necessary to produce people with initiative and capable of creative thought and action, and an independence of opinion to be able to respond to the rapidly changing circumstances. Such people are necessary at all levels of society, and it is often difficult to single them out for special treatment. It is preferable that a general atmosphere of tolerance be created which will encourage the flowering of intellect and the development of initiative at all levels. It is unlikely that mass extreme antisocial or militant behaviour is likely in the present situation because society is the great equaliser. When there are yet opportunities for individuals to be involved in the total environment, such behaviour is unlikely. It only arises when there is a strong feeling of hopelessness and alienation from society at large. When individuals feel that there is nothing to lose and something to gain, they can be driven to desperate actions.

Research is to be undertaken to understand and to learn from western societies, which have preceded us in their industrialisation and social change, to gain insights and understanding and to seek their application into our context.

With the rapidity of change, we are in danger of a moral decay within society at all levels. Moral decay is not used here in any religious or moralistic sense, which tends to be cloudy with unclear value judgements. The term "moral decay" is used simply to denote the decline of intellectual integrity. In an atmosphere of expediency required by rapid change, we are all exposed to the choice between expediency and principle as a basis for action, and each individual comes to terms within his own brand of self-deception.

Without clear criteria or principles, decisions rely more upon compromise, bargain and convenience and corruption with all its subtleties thrives in such a climate. Open blatant corruption is not easily practiced in a close society and money is not the only means to corrupt with. In a small close society, the trading of favours, information, goodwill or its opposites are more the currency of corruption. The rule of law slowly, imperceptibly is edged aside in preference for administrative procedures outside the law, but which produce results. These are acquiesced to by the public and become "customary practice". The adherence to principle becomes increasingly considered as impractical as the need to conform becomes greater. The lines between situations become blurred, the white lie becomes fashionable, even admired. Is this the inevitable outcome of progress? Intellectual honesty is vital for clear analysis which must be the basis for action. Intellectuals are only human too, unfortunately. When society rewards dishonesty and penalises outrageous or embarrassing truth, then that society must inevitably fail not because of any sentimental attachment to honesty as an absolute superlative but because it will not have the capacity to undertake action based on true understanding. Even a meritocracy is doomed if the basis for reward shows a tendency towards non-principle or non-truth. A distinction must exist between principle and truth. A principle is what is honestly held as a truth. It is preferable to having an untruth held dishonestly. Truth itself is elusive enough, but if we adopt an anti-principle attitude, then we may not even know if we have been wrong in our understanding. In such a situation, it is no longer possible to escape the circumstances created by a landslide of untruths, piled one on top of another. When the intellectual is cowed by the forces around him and abetted by an apathetic public at large, then the landslide begins, and it takes superhuman efforts together with brutal methods to rectify the situation and another phase of history is born.

Involvement in the environment is vital for social health. Economic involvement is being actively pursued in the efforts to create jobs and produce affluence, but other forms of involvement have to be provided with equal vigour. Producing wealth and having an equitable means of distributing it is in itself meaningless unless coupled with education, quality of living and the provision of the means for that quality of living.

Can Singapore produce opportunities for a high quality of living which the people will aspire to in the long run? This is the question and the case for our leaders in their planning ahead to be farsighted. This is the reason for an aggressive social and cultural programme running in parallel with the economic programme.

The physical environment being the most lasting of the actions of today has to be looked at not only in its present context of fulfilling existing needs but in its future role. The buildings and the spaces which we build are certainly the environment of the affluent future society. We should therefore be courageous, far-sighted and very conscious that we

Essays

are planning and building the world of tomorrow today. We should not be too concerned with the skyline of our city. We should be more concerned about the ground line which is more relevant to the people and to the processes of the city.

The physical environment is more than a technical problem. It is a social and cultural problem. It is necessary to decide in broad terms the cultural role of the city, the type and extent of the rural environment that we should have. The extent of recreational facilities we will need is a vital necessity for the majority of the people. In an affluent society, a number of people will no doubt be able to seek their recreation through travel, but for the majority, recreation must be near at hand. The colonial government when it first planned Singapore as seen in the 1824 map, saw to it that there were no social or community foci in the city. The ethnic groups were separated into distinct groups around the city. Chinatown itself was planned as a series of separate parallel streets each reserved for one dialect group. There were no communal or central places as it would have been imprudent should that space provide a focal point for social unrest. The colonial government planners must have been aware of the significance of London's squares which serve as focal points for socialisation. Yet, in the "European Town" which is now the North Bridge Road area, they planned for a square. One can therefore surmise that in their planning they deliberately omitted these squares for the local population. The Padang was not really a meeting place for the people. It was a promenade for the privileged. Moreover, it was under surveillance and mainly used as a military parade ground.

When we plan the city, we must consider positively its cultural implications for the new society which we are building. Similarly, when we plan our new campus, these considerations are as vital. We must create the physical environment which will work in unison and is congenial to the human activities which contribute towards greater socialisation and humanism and facilitates human interactions. We must not be over concerned with the grandeur of skylines or such preconceptions which have little relevance to human activities. We must not be blinded by development because of our lack of vision or understanding and bequeath to future generation the urban chaos, which is the curse of major cities of the world today. Nor should we in our zealous drive for simplification and clean-cut solutions build monotonous, stark and cold environments which oppress us. The city should have many places for the many undefined and undefinable human activities to take place. There must be a place for the small man. There must be places for the myriad human activities in the form of many alternative spaces and places. We must not fall into the trap of over simplified planning concepts which seek to have clear and sharp definition and zones for the broad categories of the cities' activities. This approach, 20 years out of date, has produced in western countries new parts of their cities which are cold, lifeless, monotonous and precise. They are at the same time clean, stark and orderly, and mainly reserved for big business and other large commercial and touristic activities. The human touch is missing. The cities are lifeless at nights and on weekends. There are few intimate and unique spots which in any great city, which has a long history of humanism, are found abound. These are the spaces and places that make a city great, friendly and human. Man must feel that the city is friendly and not fearsome. The city itself, in the end, must not be the means to alienate the people. We have the opportunity beyond most because of our compact size, resulting in our effective administration to actualise the ideal of the city of man. Thereby, our efforts at nation building are the most tangible affirmation of our citizenship.

Essays

SINGAPORE'S TRANSPORT DILEMMA
4 September 1974

After the government set up the Road Transport Advisory Committee in 1974 to reduce traffic congestion and improve public transport, I gave this talk at the Rotary Club.

Transport planning is not a technical problem. Transport engineers and physical planners are well aware of the interlocking relationships between transportation and spatial planning. Cooperation of many different types of specialists can produce comprehensive solutions, covering a wide area which the subject involves. Therefore, there exist many functional concepts, techniques and technologies to solve the problems. The transport problem becomes a dilemma only because of the conflicting interests and priorities in making decisions to implement a comprehensive solution. The structure of government into self-centred action-agencies each having to make a profit is in conflict when it comes to making decisions about transportation planning and implementation. Transportation planning requires detailed coordination and clear priorities to be established and a concerted will to get it carried out. In order to do this, there must be a system of coordinated decision-making. Such a system does not exist within the bureaucracy. This problem is further complicated by the procedure of accounting, that is for transport planning to be effective certain agencies will have to lose money whilst other agencies can accrue benefits. Social costs have, as well, to be included in this accounting. What is required is a total accounting system in which revenues and expenditures can be allocated and programmed rationally to produce the desired results. Moreover, the accounting process involves a change in the way in which civil servants are motivated. Even with the best of intentions, which no doubt exists, civil servants are human beings who respond to the system of accreditation, promotion and prestige. The system at present measures the performance of a civil servant in terms of his ideas and actions which produce profits for his department. Therefore, one of the major dilemmas at the base of the decision-making dilemma is how to develop a different system of motivation and of evaluation of a civil servant's performance. We can briefly discuss now the problem of coordinated planning. At present, it appears that policy level coordination takes place only in the Cabinet.

Each minister's portfolio is separated from other ministries. Each portfolio consists of various action-agencies. These are organised as self-contained units. The physical planning agency is on the same level of hierarchy as other major action agencies such as the Public Works Department (PWD), the Housing & Development Board (HDB), the Port of Singapore Authority (PSA), the Registry of Vehicles (ROV), etc. Being on the same level of hierarchy, the planning agency cannot insist on priorities. Priorities are established largely by policy decisions at higher levels, advised by the action agencies. As the size of the action agencies increase, they have a momentum of their own. Consequently, policy level decisions may become more and more geared by action agencies' requirements. Therefore, action agencies play the role of large interest groups in the decision-making process. The study by Robert Gamer on the politics of urban planning in Singapore gives documented evidence of the kinds of coordination and priority problems which arise between the interest groups. The planning process is characterised more by bargaining between the action agencies rather than by overall coordination of objectives. The resolution of conflicts between action agencies is resolved in favour of the more powerful action agencies. There are, however, other interest groups which have a play in this process.

These groups can be identified as: (1) the motoring lobby, represented mainly by the Automobile Association, (2) the public safety lobby, represented by the National Safety First Council; (3) the Ministry of the Environment; and (4) the bussing public. The fourth category is the large silent majority who has no voice except through their Members of Parliament and other small voices in the wilderness. There are also large lobbies whose presence has not been seen but can be assumed to exist. These are the oil companies, the motorcar import agencies, the Mass Rapid Transit (MRT) suppliers who no doubt are lobbying in the wings. How would these interest groups' demands be resolved? Will it be through power and manipulation or will it be through coordinated planning?

I will now proceed to examine several major aspects of the transportation problem to illustrate how and why they have to be comprehensively handled and that mere technical considerations are insufficient as value questions are involved. These value questions are questions which we, as a people, will have to reckon with as our lives are dependent upon them.

Essays

The social problems of transportation

As a crude indicator, we can assume that 60 per cent of the total population of 2.3 million people make 1.4 trips per day. This produces 3.5 million trips per day, fairly close to the estimate made by the MRT consultants who estimated 3.21 million daily trips. From this figure, if we are to subtract the total number of trips made through private vehicles and motorcycles of 1.2 million trips per day, the total number of trips required through public transport of all types would be around 2.25 million. If we estimate the bus carrying capacity at an average of 60 persons per bus, each bus will have to do an average of 121 trips. Spread over an 18-hour day, the average would be 1.44 hours. These figures of course lump on-peak and off-peak loads, and so, are probably on the low side. If we are to assume (and subsequent surveys will have to show this) that if half the population spends half an hour travelling per day, then the other half must spend nearly 2 hours. To the travelling time must be added waiting time as well as preparation time. By preparation time, I mean the family logistic problems due to staggered hours. The question which arises is: "What kind of social price are we paying when a large proportion of our people spend that amount of time travelling?" The quality of family life must deteriorate with the stress of travelling together with time spent; this means that family cohesion is affected. Amongst other contributing factors, this may well be one of the chief reasons contributing to the problem of delinquency. This is paid for in terms of wasted lives and additional costs in law enforcement. Expressed in economic terms, travel time can be costed as follows: the per capita income of Singapore at present is US$1,500 per year. At the current exchange rate of S$2.48 to US$1, this produces S$3,720 per year. The per capita income is produced by eight hours of work per day. The 16 hours of non-working time, if we are to ascribe money value to it, is at least an equal value to the productive time, because the mental and physical wellbeing of the worker is essential for his capability of producing eight hours of work. Therefore, the money value of one hour of non-working time is 63 cents. Therefore, a traffic jam of one hour would cost to those people involved, 63 cents each. If half the population were to spend two hours travelling, then the additional cost beyond, let's say the acceptable one hour, would be S$1.26 million or S$1.41 million a day or S$514.65 million a year. We can see that this is a huge amount which has to be accounted for somewhere. From the preceding statements, we can see that social value must be built into the planning process for consideration.

Fuel cost in total systems accounting

Another area which requires coordinated planning and implementation is total energy saving. In this respect, low energy spatial arrangements have to be considered. This means the allocation of activities to reduce travel and transportation of goods, services and people. Specifically, in terms of housing, low energy forms of housing have to be derived. Just for an example, it is possible to achieve HDB densities and spatial standards with six-storey blocks rather than 16-storey blocks. But this is a separate subject which I will not deal with in this paper but can be dealt elsewhere. Also, tall buildings for the sake of height have to be discouraged as these are wasteful of energy. Savings of fuel cost in a transportation system is a crucial factor, particularly because of the phenomenal fuel cost increase after October 1973. Location of employment, education, recreation and housing in which peoples' travel needs are reduced is the most basic way of solving transportation problems. This requires very detailed coordination and programming capacity which, is extremely difficult in the present bureaucratic and administrative arrangement. If people live at their workplace or very near their workplace, then the frustrations cost of travelling can be greatly reduced.

Let us assume that the present fuel cost of Singapore Bus Service (SBS) is 14 per cent of the total operating cost. If this is so, and the operating cost is S$132.8 million, revealed by the Minister of State for Communications published in *The Straits Times* on 27 July 1974, then the fuel cost is around S$18.8 million a year. This can be reduced to a third if the public service transportation system was to be converted to an electrical system. According to a study by Prof. Richard Meier of the University of California in his book on *Science and Economic Development*, a transportation system based on electric power, consumes only one-third of total fuel requirements. In terms of thermal efficiency of different systems, electric locomotive as compared to motor-vehicle is around five times as efficient. The implication for Singapore will be that buses using diesel engines should be scrapped and replaced by electrically operated trolley buses which would have additional benefits of: (1) almost total elimination of air pollution along the routes of the vehicle and (2) elimination of noise pollution. Although the capital cost of trolley buses may be more expensive, the running cost in fuel consumption will be less. Moreover, maintenance cost will be greatly reduced as there are far fewer moving parts to deteriorate. However, a shift to such a mode of transportation would represent a loss of approximately S$10 million in taxes to the ROV which, under the present system of accounting, would of course resist this strenuously. There would also be a corresponding decline in revenues through diesel fuel tax. But of course, there will be an increase in electricity consumption, from which the Public Utilities Board (PUB) can accrue benefits. This point illustrates the conflict of interests involved in making such basic decisions.

Who should run the transport system?

The question that remains to be discussed is the question of who should run the public transport system. What is being attempted is a peculiar hybrid of capital's profit interest in ownership of the bus transport system working within government controls and regulations. The Minister of Communications has stated that an annual pre-tax profit for the first three years would be limited to a maximum of 8 per cent of net assets. The question is: "Why should a private investor invest for that rate of return?" He might as well put his money in the Post Office Savings Bank (POSB) and accept a return of 6 per cent interest free of tax, which in the case of a limited company with a 40 per cent tax, actually represents 10 per cent return on investment. A further question is: If the bus transport is an "essential" public service as the minister says, then shouldn't all the profits be ploughed back into the system to provide better and cheaper service for the public, such is the case of public utilities?

Leaving the matter aside, if profits are to be maintained, SBS in the process of reorganisation will have to incur greater expenditure. For instance, the ratio of two buses to one maintenance man will have to be decreased in order to have more buses running on the road. The present ratio of 45 per cent of buses on the road is scandalous! According to international standards available from the International Union of Public Transport, the ratio should be closer to two mechanics to one bus. In Hongkong, it is 1.7 to one bus. True, with increased management efficiency, the bus service should be better, and this would encourage

A New World in the Making

more people to use the bus and swell the revenue. But this may balance against increased expenditure. And if SBS is to be a public limited company to attract the public to invest for profits, then profits can only be increased by increasing bus fares. It would not be surprising that there will be another bus fare hike, particularly with next year's National Wage Council's (NWC) recommendations looming. I would not be surprised if a one-fare system will be introduced to justify the fare hike. This move will also mean the redundancy of bus conductors, as a one-fare system does not require conductors. The present ratio of staff to buses is approximately 5.5:1. The average in many cities is about 4.5:1. This is because of the elimination of bus conductors in those cities. The National Trades Union Congress (NTUC) has already embarked on this line of reasoning with regard to hotel workers, urging that hoteliers should retrench workers in order to implement the NWC's recommendation in full.

There is a further question concerning SBS' viability as a public limited company. At the present moment, SBS revenue has dropped, not only because of declining service, but also because of the licensing of 1,900 school buses which are moreover permitted to carry adults during off-peak school hours. This move was to supplement the inadequate service provided by SBS. This has of course reduced its revenue too. Furthermore, with the introduction of the MRT, notwithstanding increased trips, SBS must again lose revenue, unless SBS is integrated with MRT as one single operation. This would of course depend on the method of accounting. One result can be that fares may be increased to offset the capital cost of MRT. I hope I am wrong here.

The finance minister's speech in April this year (1974) states this year's budget will be in deficit, to be made up through taxation on petroleum products, vehicle tax and sale of land. In view of the declining property market, land sales is unlikely to feature as a major revenue source. Consequently, taxation from private motor vehicles is likely to increase in order to offset deficits. Increased taxation of course can only reach a point beyond which, if motorcar ownership is substantially reduced, revenue for the Treasury will be correspondingly reduced, and this will not be acceptable from the budget point of view. So, we can expect an increase, but only to a point where it does not jeopardise state's revenue interest. Tough measures against motorists would also have to bear this in mind. But with the system of motivation as it exists, it is likely that individual officers concerned will be more than zealous in the execution of their duties. At a certain point, the Ministry of Finance will have to step in to prevent the erosion of revenue should the measures taken against motorists be too severe as to cause a drastic decline in car numbers. These points only illustrate further complexities of administration which require information and comprehensive policy planning. The transport dilemma represents a more fundamental dilemma. I am at a dilemma as to what constructive suggestions to make because what is suggested here is that piecemeal measures are inadequate. I hope that through my discussion, it is sufficiently clear that the transportation problem has many facets which are related to each other in a complex way. I have by no means examined all the complexities as I am sure there are many. Some fundamental premises of our society have to be re-examined too, such as the money motivation of the civil servants, notwithstanding continuous exhortation by ministers to the contrary. Also the system of symbols and rewards in which the motorcar is a status symbol has also to be changed. Transportation failure and frustrations are only the more dramatic manifestations of environmental mismanagement arising from the lack of comprehensive planning. Environmental failures in housing are not as dramatic, as human beings can adapt to adverse conditions by personal innovation in lifestyle. However, adaptation to inadequate transportation is very limited. The problem of transportation planning is only the tip of the iceberg of the failure of comprehensive planning. One of the fundamental premises of comprehensive planning is that there should be a total accounting system with a more rational way of making coordinated decisions that imply a different way of motivating decision-makers and civil servants. The characteristic of the failure of comprehensive planning is too little, too late.

IS SINGAPORE ARCHITECTURE "OBIANG"?
15 March 1990

An essay written after reading C.C. Leong's book Youth in the Army. *It was published in* The Straits Times.

"Obiang-ism" is the aesthetic of "kiasu-ism". "Kiasu-ism" is a strategy to deal with perceived cultural and situational inferiority. It is a universal phenomenon, but in Singapore it has its own special characteristics. The term "obiang" was first recorded in the book entitled *Youth in the Army* by C. C. Leong. Though it describes a certain attitude reflected in the choice of clothing and dress accessories with its characteristic maladaptation to expensive-looking-crudeness and striving to be up to date, it can apply in other fields as well.

This syndrome should be distinguished from "suaku", which is somewhat different. "Suaku" has to do with an earlier more ignorant countrified phase where there is no knowledge of world trends. The "obiang" is more advanced and urban. The "obiang" knows fashion trends but lacks the discerning ability to mix-and-match with finesse. The result of this inaptitude is a blundering over-statement in his choices. This overstatement stems from his fear of losing out.

To be on the safe side, he relies on brand names, and a good measure of them used liberally to be "with it". The characteristics of "obiang-ism" are two-fold. Firstly, he wants to have the best of everything because he does not want to lose out on anything in order to be with the "in" crowd. Secondly, he is loud. This is not because he wishes to be assertive. Far from it, because to be assertive is to dangerously identify oneself. The over-statement is inadvertent. It is a strategy deriving from the "kiasu" mentality. It is understandable that the apparently assertive expression is not derived from self-assurance or the wish to make an impact. It is the opposite. It is to merge with the in crowd. Criticism of this unintended individualism is resented. And any criticism in any case tends to be regarded as a personal attack. Thus, "obiang-ism" is a reaction against personal reaction. It is not a conviction or an assertion. It can change.

The purpose of this essay is to create awareness of this condition so that change can take place, and a more authentic aesthetic development that is sensitive to the environment and to the surroundings can come about.

As a phenomenon of cultural insecurity, we are not alone. It can be seen in all new states. It is, however, notably absent in Europe where long, continuous history and successful economic and artistic achievement have provided a stable basis for a self-assured culture.

The characteristics of such a culture stresses refinement, understatement, precision and fine craftsmanship, even though the less culturally secure segments of their society also show aesthetic characteristic akin to our "obiangs". When China also achieves economic success, Chinese culture too will upsurge. To prove this hypothesis, we will have to test it against countries such as, to name some, Japan, Korea and Thailand. In the case of Japan, it is clear that after the Meiji Period, Japanese culture experienced confrontation shock with western culture. This produced a variety of strong reactions, including a questioning of its own cultural values such as aesthetics. The Second World War and the arduous climb out of economic disaster to success is paralleled by a period of confused aesthetics in which foreign tastes were adopted and incorporated in an undigested manner, like our own "obiang" aesthetics. With economic success, however, Japan now assumes a new confidence, and this can be seen in all its aesthetic output, be it dress design, motor car design, appliances and architecture. One can conclude that besides depth in cultural history, economic success is linked to the development of authentic aesthetics. With our economic success, are we at the stage to develop our aesthetics or is our success so in doubt that we will always look outside for our aesthetic cues? Must we always remain "kiasu" and "obiang"?

Even USA and Australia can be grouped in this sense together with the new states in Latin America and the rest of the Third World in terms of aesthetic insecurity. Cultural insecurity, of course, varies in intensity but is the pervading condition. While it provides the energy for rapid change as in the USA, it also affects the development of aesthetics. Past or present aesthetics, if they form part of the choices available, tend to have a frenetic quality. Some see this as vitality and an indication of individual creativity. But with every gem, a trail of cultural discards litters the intellectual and physical landscape. This phenomenon can be seen in the aesthetics of all fields, including architecture, painting, interior design and fashion.

In Singapore, the effect of such littering in the visible landscape is harder to avoid. It is amplified by proximity. Every street is now distinguished by some new building or alteration and addition to an existing one that shouts at you. If you visit the architectural school, you will see this phenomenon in the students' work. No doubt you will see a tremendous variety of every style imaginable. Every student is trying as hard as possible to be as different as possible. Is it because there is real imagination at work or is something else happening? Bearing in mind that the school is only a microcosm of the society, is it possible that what is happening in society is also happening in the school? The tremendous vitality and diversity in design is not healthy if it is geared towards not losing out in marks. Will students lose out if their designs are quietly and sensibly sensitive? Will they be missed out and not noticed when viewed against the clamour of the rest? Hasn't competitions also tended to produce exaggerated architecture? Is this not "kiasuism" at work for the same reasons? If the motivation in the school is similar to that in society, what is the hope for the future of authentic design?

"Kiasuism" and "obiang-ism" are so complementary that they are like two sides of the same coin. We can refer to this phenomenon as the "K/O" complex. It knocks out any real creativity because it risks no ventures, and it is only concerned with superficial appearances. "Obiang-ism" wants only to be "with it". It is not interested in the intrinsic of any "ism".

For example, modernism, post-modernism, regionalism or any thorough going concept. It is only interested in its surface features to be adopted, adapted and incorporated in order to be stylish and up to date. Every concept is reduced to treatment and concepts can be mixed too. This explains why even knowledgeable developers do not spend time and money in investigating the building briefs thoroughly to define real issues and to challenge their architects. The more usual way is the simple-minded shortcut to excellence by buying ready-made talents based on published reputations. This of course assures that if anything goes wrong, the blame can be placed conveniently. This is the ultimate effect of the K/O complex. Relevant creativity is effectively knocked out by "kiasuism".

Authentic national architecture which can symbolise the will to advancement based on the specifics of our place and our time is still looking for its clients.

Essays

HERITAGE CONSERVATION'S POLITICAL AND SOCIAL IMPLICATIONS: THE CASE OF SINGAPORE
23 April 1990

A paper presented at the "Heritage Conservation: The Challenges in the Asia-Pacific Basin" conference held in Darwin, Australia.

Heritage consists of the artefacts, traditions and records which are handed down or extracted from the past. They are valued as tangible symbols and identifying characteristics of the history of a people. Accordingly, Singapore's heritage has been defined by the government-appointed Committee on Heritage formed in April 1988 as consisting of the natural heritage, the nation-building heritage, the heritage of economic success, the multi-cultural heritage and the heritage of the man-made environment. This committee submitted its report to the Advisory Council on Culture and the Arts in November 1988. This paper is in part a reflection on the salient factors underlying the report. The author was the chairman of the committee established under the ministerial council for culture and the arts in preparation for the building of the Singapore Performing Arts Centre at Marina Bay, later called the Esplanade.

Priorities

Active efforts at the conservation of heritage in Singapore is a recent phenomenon. This is not because of a lack of awareness of the importance of heritage, but because the priori ties of economic development, urbanisation, public housing and infrastructure building have been the all-consuming priorities since 1965 when the island city-state attained independent status. Conservation was viewed then as an impediment to economic and social progress.

Heritage is only part of the "glue" of society

The question of heritage conservation in Singapore has many facets, especially when viewed against the backdrop of rapid economic changes following on the heels of the political changes the island republic experienced. It was a colonial creation; it has no long history. The citizens came from all over Asia. To become an independent and self-respecting entity, it needed a new "glue" which multi-ethnicity and a plural cultural heritage do not provide.

Heritage of law and administration

Sir Stamford Raffles founded Singapore in 1819, first as a trading outpost of the East India Company and later as a full-fledged colony under the British government administered from the India Office. The Western concepts of administration were imposed on the Asian population. The whole arrangement was artificial from the beginning. The most enduring and positive effect of this artificial entity was however the establishment of patterns and standards of administration and concepts of law and justice. Despite abuses under the colonial administration, the patterns have served as a living heritage on which Singapore's future development thrived. The later transition from colony to independent status required the creation of new ties with which to bind society together, and Singapore built upon this heritage. The legal structure formed the basis for the definition of rights and responsibilities equally applicable to all citizens. But there have been modifications to the philosophy of some of the laws and some of the administrative procedures. These departures are controversial and have been argued on the grounds of necessity and context. Some would argue that they were on political necessities. Suffice it to say here that had there not been the larger Western heritage of laws and administrative criteria, the modifications to the laws argued on grounds of necessity would have evolved without any compunctions. As it is, the broader Western philosophical and legal heritage has contributed to the evolution of the political culture which is not without a conscience and urges an adherence to well-founded social and juridical traditions. This subject is far too complex to be discussed in this paper, but it represents one important facet of heritage conservation which has the most powerful effect on the daily lives and the unfolding of potentialities of a people. The trade-off between social benefit and individual rights has been stretched but not broken. The legitimacy of the ruling power has been sustained because of the obvious gains in social benefits. The processes in attaining these benefits in themselves have produced values and the working attitudes of the society. These are the main powerful contributors to the creation of the new culture which unites the diverse races and class groups in Singapore. The new ties are based on values derived from "achievement politics" and cultural unifying values. They form the supra in the nation building processes, in the economic transformation, in the establishment of universal bilingual education, in the provision of public housing, healthcare, community facilities and equal access and equal opportunities for all citizens. These have become the shared experiences and values of the people. It is now felt that because of the attainment of this layer of shared values that a return to ethnicity is possible and this is to fulfil some pent-up aspirations. There are differences of opinion on this. Only the future will tell whether the shared views are strong enough to hold the society together as it reaches for its separate roots. The fact that the roots are intertwined is not something that is readily grasped. It requires scholarship and propagation. For until this is grasped, some stresses will be felt in the social fabric.

Ancient Singapore: The heritage of place

Malay legends speak of Singapore or Temasek, as it was then known, as a kingdom. Chinese and Arab writings mention Temasek. Recent archaeological digs at Fort Canning (a hill overlooking the Singapore River) indicate that it was a sacred site where some ritual activities involving glass bead making and the use of mercury took place, which is thought to be associated with gold working. The evidence indicates a Hindu/Buddhist cultural horizon which is dated to about the 14th century. The evidence is however incomplete and tantalising. What were the relations of Temasek to Sri Vijaya, the Hindu civilisation located at Palembang in Sumatra? What were the relations with Thailand which was contemporaneously undergoing a Buddhist expansion phase? What was the character of the Malay world prior to the Islamic period? What were race relations like then? These issues are interesting in themselves, and they contribute to the making of the glue needed to hold the society together. Knowledge of place provides some depth in the appreciation of the commonly occupied territory. Place identity is reinforced by historical knowledge.

Influx of immigration

With the establishment of British colonial rule and the declaration of Singapore as a free port by Raffles, there was an influx of immigration to Singapore from the Malay world, India and China, with the most coming from the latter. This influx hugely added to the small indigenous Malay, Chinese and Orang Laut (sea gypsy) population who had settled in Singapore before the British.

Problems of race relations

Thus, from the beginning, modern Singapore was established as multi-racial, multi-cultural and multi-religious. British law and order established harmony among the races. This harmony was however always tenuous. It broke down on a number of occasions, resulting in riots and bloodshed. The question of heritage conservation in the Singapore context cannot be divorced from policies regarding the maintenance of the harmony between the races. This is a complex, yet delicate question and it continues till today. There are always tendencies in some quarters of the society to conceive it as an adjunct of some regional power. The handling of this tendency requires the most delicate of techniques.

Multicultural heritage

But the multi-racial basis of Singapore society is rich in cultural expressions. It has ethnic identity areas despite 30 years of aggressive urban renewal and slum clearance to build new housing and commercial developments. Because of cultural plurality, there is also a wide variety of food and dress styles, and many different religions, customs and rituals. All this make for a unique mix of cultural richness, but which also contain the potential of social dissension. And whatever policies regarding approaches to the conservation of Singapore's diverse cultural heritage must reckon with this fact. This is why a representative body like the government has to be the body to balance the different interests to prevent excessiveness on the part of any ethnic or cultural group who in their enthusiasm for expression may inadvertently upset other groups.

Political power and heritage conservation

There are positive and negative aspects to heritage conservation in Singapore, and no discussion on it will be adequate without discussing these aspects as they affect policies on conservation. This is because conservation is a societal process as much as it is an attitude of mind. Moreover, such a discussion in the Singapore context must deal with two additional factors, namely the tremendous centralisation of power and the manifestation of an unusually strong political will in handling the imperatives of rapid economic growth and social transformation. Economic growth is after all the engine through which the goods of society are delivered. If conservation is now to be considered as a social good, then it is this same engine with appropriate modifications which will deliver the new goods. Whether these modifications will amount to a new delivery system is difficult to say. The future is unclear at this point.

Negative factors in conservation

The abiding concerns during the rapid economic growth phase of Singapore which occurred between 1965 and 1985 had an impact on heritage conservation. The impact was mainly negative in the form of five issues that produce a benign neglect in some cases and in others actual negative actions taken against any effort at heritage conservation. It was only after the mid-1980s that positive attitudes and approaches towards heritage conservation began to build up in earnest.

1. Anti-communalism

To prevent racial conflict, the constitution guaranteed that each ethnic group could practice its own religion, customs and rituals. Multi-racialism was accepted as the basis of society. No discrimination on racial lines was permitted. Accordingly, the places of worship and other areas closely identified with each ethnic group were, broadly speaking, protected. This is not to say that there was no encroachment for the purpose of redevelopment for new uses. On the contrary, many such areas were cleared for new projects. The justification was for the general public good. Care was also taken to be even-handed in the clearing of such areas so that no group would feel that they were particularly singled out. So long as the public good was clearly demonstrated, any resentment in the clearing of heritage areas did not boil over despite the dislocation felt. While the multi-racial culture acknowledged ethnicity, no public buildings openly carried any symbols which could be identified with any ethnic group. Whether it was a conscious policy or not, is not clear but the neutral-modern look of the new buildings erected during this period attests to the pervasive modernisation zeal of that period as well as serving as an acceptable basis of expression. A National Monuments Board was formed during this period. Its record in the gazetting of buildings as public monuments was niggardly because it was slow in listing buildings for preservation. It inadvertently served the purpose of allowing or legitimising the demolition of historical buildings and whole districts as these were not included in the protected list. But the list was careful in being even-handed. A sprinkling of multi-cultural samples of historical buildings was included in the list.

Communal sentiments are, however, always present. For whilst the government's buildings were neutrally modern, some private buildings began to express the ethnic background of their sponsors. Buildings such as the Nanyang University library and the Chinese Chamber of Commerce were some of the buildings of this period that overtly showed their ethnicity. Clearly this approach was not encouraged by the government, which from time to time took measures against activities construed as communal agitation. While it is the right to express ethnicity in privately-owned buildings, the government steered away from any such expressions in public buildings.

2. Anti-communism

The actions taken to thwart communist activities led to the promulgation of rules and regulations against public assembly. This resulted in the deactivation of urban spaces which was thronging with commercial and social activities. Freedom of assembly and the normal development of a civic urban culture based on the natural conviviality of outdoor tropical living was significantly reduced. The lifestyle became sober and orderly as development progressed further.

3. Anti-gangsterism

The natural bustle of street life which characterises all Asian cities was also reduced by actions taken to curb the dominance of gangs which prey on street hawkers and vendors. A certain ambience of life in the city which constitutes a vital part of its heritage declined as hawkers and vendors were rehoused in government built and controlled food centres. The removal of this element from the streets simultaneously decongested the roads for free traffic management and for health reasons. Thus, in short the modernisation ideals of that period had a profound impact on the living culture of the city and its heritage.

4. Anti-pornography

It is difficult to determine the basis of the attitude towards activities which can be broadly classed as pornography. They could include graffiti, graphic publications and nightclub activities. The attitude towards such activities led to actions ranging from disapproval to absolute suppression. This meant that traditional activities such as taxi dancehalls, transvestite areas such as Bugis Street, and other traditional activities of a dubious nature disappeared from the public domain. Districts which developed as a result of the chain of activities spinning around these activities began to disintegrate and disperse. Thus, some of the vitality and organic interest in the city declined. This is not an argument for the retention for such activities, but a comment on the effect of policies and attitudes on the continuation of traditional activities, given the enormous capacity to carry out plans and policies in a thorough going manner.

5. Anti-backwardness

Many of the modernisation programmes meant the wholesale demolition of traditional areas and activities. The modernising zeal during the 1960s and 1970s accounts for this. This attitude underlies much of the anti-communalism, the anti-gangsterism, and the anti-pornography programmes. Indeed, during this period, any discussion on conservation was viewed as soft-headed sentimentalism and backward. A very clear indicator of this attitude was the benign state of neglect accorded to the National Museum of Singapore where it was only given the minimum financial and manpower support to protect the collection rather than to develop the exhibition programme. Only minimal funds were made available as a holding action. Another indicator of the attitude during this period was the erection of visual barriers along highways overlooking squatters and farm areas. It was evident that these areas were regarded as backward and should be blotted out. As soon as development funds and plans became available, these areas were speedily cleared for new developments.

Nature conservation

This long tradition beginning from the British days has continued. The National Parks Board and the Singapore Botanic Gardens continue to do their work despite the shift in priorities towards rapid economic development. The central nature reserve and catchment area are protected, but other areas fell under the aegis of development plans. The massive tree planting programme of Singapore owes much to the resources made available by the Gardens and by the Board. Only recently is there an acknowledgement that development plans and nature conservation are not entirely incompatible. This has as much to do with attitudes as it has to do with new technical and professional skills available.

Positive aspects of conservation

Political imperatives are always the predominant condition when considering any issue in Singapore. This factor features heavily in the negative aspects of heritage conservation already discussed. The positive aspects which we will now discuss are equally affected by political factors. It should be noted however that these political factors are themselves undergoing some change.

It is not within the scope of this paper to discuss the dynamics of power, its consolidation and its maintenance. It is sufficient to note that any conservation effort of any part of the heritage must satisfy the dynamics of power. Singapore has not yet politically reached the point where a sustained plurality of power actually exists. Conservation efforts in Singapore must be channelled through government and/or its agencies, be subject to its priorities and serve its objectives. The inherent difficulty of this however is that it is in the nature of heritage conservation to inevitably involve values and judgements embedded in society at large and in the minds of enlightened individuals. This necessitates that some political adjustments are necessary if the resources are to be incorporated to enable the flow of ideas, the articulation of values and the identification of issues related to conservation by such individuals and cultural and conservation societies and groups.

A Singapore Heritage Society was started in 1986, signifying the spontaneous rise of consciousness in Singapore on the necessity of conserving its heritage. Since the 1980s, the newspapers, who see their task as closely augmenting government policy and attitudes, has taken the initiative to highlight heritage issues too. This effort has been instrumental in accelerating the growth of consciousness on heritage matters. This is a curious phenomenon uncharacteristic in the context of a closely monitored information environment. Perhaps the ever-cooperative press took its own initiative because heritage, as defined in lifestyle and building conservation terms, is considered legitimate and not prone to raise sensitive issues.

The current situation

As Singapore moves into the 21st century, it openly acknowledges the present self-actualisation phase and adjustments for more political participation are being experimented. Accordingly, in conjunction with the ruling party's initiative to openly define a national agenda for the 1990's and beyond, an Advisory Council on Culture and the Arts was established in 1988 under the chairmanship of the second Deputy Prime Minister of Singapore. Among the different committees established was one on heritage.

This committee met over an eight-month period, drawing from a large panel of individuals who are involved in different cultural organisations and movements. It is instructive to note that the individuals were selected on the basis of their personal qualities and serve in their personal capacities rather than as representatives of organisations. They were free to speak from their own consciences and draw from their experiences. They were not subject to the dynamics of the organisations they came from. This was a useful device to separate organisational politics from the free expression of individual views. This procedure established an objective basis for the articulation of values and the identification of issues without undue pressure. Some satisfaction was still gained by the organisations to which these individuals are affiliated in that their views can still be filtered through them. These individuals did not feel pressured by their organisational affiliations as they were free to exercise their own judgements on the issues brought forward. The findings of committees structured in this manner can obtain tacit agreement only because the individuals selected to represent the various interest areas are respected persons in their own right. The system will fail if the credibility of such individuals are found wanting.

Some recommendations of the Committee on Heritage

- The establishment of a National Heritage Trust, beginning with the establishment of an inter-ministerial committee and a heritage council to prepare an inventory of all heritage items in Singapore. The council is to conduct annual audits.
- Immediate funding of existing heritage departments to enable them to play a core role in heritage conservation.

- The National Museum is to be greatly enlarged.
- To establish a Singapore History Gallery for a deeper understanding of the shared experiences in nation building.
- To celebrate cultural diversity through a Community Gallery.
- To enlarge the National Gallery and to present the artistic heritage.
- To develop a comprehensive buildings, landmarks and historic areas conservation programme.
- To conserve the natural heritage and to integrate the urban and the natural features sensitively.
- To promote the history of Singapore in the context of the region through a lively education programme.
- To urge the Singapore Broadcasting Corporation to produce historically authentic documentaries and dramas.
- To conserve and mark all historical sites throughout the island.

Conclusion

The Singapore case clearly demonstrates that political imperatives and economic development criteria predominate. As in all fields, heritage conservation comes under the aegis of the government. The politics of conservation in Singapore inevitably involves the management of race relations because ethnicity is a powerful emotional force in society. The paradox of multi-racialism as a social policy is whilst satisfying the identity needs of each ethnic community it runs the risk of developing cleavages. Heritage conservation along ethnic lines will inadvertently sharpen the cleavages unless it is handled with sensitivity and circumspection. Scholarship is crucial in establishing the cross-cultural patterns that have emerged in society, but these are unfortunately largely outside everyday consciousness. They are taken for granted. Heritage conservation has not only to make information regarding each ethnic community's roots widely available, it has also to produce information and propagate knowledge regarding how the different communities have absorbed, modified and internalised some of the values, ideas and lifestyles of other communities. To undertake this immense task, there is a need for international cooperation, especially in sustained comparative cultural and historical studies regionally. I consider this to be of the highest priority in heritage conservation in plural societies undergoing rapid transformation. If this conference can move towards this kind of cooperation, something will have been achieved.

A New World in the Making

SCOPE FOR THE ECONOMIC AND
CULTURAL INVIGORATION OF THE NATIONAL SECTOR
26 July 1990

A reflection on the talent deficit in Singapore after my involvement in the Advisory Council on Culture and the Arts.

These notes are premised on the view that we are what we do. The nature of our economy plays the largest part in determining how we define ourselves, that is our national culture and our national identity.

Singapore's economy is 40 per cent driven by Multi-National Corporations (MNC), 30 per cent in the state and private corporate sectors and the Singaporean domestic sector makes up the balance. The state and the private corporate sectors share similar attitudes and working assumptions with the MNC sector. A network of affiliations based on shared values and perceptions which are mutually supportive therefore exists. Policies and procedures are therefore geared in this direction. As such, when the state divests its corporations through privatisation, the attitudes and ties remain intact. Privatisation is therefore only a change in form and not in content.

Given the dominance of the values shared by 70 per cent of the economy, which emphasises bigness, vertical integration, global perspective, institutional rationality, and more, Singaporean activities and potentials are viewed with pessimism. This sector therefore receives scant attention. Until and unless there is a positive attitude (an act of faith) towards the Singaporean domestic sector and their associated social and cultural constituencies there is no base for the sustained development of priorities and initiatives related to the potentials of the place, the people or anything intrinsic. In such a situation, the further development of the Singapore economy and its concomitant cultural development will only lead towards the continued marginalisation and devaluation of all indigenous initiatives, priorities and sentiments. The entire administrative structure is geared this way.

A detailed analysis of the nature of the values of the Singaporean corporate sector will demonstrate the above. Similarly, detailed analysis of small and medium enterprise (SME) activities and output will, alas, show classic symptoms of short-cycle outlook, lack of internal cohesion and narrow individualism. These are classic symptoms of under-development and tend to diminish hope in the SME sector. This is despite the scope shown by other SME economies elsewhere.

Until the 70:30 ratio shifts towards at least a 50:50 ratio, there will be no real vigour in the national sector of the economy and no stimulating effect on the SME sector. The state corporate sector must truly divest a large part of its entities into truly independent and competing entities which are not dependent on or beholden to the state corporate network of affiliations for the invisible support it gets. Until this is so, there will also be no vigour in enterprise, national culture and no substance in national identity.

Positive, pointed and patient measures to encourage Singaporean efforts must come from a restructuring of the demand side. Until clear demands are expressed for Singaporean-based creativity, the supply side will be weak and inconsistent as now. The strategy is to selectively identify clusters of activities and industries to focus new demands to generate new Singaporean prototype designs and products to showcase to the world. Creativity in these will initially be for the Singaporean market with a view for subsequent export. The domestic market is not small at all for the development of creatively conceived and designed products and services. The government can and must provide the leadership, the catalyst and the scope. No one else can.

All Singaporean enterprises and all the expressive arts including architecture are affected by the above conditions and attitudes.

CIVIL SOCIETY'S CONTRIBUTION: BEYOND POWER POLITICS
23 March 2000

There was much discussion about civil society during the 2000s after the government called for the people to work with the public and private sectors to shape a sense of belonging as part of its "Singapore 21" vision.

If civil society in Singapore wants space, it has to shape it. Now is the best time because it is a time of change. Understanding context is very important. Although the principles of civil society are universal, the manifestations of these principles and the constraining factors are very different in each situation. Thus, the prospective role of civil society in the Singapore context has to be viewed against the backdrop of forces and attitudes prevalent.

In any country, social forces are always configured and do somehow conspire to maintain the status quo be it for good or for ill, for growth or for stagnancy. This is generally true except in revolutionary situations where social inequity has become so acute because order has broken down and civil authority is seen to be totally inept and corrupt.

Social classes, roles, institutions, money are the usual categories in social science analysis. The role of culture in society is more difficult. The persistence of attitudes and perceptions and how these are manifested in the motivations, methodologies and reflexes are not easily visible especially from within the culture. Viewed from outside, there are also difficulties. These are problems due to transferred perceptions and perspectives. Thus, to grasp the whole social dynamics is indeed a difficult task. This is even more so when one is emotionally committed to the culture and social system that one seeks to change.

The difficulty is clear when one considers the issue of Chinese-ness as a Chinese. Or critically considers Chinese history and culture. The emotional obligations that one has towards one's identity as well as the responsibilities one has towards one's family and friends inhibits one's understanding of being Chinese. To undertake this task, one has to, however artificial it is, step outside oneself to view oneself. A certain distancing is necessary with the attendant risks of being misunderstood.

There is another difficulty. This is the difficulty of positioning. Everyone has a position in society, especially in one predicated on development such as Singapore. In other societies, where a saturation in material terms has been reached, there is greater latitude in the acceptance of differing views. In states such as Singapore, the latitude is small indeed. Every position is affirmative or disruptive. Each position one assumes seems to presuppose the obliteration of other points of view. A condition of hyper criticality or hyper apathy thus seems to prevail.

The following sketches out the kind of positions that exist. In each situation, while the operating principles of each group are similar, the guises and tactics that are developed are to suit the situation. Thus, these broad categories are useful tools in understanding socio-dynamics in the discourses of ideas, ethnicity, class and power in Singapore.

The following are the categories:

- Dominant drivers, co-pilots and crew
- Opportunists, amplifiers and aspiring co-pilots
- Wise guys, nice guys
- Survivalists and passengers
- Innovators, visionaries and path-finders
- Idealists and dreamers
- Doomsday sayers
- Gangsters

In Singapore, the configuration of society is dominated by the three top categories. There are few idealists, innovators and fortunately, no doomsday sayers and only a few gangsters. Success up to now is premised on this dominance.

The whole array of Singapore 21 committees and the frequent voicing of need to change mindsets, promote active citizenship, encourage entrepreneurship, develop civil society, etc., are all indicators that a new culture is being contemplated. Why this new line? It is obvious that the future viability of the country, in the light of globalisation and the information technology (IT) revolution, is at stake.

An old Singapore is thus transitioning to a new Singapore. What processes are involved? How will a new space be created out of the old array of powers and perceptions? Leaders of the present Singapore know more that anyone that if we fail in engendering a new Singapore, the slide towards irrelevance is inevitable. This is the nexus in the relationship between Singapore's political leadership and others that share the wish for change. There is a shared future to create. There will be much confusion as old attitudes and methods collide with new requirements and a new spirit. How shall we go about this to get where we want to go? The calculation of political risks is very different between those who have it and those who do not. On this there is no consensus possible.

To start with, we need to understand what this old Singapore is, in terms of its operating systems, structures and assumptions before we can alter it to the new Singapore that is to be. We also need to know what the new spirit is. Current social science categories derived from Max Weber or Karl Marx have proven inadequate in our age of globalisation and IT. As the complexity of the cultural elements cannot be easily explained in terms of social classes structured along economic lines, we need new doors of perception.

Structures, cultures, administrative systems and everyday assumptions of the old Singapore:

- Chaos versus order; confrontation and consensus
- English-educated equals Western; Chinese-educated equals Asian
- Rich equals smart, poor equals dumb
- Hub, spokes and wheels: the centralisation of power and the politics of marginalisation
- Dumb money, smart money
- Constructive criticism: the politics of dismissal
- Pragmatism and progress: the politics of administration
- Censorship/self-censorship
- Modernity, modernism and modernisation: modernisation without modernity
- Democracy and the west: Concealment of the culture of autonomy
- Chinese-ness: The fictionalisation of heritage
- Confucian culture: The politics of petition
- Masses, the individual and the state
- Educating for conformism
- Structures: Top down, bottom up; elites and masses
- Grateful recipients and ungrateful dogs
- The tail wags the dog: Upgrading
- Doing it right the first time

Essays

- Collectivisation of interests versus incivility in public places
- The pyramid of perception: P1, P2, P3, and P4
- Systems: Rule by rules; No corruption, the elimination of judgement
- Language: Hot talk, cold talk, soft talk, hard talk, just talk, prattle and the mechanisation of language
- Culture of committees and boards: The politics of silent consent, ritual comment, and acquiescence in committees
- Public dialogue as ritual rap
- New Singapore, new order
- East versus west: Modernity versus modernisation
- National culture as frozen myth: The case of Japan and Malay education in Malaysia
- Malayan culture: Recovering our roots of modernity, sensibility and aesthetics; Coming to terms with our only past that means anything
- Why do the intelligent dislike the administration?
- Open society, open government
- Responsive civil service
- Government-linked companies, multinational companies, local enterprises and small and medium enterprises
- New communities: prospects for shared action
- Criticality and the autonomy of reason, aesthetics and morality
- New language: straight talk; poetic talk, humour
- Towards a new dialogue-culture in public, in committees and in boards, and internet communication; gassing versus communicating
- Press and media; beyond hype—the celebration of the trivial
- Civil society, civility and the state
- The masses: clamouring lambs to the slaughter
- Education versus Induction
- New education: cl, c2, c3, c4, c5
- Clearing the atmosphere of smoke and dust; civic urban values
- Energy efficiency: the politics of economising
- Innovators and critics

- Political risks and a risk-taking culture
- Lively and liveable city
- National Library, Bras Basah Park and Singapore Management University conservation; the politics of the Anglo-Chinese School clock tower
- Diversity in the landscape of minds
- Diversity in the landscape of place
- Diversity in administration
- Memory and the fictionalisation of history: we tell no lies; the politics of denial
- Feeling out the way ahead: creating social space, the tasks of civil society

Essays

CREATING CULTURAL CAPITAL IN SINGAPORE
7 July 2002

The equation that funding and programming will achieve the desired outcome is flawed. The fear of retribution must first be removed, dispelled and seen to be dissipating before people will become unafraid to take risks.

On increases in education and training: Yes, of course. But the hand of the government must also be reduced. Give the money, but lay off the filtering and the steering. Freedom of expression will automatically foster the necessary critical culture.

On regional culture: We should not be afraid to tap emotional ties and cultural affinities to the region. Be not afraid that Singapore's meritocratic perspective will unravel. This should replace the simplistic Chinese Malay Indian Others formula of ethnicity. This means that merit must be really seen to be. Not connections, not tarred reputations, not personal likes, dislikes and prejudices. But really to judge on the intrinsic quality of a thing in itself. It is the song, not the morals of the singer that is of concern.

Forging stronger relationships with the West than we already have: Relationships with the region need genuine magnanimity and cultural interest on our part. A Southeast Asian cultural museum was previously recommended by Dr Goh Keng Swee.

On recommendation of a national partnership to creating culture: How about freeing up media space, particularly radio and print? Why is the government so scared, given the laws of sedition and libel?

On the arts everywhere approach: Will it mean more kitsch? This is also related to freeing media space. Commentaries on the arts is presently mostly inane. Kitsch fake art should be subject to critical scrutiny.

On funding: This is certainly necessary, but must not be administered by timid and immature bureaucrats. Why can't the best artists be the evaluators of grants? Rotate them. How to spot them? Have them rank each other. Each one can rank themselves at top but this cancels out mathematically. The numbers automatically stack up and the ranking is established. Self-interest will defeat any collusion. Risking trust is the key. No trust, no spirit. Hot-housing cultural capital formation needs novel tactics. Old-style fears cannot inspire new free spirits.

The project is important, it goes beyond the economics implied. What is at stake is the rediscovery of the lost national soul!

Sorry for sounding a little tired. Cultural capital is not a commodity or a thing that can be engineered into existence. Sure, it can be accelerated by the state. But it must trust its creative people by enabling them to be managed by like-hearted individuals who can laugh and cry along with them, and not by bean-counting bureaucrats.

Essays

BEYOND CURRENT REALITY: A NEW SINGAPORE, PERHAPS?
4 August 2002

Life in Singapore has to be more than working, shopping and eating, and just duty and diligence. People must have a life before they can make culture, art, or create, invent, or want to make a new world, enjoy, be alive and believe in themselves. However, doing more for the people may actually achieve less. We need to focus on people-initiative and move away from top-down directions from the state and its institutions.

The following might be some of the ways to implement the different philosophy:

- Budget at least S$10 million every four years for a Southeast Asian contemporary art, design and literature documentation exhibition by regional and even international curators.
- Build a regional culture database for artists and researchers with intellectual and emotional linkages to the region. Let respected individuals have a free hand to run this.
- Produce and publish catalogues for each show. Include architecture models, drawings and photos with texts. Include all Southeast Asian industrial, decorative and design arts. Books, films, photos, etc.
- Have permanent exhibition spaces in MRT stations and underground bomb shelters as well as the usual venues. No need to charge market rates.
- Set aside a S$1,000,000 budget per year for each constituency to decide on community projects. The committee will consist of 49 per cent volunteers, 41 per cent by random appointment and 10 per cent direct appointees. This is the way to use money to create leadership and bond communities.
- Set aside hobby-farm plots, each with a small hut up to 12 square metre along railways and marginal lands for artists and retirees.
- Widen the range of lifestyle options in the city and the suburbs rather than only flats and condominiums. Do this by zoning to manage land rents and to keep prices affordable.

A New World in the Making

- Allow cheap, temporary occupation lofts, house boats, kelongs, jungle huts, riverside dwellings, tree houses, caravan parks, camping sites, beach huts to come about through private initiative. Let people and administrators take risks and responsibilities in running these places. Divest or reduce the responsibility load. Let people learn to take care and develop concern.
- Art schools can run public art places, cafes, restaurants, and bookshops. Employ students as part of their education to develop a service-with-style-and-care culture.
- Allow space under railway tracks and roads for creative studios. Use waste land to make space for freedom.
- Allow special jungle hides for live-in flora and fauna research. Have huts in the Bird Park, zoo; and tree houses in the botanical gardens, reservoirs, Bukit Timah Hill and Sungei Buloh.
- Turn Pulau Ubin into a nature reserve run by the Nature Society, community clubs, etc. Fees earned go to pay individuals and the club. Particular facilities can also be run by schools, the Rotary and Lions Clubs.
- Allow houseboats and kelong restaurants and riverine settlements administered by yacht clubs, nearby community centres or community clubs. They get a fee for the service. Let people row in the rivers. Stock the rivers with fish for anglers.
- Get golf clubs to run chalets and nature conservation programmes in their vicinity. They are responsible for monitoring the environmental impact of their presence.
- Establish East/West translation and publication centres in the universities. Make Singapore the intellectual resource centre of the region.
- Fund more audio/visual multilingual documentation of vanishing Southeast Asian cultures and settings.
- Establish Singapore as the operational base for an International Indo-Pacific Ocean University sailing ship. Raise an endowment fund of S$100 million from shipping tycoons with the Singapore government matching funds.

Essays

- Set up youth hostels in old shophouses and warehouses, run by Young Men's Christian Association and similar groups.
- Have beach clubs that care for the beach, run barbecues, change tents and rent out equipment. Cultivate esprit de corps from bodybuilding and life-saving activities.
- Introduce recycled art shop for creativity in use of waste.
- Organise a three month community festival to travel the island to taste, buy, see and listen to the voices and stories of other communities. This is not an arts festival but a people thing!
- Do things where the people are. Design walkways and public spaces for spontaneous choreography of events and attractions. Designs must not be monopolised by the Public Works Department, Urban Redevelopment Authority, Singapore Tourism Board or the Housing & Development Board, but through open public design competition.
- Make sure designs are fit for women with prams, the elderly, kids and the handicapped. Have plenty of shade, plants, seats, stalls, info kiosks, maps and transport guides.
- Scrap the public entertainment rules; have small places for music such as a piano in the park, drums in busy street corners. Mix noise with noise: street dancing, ballroom plazas, places for showing off, street fashion shows, art students showing their stuff, design students strutting their stuff, music jamming joints, parks for pets, experimental media cine centres. No entertainment licence needed. No public speaking licence needed. No public assembly licence required anymore. Scrap publishing licenses.
- Turn the whole island into an educational space resource. All environmental and infrastructural systems can be educational centres for people.
- Set up community museums.
- Set up yearly technical talent show centres for inventors.
- Set up investors fair in the polytechnics.
- Set up co-investment agreements with regional farmers.
- Set up eco-resorts in the region.

- Set up New Asia International University Learning Zones in the region. Allow many private schools.
- Have every student live in hostels, and run them on self-help lines to develop character, initiative and responsibility.
- Set up community-based house-help services for busy families.
- Develop showcase urban infrastructure and technologies for local use and export.
- Establish a Development Bank premised on project financing rather than collateralised financing.
- The list goes on. Add as many ideas as possible, but they should be consistent with the objective of building human capacity.

Essays

INTERROGATING GREAT ASIAN STREETS
7 December 2004

A keynote speech I gave at the 3rd Great Asian Streets Symposium organised by the Department of Architecture at the National University of Singapore.

The social science approach to interrogating the street as urban phenomenon is sectioned into sociological, political, spatial and cultural dimensions with notes on the geometry and physical characteristics. Surprisingly, there has been little attention paid to the economic basis of streets. This is serious because there is a dynamic that affects the composition, the transactions and the character of the street.

Typically, the early days of "great streets" started off as a place where small, even temporary stalls set up business. There is plenty of historical information in the form of paintings and literary descriptions of such streets. What is less emphasised is the nature of the capital and the transactions that take place—first, small capital then larger resources and now very large capital. In the beginning, small shops of more substantial construction appeared along the street or at intersections or in town or village squares. These reflect the kind of capitalisation. As capital accumulated, there was investment in more substantial establishments and provision of a wider range of goods and services. What was the mix between retail, small manufacture, craft and produce sales? What synergy among the different segments of the street economy was generated, and how were conflicts resolved or co-operation established? The architecture reflects all of these.

Petty trader capitalism was the beginning. Family businesses proliferated. These left a trace in the spatial character. The fine texture of the street is attributed to them. When big capital comes in, the scale changes and the street texture becomes coarse. The small narrow frontage buildings with store and living quarters above is the typical form of small capital. The super mall is the form of large capital. Small shops then stretch along linearly to form the street. Indeed, the street is the result of the competition for frontage.

Entrepreneurial capital was next in the evolution. They bought up or built new shopping blocks of four, six or eight shophouses. As the street filled up, depth was developed. Value was created through lower costs and

173

specialisation of goods and services. Home industries developed, bringing complexity and diversity.

As capital grew through real estate, banking and financial activities, in addition to retail, larger and larger capital accumulations resulted in reinvestment in larger spatial units which got added in between the shophouses. These grew into super blocks and later still, evolved into large stores and super malls. Then came corporate capital in the form of national or international investors with their franchise and chain stores. Small shops suffered or are absorbed into the larger units as franchisees or salaried operators. The innovation and spirit of small enterprises dies. The stage is set for the contemporary street to be replaced with spectacle and theatre. These take the place of the much loved original organic-authentic ambience.

The history of any great street is, therefore, a reflection of economic evolution. What are the dynamics of this transformation? To what extent is there inter-accommodation between the different capitalisms. Is the extent to which the dynamics of the street manifest, for better or for worse? What is the future? Will larger capital units eliminate the smaller? Is kitsch inevitable? What new transformations will occur? What is the future of the shopping street?

What is the social and spatial ecology of a Great Asian Street?

What makes great streets depends on many factors. The diversity and scale are dependent on the social ecology that is derived from such composition that establishes the culture and character of the street. What are the necessary proximities and adjacencies that enable connectivity and spatial excitement? Finally, what are the spatial tectonics of the street that contribute to its place values?

Material, financial power and ideas flow through urban spaces and streets

Primarily, it is still economics that is the first cause in the making of streets and cities, especially those which came about or grew immensely under economic imperatives released by industrialism and international trade. In Asia, it was colonialism and globalisation that shaped streets and cities. It is necessary, therefore, to grasp the quantum of material flows through a city before one can understand the qualitative implications of such flows. Quantification gives a definitive picture of the intensities and schedules involved. Financial flows give a picture of the dynamics. Of course, culture and politics are inseparable from economics and subsequent spatial formation. Measurements of flows give a picture of the inter-relationships and conflicts involved. The city is a dynamic system. That it succeeds despite its contradictions and dysfunction is a tribute to its inherent functionalities and its cultures. These affect the spatial qualities of the street, and its larger context, the city.

What are the flows that are specifically channelled through streets and why and to what effect?

Not all the flows happen in the streets. The Central Business District, the port, the factory areas, the universities and so on, are areas of internalised flows. These happen in the corridors of power, production lines and handling of goods. Only some of the flows are manifested in the street. These are retail and consumer flows although, in the economic history of a city, one can theorise an increasing trend towards greater reliance on representational transactions rather than material exchanges though finally, materials must change hands however extended this may be.

Why certain streets and passages in the city gained prominence to become primary, secondary and tertiary trade and culture venues needs comprehensive analysis. Why some transactions remain in the street in the upward process of economic integration is a question that needs study. Is there something inherent in the nature of the transacting parties that thrive off the street? If so, does it mean that the days of the street are numbered as economies move upwards? The street is a city what city is to hinterland. Who to and why the street is important is dependent on the trading partners of the street. What are the causal chains that establish the functionalities of any street and determines its mix, intensity and character? These underpin the architecture of the street.

What constitutes lively streets for the users and for the operator's points of view?

What are the different perceptions of the street from the view of shoppers, shop keepers and security personnel? What is the street to writers, artists, sociologists, politicians and public administrators?

Who maintains order: What is the power structure of the street and how do these contribute to the character of the street?

Streets are social organisms as much as they are economic entities. How is order maintained? Who maintains it? What are the limits of policing before the sense of freedom that constitutes street life becomes untenable?

What are the prospects of the Asian street as event-space in relation to the dynamics of capitalist transformations?

Given the economic underpinnings, the transactional nature of the street will be affected by changes in the nature of investment capital. The products of the street are bound to be affected positively or negatively. The history of streets is indeed a reflection of the presence of different capitalisms acting on the street. What are the prospects of different capital forms on successful existing streets? Will a preponderance of corporatist forms overturn the fine-grain nature of the traditional great street? What will the subsequent transformations be like? What should be the "right" mix of corporate capitalistic establishments with entrepreneurial capitalistic establishments and the existence of petty trader capitalism on desirable street character? Or is the prospect of the Great Asian Street to be a theme park orchestrated by corporatist imperatives?

Given the above, I would suggest that to really understand the street, one should undertake role play. Let me suggest the following characters:

- The small shop keepers
- The big corporate store managers
- The stores' purchasing agents
- The storekeeper's wife
- The son who wants to start his own business
- The money lenders
- The bankers
- The real estate agents
- The street vendors
- The wall shop keepers
- The hookers
- The policemen
- The local extortion gangsters
- The drug pushers
- The sweepers

- The refuse collectors
- The delivery men
- The shop assistants
- The coffee shop owners
- The porn merchants
- The gangsters
- The hawkers
- The city planners
- The store designers
- Flower stalls
- The news vendors
- The local hang abouts
- The old folks living nearby
- The video arcades
- The truants from school
- Mom with kids
- The salesmen
- Preachers
- The politicians

The future of the Great Asian Street will be the result of how design, economic and cultural forces interact to make the story with the planners and the architects. The story is an ongoing narrative that all the actors and planners make together. Is there a methodology implied? Certainly. For great streets to be sustained, design cannot anymore be the result of design object focus. Design has to be an on-site organic process of collectively imagining the narrative and matching ambitions to realities consistent with the narrative. A new kind of planner and architect is needed to understand the forces and to stimulate the narratives that can capture the imagination of all parties concerned.

A New World in the Making

HANYU PINYIN AND SINGAPORE STREET NAMES
12 October 2005

In the 1980s, I served on Singapore's Street and Building Names Board that considers and approves naming applications for buildings, estates and streets in the city.

I was surprised to be nominated to serve on the committee for naming streets. Though I knew that it had existed for some years, I did not give a thought as to what its importance was. I came to realise that naming streets and places is serious business as there are sensitivities involved. Names are part of the politics and culture of a place. There are traditional names to be respected and new ones to be coined, but everything has to achieve a delicate balance to maintain social harmony and reflect history.

There was a push by the Singapore Tourism Board to bring back the name Bugis Street when in fact the street had already been expunged through urban renewal. I refused to allow the new street to be named Bugis Street. I agreed for it to be named Bugis Place. There will always be attempts to rewrite history.

Many key issues stem from the need to have parity among the races. The sensitivities of the Chinese, Malay, Indian and Others had to be respected. I did not realise that the partitioning of society this way is not straightforward. While there must be parity and legitimacy in the decisions, the very fact of compartmentation creates special problems. And so, the committee had to be credibly represented by prominent persons from the different races. I was appointed because I was on the National Museum Development Committee then. I suppose I was to represent "heritage".

There were long lists of new roads, streets, links, centres that had to be named. The rapid change of the landscape demanded it. We ran out of categories and had to invent new ones beyond the usual road, street, avenue, close, crescent, place and lane. Instead, we had point, link, boulevard, passage and one wonders what! There were a few "standard" features. All names have to be in Latin script. That was part of the colonial legacy that everyone was used to. Had that not been so, what a clutter of signs there would be on our streets!

There was also to be no names after living persons. This was quite a departure from the practice in many developing countries where

Essays

personality cults were rampant. I think Singapore's leaders in their wisdom decided it was unbecoming and the word came down that the practice is a no-no. But this was not always the case in Singapore. It will be recalled that during the heady days of rapid private housing building during the 1950s' Korean War boom, Sennett Estate's roads were named after persons associated with the development either as directors or financiers. Some of these like Yap Pheng Gek were prominent in politics. This may have been another reason why there was the prohibition.

As it happened, this fact became an important plank in my argument against the "hanyu pinyin-isation" of place names, which was gathering momentum among the Chinese-educated political leaders in Singapore. Chng Jit Koon and several like-minded members of the committee had already done so for several place names before I came onto the scene. "Tekka", the Hokkien name for Kandang Kerbau Market at the junction of Bukit Timah Road and Serangoon Road, had been changed to "Zhujiao". It was Mandarin for "bamboo base", which is what Tekka means in Hokkien. No one could say anything because it was presumed to be a Chinese matter. Why this is so reflects the poor understanding of cross-cultural realities within the state-endorsed cultural concept defined exclusively as consisting of Chinese, Malay, Indian and Others.

China was on the ascendancy, and those Chinese-educated Singaporeans who were inclined to look towards it for intellectual and cultural cues were eager to emulate the country's new developments. To accelerate China's modernisation after the Cultural Revolution, one of the first steps it took was the renovation of its language. The simplification of the script was already done, the Romanisation of the language was the next step. They wanted to distinguish themselves from the Japanese Romanisation system. That was the underlying motive shared by Singapore Chinese intellectuals who remember the Japanese Imperial atrocities all too well.

Names in the school registers were required to be in hanyu pinyin. My sons refused as their family name, Tay, would have to become Zheng. They revolted. I was perturbed. But in the committee for naming streets, the "Chinese" wind was blowing strong and the others kept their own counsel.

Nellie, the Eurasian committee member, and Edwin Thumboo, a professor of English at the National University of Singapore of mixed

Chinese and Indian descent, felt helpless. They were uncomfortable but must have felt restrained to voice strong objection to the erasure of familiar place and street names formally in the vernacular Chinese dialect.

Such is the psychological framework operating in committees arising from the racial categorisation of Singaporeans. The non-Chinese felt and still feel it inappropriate to "interfere" in the matters of another race. There is a tacit agreement not to cross ethnic boundaries. The laws of sedition and common acceptance were the norms everyone abided by. Whereas, an inclusive ethnicity would have led towards an easy recognition of "street" multi-culturalism, the State-endorsed distinction of ethnicities led instead to an artificial exclusivism. Thus, no one felt comfortable to "transgress" into the cultural territory of another and the mutilation of Singaporean names and place names carried on. The hanyu pinyin movement was seen as exclusively a Chinese domain, their right and theirs alone.

It was, and still is, little understood that language, place names and food are cross-cultural facts of Singaporean culture—a fact so obvious as to be hardly conscious. And so, the unconsciousness of Singapore's own cross-cultural character remained in the shadows of the mind. It took Kuo Pao Kun, Singapore's true son, to give expression to this reality through his many beautiful and significant dramatic presentations of our unique culture.

"Tekka" was and is not only a Chinese term, it was and still is a name used by Malays, Indians and other Singaporeans. In their enthusiasm to regain lost ground after the closure of Nanyang University and smarting from the clampdown on "Chinese chauvinism", the Chinese lobby failed to realise the implication of name change to others. This is the problem of cultural naiveté in a young society lacking self-reflection. The phenomenon can be seen in exactly a similar manner in neighbouring Malaysia. There, the Chinese, Malay, Indian and Others (CMIO) formulation, an administratively convenient British creation, more appropriately rendered CIMO, also prevailed, given Malay dominance. The difference is in the eagerness to adopt Arab signs and symbols. There is a penchant for the Arabisation of names. The names of whole towns and states were rendered in Arabic without realising that these terms are totally alien to the other races. Johore is given the Arab honorific title, "Darul Ta'azim". Many personal names have lost the usage of Malay in preference for Arabic also. The same cultural dynamics is at work. Place names in a

Take the name change of Nee Soon, a district in the north of Singapore named after the illustrious pioneer rubber planter there. When the name was replaced by Yishun, it brought much dismay to Nee Soon's progeny. When I was chairman of the Heritage Committee, one of five within the Arts and Culture Council in 1990, I received an irate letter from Mr Lim Nee Soon's grandson urging me to help restore his grandfather's name. I tried in the Committee but was told it was impossible. The reason: All the title deeds had already been printed and issued for that whole district. So that was that.

Then there was another case of "Boh Sua Tian" (Hokkien for wireless), an area off Yio Chu Kang Road that was so coined after the BBC transmitter repeater aerial farm located there. The hanyu pinyin lobby wanted it to be given a "proper" name, saying that the vernacular was very "uneducated". Here, Edwin Thumboo argued strenuously against it. I supported him.

This case reflects a deep issue within the Chinese community. There is an interesting cultural attitude at work here. The Chinese-educated, certainly, and perhaps the Chinese who speak in dialects also share this same attitude in Singapore: that the vernacular is inferior to Mandarin. It is also an issue of class status. One able to speak, read and write Chinese is of high status. It was, after all, the language of the ruling class in China.

The significance of Mandarin is associated with the nation-state. It is, historically, a product of the Republic of China. Mandarin was referred to in Republican China as "guo yu" that is, the national language. The term was loosely applied by overseas Chinese as well. It was appropriate after Singapore got independence to change the term to "hua yu", that is, the "Chinese language". Though the correct distinction was made, attitude towards the vernacular dialects remained. Thus, when the Speak Mandarin Campaign began to eradicate the Hokkien, Teochew and Cantonese dialects, there was little difficulty in convincing people to change. This was despite the dislocation it would cause to many families where children would not be able to communicate with their grandparents.

And so, I started to object and tried to argue a general case against the use of hanyu pinyin in place names. The difficulty was how to make the case in the face of the sensitivities involved. The protagonists were undoubtedly sincere Chinese culturalists who were aggrieved at the erosion of Chinese language and culture. It was difficult to argue against obvious myopia especially as the protagonists were highly educated persons. One had also to be cognizant that the highest authority in the land had given tacit approval, especially as a campaigning of Asian values and Confucian ethics was on going.

I decided on a different tack. I asked for confirmation that the name of a living person cannot be used for a street or place. It was confirmed that this was the case. I then asked how the name of Dr Goh Keng Swee, the architect of the Singapore economy, a much revered person, would be rendered when the time came to honour him by naming a place or road after him. It would have to be in hanyu pinyin, and his name would be presented as "Wu Qing Rui"! It was a shock to everyone in the committee. No one would recognise the name except Chinese scholars! And so, the movement to change names in Singapore to hanyu pinyin was quietly dropped. I sensed a sigh of relief from the non-Chinese members of the committee, and my own Malayan-ness rose a few notches. I eventually drifted out of the committee with some satisfaction.

Essays

SINGAPORE COLLOQUIAL VALUES THAT STRIKE A CHORD
11 August 2005

Do also wrong
Don't do also wrong
Talk also no use, pretend *gong* is best
As a result what?
Say also not listen,
Listen also not understand, don't understand also don't ask, ask also don't
do,
Do also do wrong,
Wrong also don't admit,
Admit also not happy
Not happy also don't say.

SINGAPORE: A PARADOXICAL PARADISE
19 April 2006

It is a strong state but a weak nation.

It is a democracy without democrats.

It is a modern state without modernity.

It takes good care of its people but has a dim view of human nature.

It wants its young to be innovative yet conservative like their elders.

It wants change but is structured for conformity.

It is fully networked but has little free communication.

It justifies a non-level political playing field by world norms yet bucks the trends by deciding to be non-corrupt.

It wants an innovative culture but is run by rules.

It is fully informatized but has no flow of critical ideas.

It is an open society, but critical individuals fear jeopardy to their careers.

It is multiracial but is very colour conscious.

It has full home ownership, but people cannot plan their common spaces.

It has full education but there are no private Singapore schools.

It seeks foreign talent but is prejudiced against its own.

It wants exceptional quality but rules out exceptions.

It is illiberal, yet it has numerous committees and feedback mechanisms.

It wants public participation, but pressure groups are discouraged.

It is farsighted, but trains its people to be near sighted.

It is clean and green, but its people are untidy.

It plans and controls everything, yet it wants spontaneity and vibrancy.

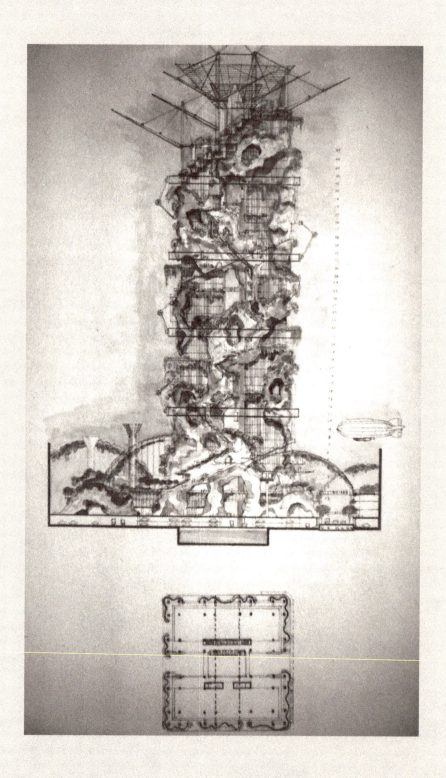

Ideas and Proposals

This landscaped tower was part of a tropical city concept I developed in 1990 with a multidisciplinary team for the Kampong Bugis Design Guide Plan. The building façade has horizontal tracks for maintenance cranes, ramps and staircases for public access, as well as tea houses, waterfalls and lookout pods. Why shouldn't the outsides of a building be usable?

07

Ideas and Proposals

Proposal for "South Sea Lagoon Project" at East Coast Reclamation
October 1968

I wrote this for the Singapore Planning Urban Research Group after visiting Honolulu, Hawaii, and seeing how the beachfront was used for development.

The project is located on the reclamation site along the full length of Marine Parade, stretching from Katong Convent in the east to the SEACOM cable in the west, over a distance of one mile. It would involve an area of approximately 180 acres, but this represents only 18 per cent of the total reclamation area of 1,000 acres.

Brief description

The project consists of the creation of two or more large internal swimming lagoons, with natural beaches and filtered sea water. The filtering process would utilise the tides, with some power assistance. The existing Marine Parade Promenade will be enlarged, providing space for increased recreational facilities, restaurants, carparks, and shops, besides of course, enhancing swimming and water sport facilities. On the opposite shore of the internal lagoon facing Marine Parade, the land will be sold for the development of hotels, nightclubs and other tourist facilities. It is probable that, resulting from this, properties adjacent to Marine Parade may in future be developed as tourist facilities.

Social benefit

The immediate hinterland of this project is the Katong and Siglap areas which, at the moment, are densely populated with about 1/3 of the total population of Singapore. Recreational facilities in this area are generally rather lacking. The only major open spaces available are Katong Park and Marine Parade Promenade. This project will certainly be a boon for the residents of this area.

Economic benefit

This development will enhance land values in and around Katong Centre and particularly along Marine Parade. Indeed, properties along Marine Parade will have a windfall, and may convert the present master plan zoned usage from residential to commercial development. The State can accrue a portion of this increased land value by a special-zoned development charge levied at a higher rate than at present provided for in the development charge rules.

Tourist attraction

Singapore, by and large, is lacking in tourist facilities and such a scheme can become its number one attraction for visitors. It is ideally located in relation to the airport. The high-speed road places it within easy communication with the city. Its proximity will benefit the existing Katong shopping area while also providing tourists with shopping and other urban types of services. From a town planning point of view, this project will help decentralise functions away from the city centre and Orchard Road areas, thereby reducing crowding and traffic congestion.

Increase in reclamation land value

Of course, as a result of this project, the land value in the project area, as well as in the immediate surrounding, will be enhanced considerably. The cost of land lost to the lagoon will most definitely be offset by this increase in land value. This would mean a profit to the state. Development is likely to be rapid. All the energy being expended both by the government and the private sector in tourist promotion can be brought to bear upon this project, and by this concerted action the project can take off in a very short time. It has a powerful inherent image and Singapore's tourism can be "sold" on it.

Financing of the project

While it is not possible at this stage to precisely state the costs involved, a favourable factor is the commitment already made on the reclamation and with a little more capital, the project can come into fruition. It can be seen that some of, if not all, the cost can be recovered by various measures, such as:

- Localised development charge
- Enhanced land value
- Foreign exchange earnings from tourism
- Letting of concessions for recreational facilities, (restaurants, nightclubs, marine land [marinas?], etc.)

Technical feasibility

This has a direct effect on the cost of the project. At this stage, major technical problems are not envisaged in the formation of the inland lagoons. These, in fact, can be created by omitting the earth filling where the lagoons are to be. As sand is plentiful in this area, it will cost very little to line the entire lake with sand, which will provide good beaches, as well as maintain the clarity of the water. Natural tides can be used to minimise the power required for delivery of the sea water. Some treatment will probably be needed to bring water quality up to levels required for bathing. Possibly filtration plus chlorination will be sufficient. Some control may be required to operate various mechanical devices in this process. A sanitary engineer should analyse the water and conditions of use to determine the extent of treatment required.

Urgency of action

The reclamation is, at this date, already at Siglap opposite Katong Convent. A quick decision will be necessary to divert the reclamation, and for proper technical and economic studies to be undertaken. The present process of reclamation, in fact, makes this diversion possible. If, however, due to unforeseen technical and economic reasons the project needs to be abandoned, the hollows for the lagoons left unfilled by the reclamation can be subsequently filled up and the area reverted to the originally intended state.

Cost benefit

It is difficult to analyse costs without fairly detailed plans of the lagoons plus appurtenances. However, engineers can make preliminary plans from which costs can be estimated. Benefits are even more difficult to estimate. They will come from recreation and enhancement of property values.

Projections of use of the recreation areas can lead to estimates of present value of P.Q. where "P" is the price people pay per visit to similar facilities (i.e. admission fees for sport events or cinema), and "Q" is the estimated number of visits to the lagoons.

Real estate valuators can estimate land values with and without the proposed facilities. The difference would represent enhanced value of properties.

Ideas and Proposals

HOUSING FOR INDUSTRIAL CENTRES
5 October 1969

A paper I presented at a seminar on new communities in industrial estate, using Jurong as a case study. It was organised by the Singapore Planning and Urban Research Group and involved speakers from the government, including George Thomson of the Ministry of Foreign Affairs and Fong Tiew Weng, a senior planner of Jurong Town Corporation.

Singapore is entering a new phase of development which will have fundamental effect on the evolution of its social fabric. From a basically trading community, it is rapidly evolving into a modern industrialised community and this has effect on the physical environment, particularly that of workplace and dwelling place. In the past, traders and commercial workers lived adjacent to their place of work in a natural relationship. The shophouse with the commercial premise below and dwelling accommodation above, is a typical example of the unification of workplace and dwelling place. The city is also characterised by this very close relationship between workplace and dwelling place, though this is rapidly changing as a result of urban renewal and the intensification of commercial premises within the city. The situation of close relationship between workplace and dwelling place is possible when the population is relatively small. With an increasing population demanding more dwelling spaces and the corresponding increase in the demand for commercial spaces, the conflict of these two demands, particularly when viewed as a single-level utilisation of land use, becomes incompatible. This results in a drift of widening proportions between the location of workplace and dwelling place. A major factor which contributes to this drift is the idealised town planning concepts which have been exercised to neatly compartmentalise different activities and land usages into distinctly separate zones as contained in the 1958 Master Plan of Singapore and its subsequent revisions. These factors among others, set the scene for the development of dormitory residential estates such as Serangoon Garden Estate, Frankel Estate and numerous housing estates located around the city centre, including those developed by the public sector.

The city centre was reserved largely for commercial and semi-industrial usages. The existing road system was enlarged and developed to provide a transportation network to shuttle people between places of work and places of dwelling. This situation is tenable up to a point, but we are now approaching a point of saturation and we witness increasing strangulation of vehicular movement on the roads. Road transportation by means of private vehicles is defeating itself, and land use controls as they exist at present, tend to perpetuate and aggravate the transportation problem.

So long as industry is largely based on the utilisation of manpower, and this is likely to be the case for many years to come until it is economically and socially possible to automate industry, the relationship of the place of work and the place of dwelling will be the central problem in planning land use and transportation. Severe dislocations can impinge on the efficiency and productivity of industry. It is erroneous to consider the manpower situation in Singapore on a pan-island basis without considering the location of the manpower supply in relation to the demands of industry and the location of industry. When transportation costs amount to 20 to 30 per cent of the worker's income and particularly when income is relatively low in the region of $100 to $150 per month, which is the normal wages available for industrial workers, transportation cost becomes a major deterrent factor for potential workers to accept jobs at a great distance from their homes. Another serious implication of the dislocation between place of work and place of dwelling of industrial workers is the travelling time involved. Industrial workers living in Toa Payoh and working in Jurong have to spend approximately four hours of travelling time every day. This has a serious impact on the physical and mental health of the worker which will no doubt affect his productivity. This is not to mention the serious implication this will have on his family life, when one adds to this figure the 8 to 10 hours of working time demanded by industry.

Family structures as they exist today, are largely those which have evolved and persisted from that of a trading community which Singapore was until the recent past. Industrialisation can cause serious strain on such family structures as they impose different demands on the individual members of families. Large families with many adherents sharing a dwelling premise is common in a trading community. A large family involved in a family business is a definite economic advantage in a trading community, but this is a disadvantage in an industrialised community where individuals have separate employment which may be located in different parts of the island and may require different working

Ideas and Proposals

times. The roster and night duty shifts must seriously affect family organisation. Young single members of a family, because of job demands, often have to work away from home and live in dormitories. This creates problems for the individual in adjusting to the new environment as well as creates family tensions. Superimposed on this situation is the demands by the children of such families for education and recreation which are not fully developed in the new work centres. We are already witnessing the proliferation of small households and this is evidenced by the tremendous demand by young couples, married or about to be married, applying for Housing & Development Board units. Such young couples have increased mobility, and this is certainly one of the implications of a modern industrialised community which has great disincentives for larger family units. This, of course, indicates that family structures and relationships are not static. It may well be that we may evolve a social system in the future to provide for greater individual freedom and for children to be reared and educated collectively.

Development of creches and kindergartens is also an indication of the demands which are made on the individual members of households. Womenfolk are increasingly sought after as female labour for industry and this will seriously affect family structures as we know them now. With employment opportunities for male and female members of the household and the trend towards the formation of small households, there will be a need for retirement homes for the aged as work demands may create disincentives for immobile family members. The evolution of western industrialised societies has been imperfect mainly because of their religious fixations. However, we are on the threshold of an industrialisation and modernisation programme, and we will have to be mindful of the social implications of this programme. These are the long-term implications. However, for the present and immediate future, it will be necessary to have an integrated approach towards the development of industrial and urban centres which will provide employment as well as dwelling places, recreation and all the amenities associated with living. From the point of view of industry, this has the advantage of increasing efficiency and productivity of the workers. And from the social point of view, it provides for better living, catering to rising expectations.

In the development of new towns which have an industrial base, after infrastructure, roads and utilities have been installed, factories are often the first structures to be built. Housing for industrial workers then comes in as a second stage of development and this may well be a mistake because without recreational and civic amenities, people are reluctant to live in the houses which are provided. The converse is true that the recreational and civic amenities will not develop because shopkeepers and other service industries are not prepared to operate without a captive clientele. The question is to break the vicious cycle. We have witnessed the phenomenon of the car-owning middle-income group's preparedness to live at greater and greater distances from the city, which is often their place of work and entertainment. Clementi Park and Faber Hill are examples of this trend. This is because of the increasing land cost for private dwellings caused by the general unavailability of residential land. This willingness to live away from the city can be used constructively as a genesis for new industrial and urban centres away from the city.

Middle income housing can be built in large quantities in locations such as Changi, Lim Chu Kang, Sembawang, Woodlands and Jurong, where new industrial and urban centres are planned. However, housing developers because of the many problems which they face, have begun to lose interest in housing development and are branching out into other forms of investment. This trend can be overcome by recognising such problems and taking steps to alleviate them. This is justified when it can be seen that housing developers can play a positive role in the provision of a wide variety of houses needed in new industrial and urban centres.

The main problem faced by housing developers is the difficulty of obtaining land at a reasonable cost free of squatters. They also find considerable difficulty in obtaining approval for their developments. The government may assist by releasing land for housing development with appropriate stipulated conditions, similar to those provided for in the government's sale of land under the urban renewal programme. It is established that if land is available at $1.50 to $2.00 per square foot, it is possible for developers to construct houses for sale at a price between $20,000 to $30,000 and yet make a reasonable profit. Another category of developers may appear on the scene when favourable conditions are available. These developers may take the form of managers or project management companies. These management companies will undertake to build houses for a professional fee and in this way would achieve what the housing co-operatives have largely failed to do. Housing co-operatives

Ideas and Proposals

themselves can be given encouragement and be more effective if land is made available and if the government can assist in the financing of housing projects either directly through loans from the Development Bank of Singapore or any other appropriate agency or by instituting mortgage insurance to underwrite loans.

With the trend towards the proliferation of smaller households and with the possibility of middle-income housing serving to catalyse the development, the new industrial and urban centres will become truly viable centres both for living and working. In order to achieve this, however, a wide range of work opportunities besides industrial employment will have to be provided. Commercial, entertainment and the numerous servicing types of employment could also be created. A viable new town or urban centre should provide a 1:3 work ratio between primary and secondary jobs. That is for every industrial job, there should be about three other jobs in the professional, servicing, entertainment and food sectors. This would also require a deliberate central area development policy to decentralise such functions which are not associated with the city centre. This would also require a deliberate policy on the location of hospitals, schools and other social amenities away from the city centre and into these new centres. A full range of housing types should also be provided, not only industrial dormitories and low-cost public housing, but also upper middle- and middle-income housing. Not only flats, but also bungalows and terrace houses. In this way, we should be able to build viable new industrial and urban centres in Singapore.

A New World in the Making

LOCATE AIRPORT AT CHANGI
23 February 1971

A statement for the Singapore Planning and Urban Research Group that followed up our earlier concerns about the government's plans to expand Paya Lebar airport. In 1975, it was announced that Singapore's new international airport would move to Changi instead.

The recent announcement in the local press by the British Air Chief Marshal that military air operations in Singapore will be located at Tengah base, and that Changi airfield which is now the Royal Air Force main transport base, will be handed back to Singapore at the end of this year, reopens the issue concerning the expansion of Paya Lebar Airport as Singapore's main civilian air transport centre. The Singapore Planning and Urban Research Group has had misgivings concerning the large-scale expansion of Paya Lebar mainly in view of the adverse environmental effects this would have on the Geylang/Katong area. The prime minister's previous announcement of the intention to develop Changi as the civilian airport within ten years served to reassure the public that the government was aware of the adverse environmental effects on Paya Lebar. We are, however, unsure as to the extent the Paya Lebar expansion now at hand will pre-determine the desirable long-term objective of siting the airport at Changi, and the extent of other intermediate environmental problems before a transfer is achieved. The recent announcement opens the possibility of Changi as a civilian airport and it is hoped that the authorities will be able to divert resources for the Changi development in spite of committed programmes and administrative arrangements at Paya Lebar.

The authorities should be encouraged to build up the Changi airfield into Singapore's international airport in view of the following adverse considerations related to Paya Lebar:

- That the investment in Paya Lebar may reduce the impetus to develop Changi because of continuing investment necessary to keep pace with increasing air traffic demands.
- With the increasing air traffic and with the introduction of noisier aircraft such as the jumbo jets and supersonics, and should additional runways be introduced to the east or west of the existing Paya Lebar runway, noise pollution along the

Ideas and Proposals

aircraft approach corridor will be intensified over a large, populated area.

- The expansion of Paya Lebar will also require as a consequence, the re-zoning of land use pattern along the aircraft approach corridor for usages such as industry and commerce. This would be very disruptive to the land usage and existing facilities. Unfortunately, three large residential areas already lie within the aircraft approach corridor and are subject to intense noise pollution. There should be no more residential development permitted within the zones affected by noise pollution both by private and public sectors.

- Noise control measures to be taken in existing residential buildings within the aircraft approach corridor. This will involve alterations to the buildings, such as provision of double-glazing windows, air-tight doors and ventilation systems, etc. These are expensive.

The plan of the existing Paya Lebar Airport shows the aircraft approach corridors for landing and taking off from the runway (increased length of 13,200 feet) and corresponding noise intensities generated by aircraft at various distances from the runway. Aircraft approach corridors and corresponding noise intensities are also indicated should there be additional runways constructed in the future either to the east or to the west of the existing runway or both.

International design standards and statistics provide the following:

- New York Airport restricts noise level to 100 decibels (internationally acceptable noise level measurement for aircraft noise) for night operations and 112 decibels for day operations. Corresponding figures for London Airport are 100 decibels for night operations and 108 decibels. for day operations. Where noise level exceeds 90 decibels, human comfort and well-being are affected.

- International standards for airport planning recommend that no residential buildings, schools, hospitals and places of worship should be located where noise level exceeds 100 decibels.

- A half mile within each end of the runway and approach funnel is usually considered as accident prone and there should be no development within this area. A 11-mile radius around the approach funnel is also considered as accident prone and where avoidable, there should be no development in this area.

It is appreciated that in view of the future of the Changi air base being uncertain at the time when decision to proceed with airport facilities to cater for projection of increased air traffic urgently required by the Republic, the Paya Lebar expansion programme was embarked upon. With the latest announcement of Changi, however, we hope the authorities will not be unprepared in view of commitments, to divert the expansion programme to Changi which would be the most beneficial location for the people of Singapore as most aircraft noise will be over the sea.

Ideas and Proposals

LOW-RISE HIGH-DENSITY HOUSING: TOWARDS A MORE SOCIABLE HOUSING FORM
27 September 1978

My reflections after completing a low-cost housing project in Cheras, Kuala Lumpur, in 1976.

The problem of sociability in housing has attracted the attention of the general public and has been constantly mentioned by politicians and social commentators. They imply a link between the social behaviour of people at neighbourhood level and national culture. Since they desire a cohesive national culture, they believe that neighbourliness is the cornerstone in the nation-building process, that national culture in its evolution must also be reflected and stabilised at community level. They feel that it is difficult to attain a cohesive national culture when there is little cohesion at the neighbourhood level. The problem is of course a complex one, and there are contradictory factors at work; the chief of which is the growing self-centeredness arising from meritocracy.

The process of economic growth, together with the trickling down of economic benefits and social amenities, including housing the people, if successful, also provides for a more self-sufficient way of life, which can easily become a more selfish way of life. Indeed, in motivating the workforce towards greater efforts in securing, in a meritocratic system, personal progress measured in terms of more income, and greater accessibility to more and better goods and services, the process, including the breakdown of the extended family, and the setting up of nuclear families, automatically creates a culture of more self-centred individuals. Additionally, rapid economic development demands a great deal of time devoted to work and preparation for education. The quality of family life is affected, more so when both parents work. C. C. Leong in his book, *Youth in The Army* portrays a picture of impoverished home life of the masses, resulting from the demands of work. Parents tired out by their work, traffic jams, pollution and a general humdrum existence have little wherewithal to explain things to their children. Discipline is usually delivered without explanation and family conversation as a means of sharing experience is substituted by entertainment diversion. Children tend to be left on their own, with a minimum of parental guidance. The Housing & Development Board (HDB) Sample Household Survey of 1973 shows that 63.3 per cent of children living in HDB flats between the ages of 6 and 12 play indoors, whereas 22.2 per cent play in the corridors, void decks, playing fields and community centres. The HDB study notes that there has been a significant shift in behaviour since the 1968 survey in that parents generally discourage their children from playing outside the house in order not to distract them from their homework, and to avoid mixing with bad company. Probably in the intervening years, the massive increase in the female workforce has also contributed to this behaviour. Nevertheless, it is significant to note that of those playing outside the house, more play in the public corridors than in the public open spaces for this age group. Leong notes that in an impoverished home environment, the peer group influence on the morals, values and general attitudes of youths plays an inordinately large role, and not necessarily a healthy one. He advocates that there should be more organised youth groups to cater for the developmental needs of youngsters, of whom the majority now live in high-rise flats.

The question in housing design is how the housing form can accommodate the sociability and organisational needs of such youth. The kampong kind of social interaction which many social commentators and ex-kampong dwellers fondly remember are no longer replicable when the socio-economic conditions of the individuals concerned changed radically when they moved into public housing, and especially when they are more and more absorbed into the mainstream of economic life in urban centres like Singapore. The warm neighbourliness of the kampong stems from a system of social obligations and a sense of shared destiny, fear of fire, of intruders and the borrowing and lending of daily necessities. The physical environment of the kampong is conducive for the mutual surveillance of common territory, and easy accessibility to each other's homes, together with visual and acoustic proximity, aided the setting up of a warm neighbourly feeling. This is reported by Michael Walter in *Design and Territoriality in Public Housing in Singapore*.

Aside from the socio-economic variables in the complex forces which produce neighbourliness in its positive connotation, those living in public housing, who are well plugged into the mainstream economic system will still require the satisfaction of their basic social and psychological needs to relief boredom and to exercise their social selves. What are these? Undoubtedly, workmates and schoolmates provide for some satisfaction

Ideas and Proposals

of the social and psychological needs of individuals. Greater personal mobility, access to other sources of information, travel, intellectual and emotional stimulus with greater affluence also fulfils some of these needs. There is no substitute within the family and in the neighbourhood for the daily exercise of intimate and neighbourly relationships, which form the most tangible steps on the ladder towards a cohesive society. There is a great deal of truth in what Leong says about the bored but hardworking Singaporean who kills his boredom by gambling, eating and sleeping. The older people left at home, or mothers who are not yet drawn into the workforce, or do not wish to be drawn into the workforce, have social and psychological needs during their long hours at home attending to the household chores. They need to talk to other people; they need to be exposed to more stimulating events other than repetitive household chores. Children need to have playmates in the neighbourhood other than their siblings. How can the housing form provide for these?

The negative connotation of neighbourliness that is non-interference, and not creating a nuisance, or impinging in any way on the neighbours' privacy, tends to flow from the spirit of greater self-sufficiency. The cry for greater privacy is also an expression of the daily exasperation with the problem of high-density living and working. People want to escape from it all. They want to wall themselves in. When neighbours do not know each other, any intrusion, whether accidental or unintentional is exaggerated in the mind of the offended neighbour. It is embroidered and imagined into a deliberate provocation requiring an aggressive response. More often, the reaction is a passive aggression expressed by snubbing and a growing conviction of the badness of human nature. With improved familiarity, many of these provocations can become accepted as an unavoidable consequence of high-density living and some of them can be eliminated if they are made conscious.

The high degree of tolerance shown by the residents of the Sambahayan condominium project—a low-cost housing scheme in Rizal, Philippines, where the apartments are 350 square feet, each containing approximately 7 people, and there are 358 families housed in a series of 5-storey blocks of walk-up apartments in 1 hectare of land—is impressive. The ambient noise level was higher than many HDB flats. The population density is more than twice that of HDB being 1,000 persons per acre (ppa). There is no individual refuse chute attached to the flats. A centralised refuse chute was provided, and yet it was scrupulously clean (attesting to the strong sense of community cohesion and co-operation). They have their own community organisation, with full time staff employed on a nominal basis, drawn from some of the housewives and older people living there. Committee members are all elected among themselves, and they have very active sub-committees dealing with education, recreation and so forth. In spite of the very high-density, there is hardly any scribbling on the walls, the refuse chute area is remarkably clean, the public areas are not vandalised, the play spaces along the corridors and the ground floor are well maintained and used by the children. One has the feeling that this is a functioning community as close as one can get to a kampong.

Thus, one of the chief variables in the sociability of housing is that there must be community participation in the management of community affairs. This will not be easy, nor will it be automatic. It will not be easy, especially in a social environment which has largely neglected and even punished the development of the altruistic conscience, to transcend selfish barriers accumulated and reinforced by a poor view of human nature. The style of government has a lot to do with the endorsement, confirmation and consolidation of the negative view of human nature. When the stick and carrot is always used, then voluntary participation declines. And yet if sociability in housing is to be achieved, steps must be taken with the necessary skill to encourage community initiative in community formation. The physical provision of appropriate spaces in the design of housing must aid and assist the process of community formation. The organisation of street camps in HDB estates by the Children's Society is truly a positive step and it must be given every encouragement and space for its success and future growth.

The temptation to seek a more "efficient" method of creating neighbourliness must be resisted, for voluntarism and the warmness of human relationships can only be nurtured through trial and error and personal involvement and experience cannot be legislated nor bureaucratised.

Options for housing forms

The criteria for designing physical structures to house families in a way which provides for the sociability needs of the families is clear. Can high-rise housing forms fulfil these criteria? Is it possible to build alternative housing forms within the same density and space and population requirements? Does high-rise housing encourage or discourage greater sociability? Can alternative housing forms of medium-rise or low-rise better fulfil the needs of the residents? Of course, all these questions must be underscored by a common low-cost criterion, otherwise it is not possible to discuss alternatives sensibly.

Of the high-rise housing forms, the point block is the most private and the least sociable. The slab block with skipped-floor corridors provides for a diminished corridor-doorstep play space for the children but it has increased privacy. Slab blocks with common corridors on every floor is a housing form that provides scope for some social interaction of children and neighbours on the same floor. It is the most sociable of the high-rise housing forms. Then why not continue to build high-rise slab blocks with enlarged corridors and possibly social facilities such as reading rooms, games rooms and space for clubs within the slab block? All these of course can be done but with much increased cost. Also, the effectiveness of the corridor as a play space, with its safety problem, is not easily resolved. Can enlarged and better designed corridors provide the quality required of play spaces suitable for youngsters? Younger children in their play require a more stimulating physical environment other than concrete surfaces and the paraphernalia commonly found along corridors.

The number of material objects and things in the corridors as compared to the number on the ground space with grass and planting and with nature closer at hand is drastically lower. The total number of stimulants in the play environment on the ground is enormously larger and offers that much more scope for imaginative play. If in the face of the low-rise alternative it is still insisted that high-rise housing should be the housing form, then the high-rise policy is not founded on cost criteria nor on the desire for a healthier and stimulating environment for children and domicile adults. Based on the realisation of the socio-psychological and cost limitations of the high-rise housing form, we must proceed to investigate the other housing forms.

Alternative housing forms:
low- and medium-rise high-density housing forms

The physical design of housing forms for densities up to 371 ppa at a plot ratio of 1.2:1 offers many design possibilities, ranging from low-rise high-density (LRHD) to medium rise high-density (MRHD) to high-rise high-density (HRHD).

The experience of design solutions for this density has been pre-dominantly that of the high-rise form. This is partly due to the misconception that for densities up to 371 ppa, high-rise means high-density, that is it is impossible to have the same high-density with building forms of two to four-storeys in height with the same distance to height ratio. Designers generally have not explored the design and geometrical possibilities for LRHD design solutions, and this neglect is aided by sociological research on the housing environment which has tended to confirm the adaptation that has taken place in a no-choice situation of the dwellers of HRHD housing. Such research has tended to encourage the high-rise policy.

It is not the intention of this paper to deal in detail with the physical design alternatives to high-rise housing for that would involve a detailed study of the mathematical and geometrical aspects of building form. This subject has already been well developed by the Centre for Land Use and Built Form Studies at Cambridge University by Leslie Martin, Lionel March and company in the early seventies. It would be sufficient here to illustrate the point by a simple example, that is the following:

The average plot ratio of HDB housing in Singapore is 1.2:1, that is the total floor area of the housing blocks is 1.2 times the area allotted for housing. The site coverage of these blocks, that is the area of land built on, is approximately 12 per cent. The average height of HDB blocks is between 10 to 12 storeys. If the design requirement is to reduce the height to say four storeys, then the site coverage would automatically increase to 36 per cent or three times the average HDB site coverage. To reduce the height, however, to say two or three storeys would entail an increase in site coverage to approximately 45 per cent.

The detailed architectural design problem involving the design of the housing unit and its collective form is how to design dwellings with sufficient ventilation, lighting and privacy with high site coverage. It is not a very difficult problem. It only requires a moderate degree of architectural competence. It must be stated, however, that the reduction in height to four storey and below, besides entailing an increase in site coverage, would also involve new environmental and spatial relationships and their corresponding psychological adaptations.

Ideas and Proposals

Toa Payoh Neighbourhood II can be redesigned with four-storey ring blocks with the same accommodation as the existing slab block arrangement with an average of 10.75 storeys. A ring block can achieve this by virtue of its increased perimeter length. It should be noted that there is a corresponding increase in site coverage, but this is ameliorated by the increased ground accessibility from the flats. The ring block also involves an increased building depth. The existing HDB slab blocks are approximately 35 feet in depth. In ring blocks, this will increase to approximately 50 feet. This would pose a design challenge which should not be insurmountable to architects. Of course, some form of air wells will have to be provided. This would of course involve a certain reduction in privacy.

But it should not be assumed that the kind of privacy aggressively defended with a suspicious attitude towards neighbours is something that is not changeable. It can be changed, and it will be changed through good design and community participation in the development of neighbourliness, not of course, without difficulties.

Cluster link houses are another housing type. It is basically a back-to-back arrangement with penetrating breezeways to achieve better ventilation and accessibility. The cluster link house can achieve densities of approximately 60 dwellings per acre or 300 ppa. There are many other forms of high-density low-rise housing forms within the range of densities required in Singapore, that is up to 371 ppa.

Cluster court houses are another building form that can achieve an even higher density with two-storey houses. It can achieve densities of up to 80 dwellings per acre or approximately 400 ppa. But its application will entail greater changes in concepts of privacy and require greater efforts at community development. These new housing forms entail a slight revaluation of internal floor space. In being able to use the ground space around the house, it is possible to reduce the internal floor space. Probably a mixture of four-storey and two-storey housing forms will provide the greatest flexibility in design.

The aesthetic problem

Before examining further the case for LRHD housing, it would be necessary here to interject some remarks on the problem of the aesthetics of low-cost housing. Many architects and policymakers are obsessed with neatness (meaning "visual order"). Lack of visual order is often termed pejoratively as "slums". Architects are also instinctively pre-disposed against regularity. What they want is a combination of visual order but variegated in an artful manner. They dislike symmetry and they also dislike simple lineal repetition. This prejudice of architects finds its way into the different policies and designs of low-cost housing.

Assuming an a priori superiority in their architectonic preference, they judge design solutions out of the socio-economic context. The unsatisfied aesthetic sense of architects has led most to avoid designing low-cost housing that is really cheap and sociable. Architects that are concerned with low-cost housing must develop a design approach that can solve problems without unnecessarily burdening the housing situation with unnecessary architectural embellishment gleaned from the architectural fashion magazines. Some favourite ideas which are constantly cited in justification of variegated layouts is that of "identity" arising from visual variety. Kevin Lynch in a study of Victorian industrial housing, which consists of extensive repetition of parallel terrace blocks and was much condemned by architects for their monotony, shows that the residents far from losing their way due to the monotony and lack of identity in the housing area in fact have a rich system of non-architectonic symbols in their minds together with some landmarks and features meaningful to them which constitute their mental maps and sign posts. Modern architecture's penchant for neatness and precision is not automatically valued by householders. Very often, modern architecture is much altered and adorned with decorations by householders in their efforts to personalise and humanise the space. These efforts have drawn the scorn of architects of the lack of taste and "education" of the ordinary man. In low-cost housing, it is necessary to sympathetically understand people's needs and to devise an architecture that can fulfil these needs rather than wilfully imposing a pre-ordained architectural aesthetic, whatever the virtues of that might be. The architectural challenge in the design of low-cost housing is to invent a new aesthetic which can express the community grouping and symbolise its sociability through its collective form. This calls for the highest levels of imagination and skill in evolving an aesthetic out of the reality of low-cost housing rather than borrowed from other sources.

Ideas and Proposals

A case of LRHD housing

Arising from the technical studies conducted by the writer, an experimental LRHD housing project was built for City Hall in Kuala Lumpur, Malaysia, in 1976, consisting of 676 dwellings on 11 acres of land. Construction took a period of eight months. The project consisted entirely of two-storey back-to-back cluster link houses, each with two bedrooms, a living/dining space, a small kitchenette and a toilet/bath. Four dwellings share a common eight-feet wide breezeway and each dwelling has a small private garden. Twelve-feet wide emergency service roads within 20-feet reserves are located at every two blocks, providing vehicle accessibility as well as play spaces. (Yes, roads can be play spaces too if the traffic density is low!). A sociological study conducted by Chong Yoke Choy from the Department of Anthropology & Sociology at the University of Malaya three months after the houses were occupied, produced valuable information on this project. To the writer's knowledge, this is the first modern LRHD project in the Malaysia/Singapore area. Studies of its achievements, problems and its consequences are vital for the future of LRHD. Undoubtedly there are errors and mistakes, and it is from these as well as from its achievements that lessons for the future of LRHD can be drawn. The rest of this article will highlight features of this study which is of direct relevance. It will also quote some unpublished data by the same researcher. The writer understands that a subsequent study was also conducted by MARA Institute and this study was concerned mainly with the resettlement of Malay families within the Cheras pilot housing project. Findings with regard to the adaptations of these people to the new housing environment are very similar to the University of Malaya study.

The pilot low-cost housing project that was built in Kuala Lumpur at Cheras proves that the construction cost was significantly reduced due to low-rise design. An alternative scheme was proposed, using four-storey slab blocks, and it proved to be approximately RM$1,600 more than the RM$5,000 cost per unit of the cluster link house. This cost does not include the cost for roads, drains, sewer, which works out between RM$600 to RM$800 per unit at 1976 prices. With the completion of the project, it is felt that an additional expenditure of approximately RM$800 to RM$1,000 can make vast improvements in the form of better finishes and workmanship, increased ventilation, more electrical power points, bigger toilet, etc.

Some of the baseline issues which the Cheras project attempted to provide answers for are those problems commonly highlighted in the survey conducted by the HDB on residents' reactions to high-rise living. The common complaints with regard to the physical environment are:

- The generally high level of ambient noise.
- The problems of unreliability of and vandalism to the lifts. Added to this is the dangers of rape and crime being committed within lifts.
- The problem of noise generated by children playing along corridors.
- The generally high level of vandalism to public areas notwithstanding the high degree of surveillance and maintenance provided by the police and HDB wardens.
- Problems associated with the cleanliness of the refuse chute and its abuse due to inconsiderate throwing down of bottles and other heavy objects.
- The problem of the lack of neighbourliness.

These are the findings from the Cheras pilot low-cost housing project in relation to the above points:

With regard to the level of ambient noise, LRHD in the Cheras pilot low-cost housing project shows a greatly diminished noise level. This is apparent to any visitor to the site. Survey result confirms that only 8.9 per cent of the population consider the noise level very disturbing, and this group complained of the noise from children playing nearby and not from television or radio noise which features highly in the HDB situation. The remainder consider it sometimes disturbing and not disturbing.

In the case of LRHD, lifts have been totally eliminated together with its problems. Accessibility to the houses is by footpaths at ground level. This subject of course requires more detailed evaluation, although a visit to the site will reveal that accessibility is exceptionally good through the service roads, rear footpaths and breezeways. In fact, a matrix of footpaths is achieved throughout the entire scheme so that accessibility for pedestrians and service vehicles is rather high, with a choice of many alternative routes. There is no complaint on this score.

In developing LRHD housing for larger sites, more detailed studies will have to be conducted on accessibility requirements to establish the different acceptable travel distances in order to establish the size of the housing environmental area, serviced by perimeter roads.

The problem of noise created by children playing along corridors of course has two aspects: that is the conflict between household privacy and the children's play demands. Noise generated by children's play in the breezeway has not arisen as a significant problem in the Cheras project. This is especially striking in that approximately 75 per cent of the children of the age group 6 to 12 play in the breezeway and around the house and undoubtedly, they do create noise and nuisance. However, probably due to the higher degree of social interaction and friendliness between neighbours, this problem has been ameliorated so that only 8.9 per cent consider this activity disturbing.

Interviews show that most of the neighbours were newly acquainted from the resettlement.

Location of children's play spaces in complex by racial group (Chong's notes)

	Location	Malays (%)	Chinese (%)	Indians (%)
a)	In breezeway	32.4	32.0	50.0
b)	In house	S.B	32.0	25.0
c)	Around house	55.8	28.0	12.5
d)	Others	-	4.0	12.5
	Total	94.0	96.0	100.0

The location of friends and neighbours most frequently visited shows a slight bias for visits within the scheme instead of outside the scheme.

The writer has made many visits to the site and talked with residents. Most residents feel that the chances of their forming a community organisation to look after the general maintenance of the scheme and to provide them an informal means of grouping is extremely optimistic. One resident claiming to represent 100 families voiced the opinion that he has advised the group not to allow themselves to be drawn into racial party politics. He felt that he was speaking for the majority when he said that there should be no racial politics but there should be an organisation to look after the welfare of the community as a whole. The writer was struck by the optimism of the respondent in identifying the community as a single entity.

Respondents' confidence in forming of a community association by racial group (Chong's notes)

	Confidence in formation	Malays (%)	Chinese (%)	Indians (%)	Total (%)
a)	Yes	97.1	76.0	100.0	89.6
b)	Maybe	2.9	24.0	-	10.4
c)	No	-	-	-	-
	Total	100.0	100.0	100.0	100.0

Reaction and response to the house structure itself reveals some areas of dissatisfaction. The residents are dissatisfied with the smallness of the toilet and wash area. They also feel that generally the house of 520 square feet enclosed area is too small. They also feel that the house is rather hot. It must however be noted that their views are coloured by their dissatisfaction with the rental charged. They were charged RM$80 per month. Similar accommodation in flats range in rental between RM$36 and RM$68 per month. When asked to suggest what they thought would be a reasonable rent, they mostly nominated a figure of RM$60 to RM$65 per month. It is gratifying to note that similar accommodation in the adjacent four-storey walk-up flats is RM$45 per month. The additional RM$15 to RM$20 volunteered can be taken as a vote of confidence in the house form. When polled as to preference for housing type, the overwhelming majority preferred the type they are living in.

Reasons given for their choice were the following:
- High-rise flats are inconvenient because one has to move up and down all the time.
- High-rise flats are quite unsafe for young children to play and run about.
- Flats are rather noisy.
- The cluster-link provides for more orderly living; is not so "mixed" as flats.

Thus, on the whole the general picture is a positive one. The evidence point to a positive level of integration in and among races. Apart from dissatisfaction with the spatial aspects of the cluster-link unit, most respondents perceive their new home as an improvement over their former home and would like to stay on. The location of the scheme was also generally well received, and an overwhelming majority would want to own the cluster-link units. The Malays in fact represented the largest group wanting to stay on. Noise was perceived to be on a low level in the scheme. The rental in the scheme was perceived as not very reasonable and most respondents suggested a reasonable amount would be between RM\$50 to RM\$60. The cluster-link was generally preferred when compared with four-storey walk-up units or high-rise units. What people say must be viewed against what they do. Many residents have renovated and decorated their houses with partitions, panelling and other decorations. The gardens are also well planted with decorative as well as useful plants. These activities indicate a sense of permanence.

Recommendations

Undoubtedly, the pilot low-cost housing project at Cheras is an experiment. Reflecting on the results of the surveys and from direct observations of the way space is being utilised, the following recommendations and conclusions can be made:

Ventilation and heat

With a small additional expenditure, roof ventilators can be installed, but this must be provided with easily operable flaps to prevent driving rain entering. The roof should be provided with aluminium foil paper to reflect away radiant heat. Perhaps additional insulation in the form of rigid insulation boards should be fitted as ceiling. Additionally, non-see-through concrete ventilation blocks should be installed below and above windows and in other possible locations.

Weather proofing

A translucent plastic roof should be provided in the breezeway at roof level. This would provide better shelter in the breezeway and also create a space at the upper part of the breezeway for the drying of clothes during wet weather. The drying of clothes on clothes lines in the garden space is visually unsatisfactory and interferes with the use of the garden and this should be relocated to the upper part of the breezeway. For this purpose, bamboo poles will have to be made available to residents. Bamboo poles are not generally available in Kuala Lumpur.

Size of toilet

Size of the toilet should be increased by another two feet. This would mean that the entire ground floor structure would be enlarged by that amount. It seems to me that this would be acceptable, especially when the clothes drying in the garden space can be removed. Alternatively, the garden space of 15 feet can still remain with the reduction of the 20-foot services roads to 12-foot double-track single-way footpath which allows emergency vehicles access. This way, the density and space relationships remain the same. These modifications would cost not more than RM$1,000 per unit at 1978 prices, but the nett result would be well worth the while.

Territoriality

Observations and direct conversations with residents reveal that the breezeway is considered as a common territory of the four families. They are particularly annoyed by bicycles and motorcycles driving through it. To prevent these, bollards can be erected at critical positions. The need to identify and personalise the garden space is highly developed. There are some gardens that are extremely well laid out. In general, planting and landscaping of the garden space has been a matter of necessity and of pride. All gardens are heavily planted, fertilised by the effluent from the temporary septic tank! Low fencing and other means of defining the garden plot should be allowed. A certain amount of visual disorder can be accepted in preference for a greater degree of rootedness and belonging.

Other general aspects of LRHD arising from the Cheras project

The basic theory that low-rise houses will increase speed of construction was proven in the Cheras project. The project consisting of 676 units was completed in eight months, notwithstanding the unfamiliarity and teething construction problem. Basically with low-rise construction, many more workers can be mobilised simultaneously to perform the various building functions. There is a greater degree of overlap in the building process which a high-rise structure will not be able to afford.

Ideas and Proposals

Maintenance at Cheras is minimum. The environment is capable of absorbing, for instance, a delay in refuse collection. Such a situation would rapidly become intolerable in high-rise flats.

Total energy use during construction and during the life of the building is at a minimum. The public footpaths are lit by stray light emitting from the surrounding houses at night.

Accessibility in and out of the house is satisfactorily. Although the services roads were intended only for service vehicles, and parking was intended to be at the fringe carpark, those who own cars of which thankfully they are a minority, do sometimes park their cars in the service road which is only 12 feet. It is interesting that notwithstanding this, other vehicles are still able to pass through without mishap and an additional benefit is that vehicles passing through have to drive very slowly, thereby adding to safety.

Inevitably, housing especially for the lower income groups is not only a problem of shelter, but the house is also an economic space. Of course, regulations are necessary to prevent excessive abuse. The house together with the plot on which it sits can provide some economic returns to the households. The garden herbs and the carrying out of home industries such as tailoring and other such activities can attribute to the household income and these can surely be integrated into economic planning as a positive input rather than to be treated purely as undesirable activities. The low-rise form gives more options for such fringe economic activities. The added benefit of such fringe economic activities is the enrichment of the learning environment for the children living there.

The provision of social space to fulfil those social needs notwithstanding, greater independence of the residents can be provided for more cheaply in low-rise housing forms. What is needed is a new design approach and a re-orientation of attitude towards community initiative. At Cheras, three months after people moved in, a sepak takraw club had started in the neighbourhood space. It enjoys an active support from the community.

The acoustic effect of noise reverberating between slab blocks is a phenomena all are familiar with in high-rise flats. But the acoustical environment of ring blocks or LRHD housing is unfamiliar. There are, however, existing ring blocks which can be visited, and measurements can be made. The ring block built in 1936 by the Singapore Improvement

Trust (SIT) at Moh Guan Terrace in Tiong Bahru, Singapore, with a fairly high-density is notwithstanding rather quiet. Any visit to Cheras will also confirm this impression.

High-rise slab blocks must be laid out to avoid direct sun. In this, the layout planning is restricted. In LRHD or MRHD high-density layouts, there is a greater latitude in layout planning to depart from the east-west orientation by planting of trees.

Lower intensity of servicing and garbage collection, which in the event of breakdown or slowdown of essential services will not lead rapidly to an intolerable situation.

Maximum fire escape options. In the event of redevelopment, much simpler to demolish. With the enormous savings, the roofs can be turfed so that huge additional open spaces can be provided.

The case for LRHD housing, however, does not argue that all housing within a housing scheme must be low-rise. It, however, argues that the predominant form of housing up to densities of 371 ppa or plot ratio of 1:2 should be low-rise or medium-rise. For reasons of aesthetics and landmarks, there should be some high-rise blocks within a housing scheme to help orientate pedestrians and give character and meaning to spaces and places. Undoubtedly, in all cultures throughout history, the desire to build tall buildings and to ascend them is deeply satisfying. For this reason, there should be some tall buildings.

SYNOPSIS OF CONCEPTS OF THE INTELLIGENT TROPICAL CITY
23 September 1989

A condensed version of my 1988 essay on a new planning model for cities in the tropics, which have long relied on concepts from developed nations in the Northern hemisphere.

Climate

The climate should be studied in terms of the effect on the human habitat, lifestyle, use of space and land and the behaviour of materials. The physics of design and the ways the natural and artificial realms are articulated and made to relate to each other, will give insights into the way humans shape the environment and how in turn the environment shapes human concepts and behaviour.

Architectural precedents

Early human settlements, contemporary aboriginal settlements, village groupings, colonial urban adaptations and the immediate post-colonial period should be analysed for evidence of lifestyle and building forms which were a response to the ambient climatic and geographical conditions of the tropics. This study is to distinguish the modifications of the basic architectural and spatial forms as the result of new ideologies and typologies. Such studies should result in setting up an "arche-typology" of forms as distinct from the architectural and stylistic typologies which are always bound up with style and temporal cultural symbols that are attached to ethnic or community sentiments. The search for the underlying basis of order has to cut through cultural barriers to a deeper level of understanding.

Documentation of settlement patterns, building forms, grouping of buildings, relationships between artificial and natural settings would also be analysed to give insights into the strategies adopted towards environmental adaptation and its celebration. Result: arche-typology of space use.

Social and cultural responses

It is essential to establish a background by examining the traditional beliefs, customs, lifestyles, attitudes, values, patterns of space use and ultimately gain insights into the strategies of achieving equilibrium as adopted in the past given the resource and technological levels available then. This section is to prepare for a discussion of the current disequilibrium caused by the impact of new ideas and technologies imposed upon tropical peoples during the colonial period extending till now. The present period of rapid modernisation and economic change is both the cause and the effect of the present disequilibrium and is the precise reason to embark on a re-examination of the geographical/social/cultural conditions of tropical living. This is to rediscover the authentic and organic basis for a more relevant basis of order and of convenience in the city, giving coherence to the lives of people trying frantically to catch up with northern standards in all things.

The Tropical City concept is seen in the context of colonialism, northern technological, economic and intellectual dominance with its needs for raw materials and captive markets. The high resource to low population ratios and the low living standards (measured materially) of tropical countries was the result of prevalent natural order and resulted in the natural equilibrium. This was altered irreversibly by colonial plantations and other mass labour projects. Systematic administration, law and order, tropical hygiene and the necessary basic educational infrastructure altered the prevailing conditions of life and fostered great population concentrations and growth in tropical cities. The institutions brought by colonisation later became the basis of the institutional order in the new postcolonial states after the Second World War. New states that were more successful in integrating traditional attitudes into the institutional order advanced rapidly. Precisely because of this advancement, it is all the more necessary now that new states adopt fresh thinking on tropical realities in order to derive new planning concepts and social, cultural and economic objectives.

Two aspects must be examined: The characteristics of the expending of human energy in the tropics and the patterns of fuel use. Architects and researchers have paid attention to designing for comfort in the hot humid zones, and a reasonably large literature exists on the subject. The social and productive implications of climatic optimisation through town planning have received insufficient attention and have not been subjects of national policy nor of social engineering. It is the intention of this section to lay the foundations for a focus on the subject in the design adaptation of existing cities in the tropics and in conceptualising the planning of tropical cities of the future.

The town planning concepts of the tropical world are, at present, all mere versions of the Town and Country Planning Acts of northern countries introduced during the colonial period, and continue to be used with minor modifications. There has, however, been no fundamental review of the assumptions built in. The conflicts caused by intensive and rapid developments in the postcolonial period are exacerbated by their maladaptation because the assumptions within the town planning concepts are simply not meant for the intensities encountered in the tropical cities of today. Review is necessary. But the problem of conceptual review is difficult as there are no planning precedents. Everywhere, as populations expand and economies advance, we see exponential increases in the use of energy just to ameliorate the negative acts of heat, noise and dust. Tropicalised design of individual buildings cannot resolve what has to be basically solved in the planning and management of the urban environment, in layouts and in the mix of land uses.

Some possible new and architectural responses for the tropical city

Reducing the need to travel and to move about is the first basic strategy in the planning of the tropical city. A basic strategy of energy optimisation, use of the sun and the rain, developing and utilising new technologies and spawning new research into energy efficient designs has to be brought into focus and implemented. This process is accompanied by a whole host of issues related to the correct mix of uses, including the need for compact geometries; the provision for privacy and community in close proximity; the optimisation of human contact and the potentials for creativity and conviviality; the optimisation of time-use, including night time and early morning schedules; the problems of administration and creation of new identity. The layout and form of the city itself needs to be reviewed and new proposals made to capture the public's imagination.

While the practical issues are being addressed, there are also many challenging poetic and artistic questions too. The Tropical City concept is the new challenge, not just tropically-styled buildings.

A New World in the Making

The problem of incrementality

Apart from compact form, the parcellation of land and the provision of roads, and other essential services imply a geometry which must give scope for incremental growth and also intensification. Large covered outdoor areas, however, require coordinated implementation. The weaving of physical linkages between buildings and open spaces requires smooth implementation and large-scale coordination. This imposes special problems on phasing which require special design and management strategies to ensure incrementality. New forms and new methods are required.

Artistic and lifestyle possibilities of the tropical city

The artistic possibilities of using the sun, rain and vegetation in the built environment as positive features to be exploited and enjoyed rather than to be avoided is an important artistic challenge if the Tropical City concept is to have more than an intellectual appeal. For it to succeed, it must be able to captivate the imagination to overcome the unconscious but prevailing northern conceptual biases which are locked into the personal career paths of architects, planners and managers of cities in the tropics.

Intelligent city

While we ponder the tropical city, we must also think about, making it more intelligent. The information content has to be increased. All cities came about because of the need to transact ideas, goods and services. Therefore, the natural emphasis is on communications and logistics. Increasingly, the transactions are speeded up through the use of information and communications technology. We can expect such communication networks to be further intensified with additional features which will enable remote working, shopping and even manufacturing. A certain degree of decentralisation of the workplace will be possible and the extent to which it will actually happen will depend on provisions made for the social and cultural aspects of work and recreation which a more information-intensive system will imply the need for.

The demand for intensive human face-to-face interaction will correspondingly increase as urbanisation and economic development advances. Face-to-face communication cannot be substituted as it has advantages over electronic communication systems in that it is

Ideas and Proposals

unpredictable and unplannable. Its importance lies in the serendipitous stimulation of ideas and initiatives. In research areas such as in Silicon Valley and in the Massachusetts Insittute of Technology's "most intelligent triangle", the restaurants and watering holes are the important meeting places where researchers meet after work to exchange ideas. This spatial pattern has important implications for the planning of cities of the future where proximity of critical activities to the location of social nodes are needed to provide scope for a wider range of human transactions which enhance the city as a multi-transactional, information and ideas centre. This fits in well with the essentially compact planning of tropical cities. Greater stress will be made of information exchange in this late stage of the Industrial Revolution and tropical cities like Singapore and other cities of the tropics are fast swept along this route. The combination of Electronic Information Systems and intensified human interfaces produces the challenge to consider an enhanced role for the city. The city can be a campus wherein lifelong learning is entirely feasible and desirable and the lines between work, study and research can and need to be closely inter-related. New spatial implications challenge architecture and urban planning.

Yet another aspect of the intelligent city is its ability to transmit and carry cultural cues. One of the most powerful but subtle means by which culture is carried is through ambience. The design of the urban nodes should ensure that the ambience created is conducive to the animation of social and cultural activities within such nodes. Ambience is produced through subtle and complex mix of factors. These factors include the mix of activities, the qualities, the appropriateness and the pace of activities modulated by visual scale and the textures of the place. To achieve conducive ambience would require a much more sophisticated process of planning and design and implementation than at present employed. More user participation, dialogue with and design by different designers and entrepreneurial groups have to be allowed to create diversity and vitality.

Another aspect that contributes to the intelligence of an environment is its ambient sense-data level. It has been found in child psychology that visual and formal complexity of the lived-in environment contributes to the development of mathematical and spatial skills. Freedom of physical movement, tumbling and touch contribute to the development of an individual's confidence, physical coordination and conceptual capacity.

The environment must be designed to be rich in texture, be variegated and with space for stretching limbs and involving the senses. To stimulate the mind and the senses, the ambient data level in terms of activities and sensations should be high. Clean and sterile buildings and spaces separated from nature and from human activity should be avoided or ameliorated. This is an urgent agenda in environmental and architectural design. Existing environments can and must be enriched through modification to make them conducive for the growth of intelligence.

Philosophical issues related to balance between the artificial and the natural: problems of environmental and aesthetic equilibrium

In order to live in high human concentrations in the tropics is itself a confrontation with natural order. To sustain viable and creative human concentrations in the tropics requires a high level of artificial infrastructure support and environmental management. Where do we draw the line? Since we cannot go back to the idyllic village or small town, why not artificially control the living environment altogether? Can a new equilibrium between the artificial and the natural be achieved and to what effect? These are the questions which arise.

Ideas and Proposals

THE KAMPONG BUGIS CASE STUDY
23 November 1990

My account of leading a team of architects, planners and sociologists to reconceptualise the relationship between architecture and city planning at the metropolitan scale in a sustainable ecological manner.

When Mr S. Dhanabalan took over the role of Minister of National Development (the government ministry in charge of planning) after the demise of the former minister, Mr Teh Cheang Wan, he set about amending the planning and development control procedures to be more transparent and principled. He also instituted changes in the premier government agency the Housing & Development Board (HDB) to prepare the way for greater sensitivity to consumer requirements and to provide greater variety in housing types for the future.

Among the many changes the minister began was to invite more public involvement in the planning process. In this context, he asked the Singapore Institute of Architects (SIA) to appoint two teams to undertake alternative plans to the government's Development Guide Plans (DGPs) for two different sites for public exhibition and discussion. The two sites were one at Simpang, in the northern coastal part of the island, and the other in Kampong Bugis, a fringe city centre location on the site of a gas works to be vacated in the near future.

The exercises were to obtain public feedback. Accordingly, the procedures adopted were designed to allow the two teams to freely consult members of the profession and any others so needed. The results of the studies both by the private sector and the government were exhibited and publicised for public dialogue later. These procedures are entirely novel in the context of planning in Singapore. For the first time, planning exercises were as open as this.

A note on planning in Singapore. The state is the largest single landowner. It has extensive powers over the acquisition and utilisation of land in the Land Acquisition Act and it has been the single most essential basis for the success of the housing program. Large tracts of urban and rural lands were acquired during the last 30 years to build the new towns and to implement urban renewal schemes in the city. The act provided cheap land for the government as financial compensations to landowners are far below the market rate. Market rates are also determined by potentials to which the land may be put, and since this is entirely in the hands of the government, exercised through the planning department; land value is to a large extent determined by the government. The powers to zone the usage of land is provided in the Planning Act. Clause 9 Part 14 of the Act provides incredible powers; the Minister may take a decision on a matter and this decision may not be challenged in any court! This clause exists since the rationale is political. It is argued in its defence that the ultimate discretion in the political system rests on the elected representatives. It is incumbent on the electorate to elect honourable persons to office, failing which to replace them in the next elections. There is no need to enter into a discussion on the subtleties and complexities of the political system itself here but, suffice it to say, that this law has both been the instrument for rapid infrastructure and public housing development in Singapore and the relative under-utilisation of the building professional in the private sector. The Act virtually transferred the entire priority and professional initiative into the hands of the government professionals. Seen in this light, the moves by the new minister to open the system to private architects and others is revolutionary!

The terms of reference for the Kampong Bugis site were an open brief. This enabled the SIA team to address fundamental issues on type of uses and quantum to be introduced into the site. Prior to the Kampong Bugis DGP exercise, I had already been investigating the "Tropical City" concept in various academic papers, design workshops with students at the National University of Singapore, and publicising the ideas generated through the local newspapers.

The strategic land use issue in Singapore

Just prior to the announcement of the DGPs in 1989, a special Committee on Quality of Life in Singapore was established under the chairmanship of the Minister of State of the Ministry of National Development Mr Lee Boon Yang. This is an example of a shift in style of the new emerging political leadership in the government who will take over from the current leadership in November of 1990.

This committee, consisting of a select group of persons reputably associated with relevant fields, commented on several working papers generated by the Planning Department in charge of the current Master Plan Review. Among the main issues raised was the dangers of creating an even spread of urbanised developments throughout the island, threatening to make the landscape too uniform and monotonous. The committee agreed that efforts must be made to ensure that there will be rich visual variety and contrasts.

This can only come about through a fundamental review of the assumptions built into the land allocation criteria, which are in turn dependent on the building floor space design assumptions. It was noted that there has been no review of these due to disinclination to tamper with the success formula of the HDB's public housing designs. Without such a review, the building of new towns will continue unchanged, with disastrous consequences to the eventual landscape of Singapore.

As it is the plan is to provide for an eventual population of four million, an increase of 1.4 million from the current population of 2.6 million. The initial concern was that Singapore's basic limitation is land and water. Within a short time, investigations revealed that land shortage is not as severe as originally thought. Industrial restructuring, due to more capital intensive and multi-storey factories, and the shift into greater emphasis on financial and other services, meant that major economic claimants on land were less. The only major land consumer remained housing. No new projections on intensification were undertaken. Indeed, it is perceived that densities in housing would fall as homeowners demanded more floor space. Combined with the tendency to have smaller families, floor space translated into land area demands would increase. Currently, the per capita floor space in the new towns is about 25 square metre. Given affluence and higher expectations it is expected that this ratio would increase to 30 square metre. On the medium fertility model of population growth, it is assumed that average family sizes would be 3.11. These are justifications for the building of more new towns, further away from the city centre. As a concomitant to this, the Master Plan Review recommends the establishment of four more new regional town centres, away from the existing urban core, to provide commercial, entertainment and employment facilities.

The Kampong Bugis strategic land use review

The Kampong Bugis DGP study re-examined these assumptions and proposed a different scenario. The basic proposal arose from an examination of six alternative scenarios, ranging from the extended new town policy to the total halt to new town expansions with intensification through development on all available urbanised sites, and redevelopment of such urban sites, which are currently undeveloped, or are ripe for redevelopment. The scenarios in between are also projected with additional sites identified in the existing industrial site at Jurong and new sites created on the East Coast Dike. In all, approximately 1,500 hectare of urbanised sites were identified in the study. The average density in such sites would produce development densities of a plot ratio (floor space ratio of site area) of approximately 4.5 to accommodate the new population including residential and non-residential quota of floor space.

Due to non-availability of data on the per capita non-residential floor space in Singapore, the planning team computed the average floor space built in a 10-year period. It was estimated that approximately a third of all floor space was devoted to non-residential use. Although this rate might change in the future, it was the best figure available and it was adopted as the planning criteria for Kampong Bugis.

Next, a study of compact high-density building prototypes was conducted to provide the fundamental building space concepts for input into the planning process. The team realised that this was a novel procedure as most planning processes focussed on the economic, transportation and social parameters using existing building norms. Building norms extracted from the field form the space allocation assumptions of the plans which when adopted are translated into development control rules. These regulate all subsequent buildings, which are again confirmed in subsequent planning reviews.

Thus, the following are some of the studies undertaken. The basic method is that "openness" factor, in high-density designs, is taken to be a function of the distance between buildings in relation to their height is expressed as a ratio. The ratio is taken to be one. That is the distance apart is equal to the height of the buildings. Modifications may be made in cases of buildings of unequal height. In any case, these assumptions can be verified by model tests before being adopted for actual tests. Surely, if we are going to be able to build environmentally and ecologically better cities in the future, these procedures and attendant costs are small prices to pay.

The departure in the Kampong Bugis built-form studies is the introduction of the "grid stack" model, where usable floor space losses in the intersection is avoided. The departure is that usable floor space losses of blocks, at the corners, is avoided by stacking across the corners, rather than allowing the corner spaces to increase in size, thereby blocking off more and more floor space at the corners from light and air, as the quantum of floor space at the corners increases due to horizontal compaction. This resolution of the corner is particularly viable in the tropics where the priority is shade. Ventilation is not at all affected due to stacking. The only constraint is in the overhang and subjective feeling of visual oppression. These legitimate concerns have to be evaluated in actual test cases, where the socioeconomic aspects are favourably structured, otherwise the wrong reactions may be obtained for the wrong reasons.

The case of the Pruitt-Igoe apartment in St. Louis, USA, is a case in point where unjustly high-rise developments was falsely maligned. The causes of the situation there were due more to socioeconomic detriments rather than the mere consequence of height. The fact that the high-rises there were dreary in design was also targets for easy criticism.

With the grid stack model, the prospect of a high-density urban form of life is entirely feasible. The stacking of blocks across each other also provides opportunities for the creation of public gardens and other facilities, which hitherto had either to be on the ground or on rooftops. These are somewhat dislocated from the residential apartments or workplaces.

The mental model of Le Corbusier's towers in a park and later his gardens on the rooftop of the *Unite d'habitation* housing still serve as the haunting images of the city of the future, when they patently fail in creating the urbanism which they sought to replace in the first place.

With the grid stack system, rooftop spaces can be more closely interwoven into the vertical fabric of the urban building clusters. Vertical and horizontal connectivities are both visually and physically possible. The introduction of the new vertical element into the urban fabric should make urban life even more vital when densities are high. The vertical surfaces of buildings need not, in principle, be isolating architectural elements serving as display features. They can become accessible! The fine texture of the urban tissue with its inherent diversity and visual coherence can still be recreated at the new densities contemplated—limited by design skills only. The basic criticism of the postwar developments is not inevitable, nor is a desperate return to the vernacular necessary if the grid stack form is seriously researched and implemented.

In ameliorating the negative aspects of high-rise high-density development in the traditional design of urban forms, a much higher degree of both vertical and horizontal separation has been necessary to avoid its ills. This has been to the detriment of reputations of these new dense developments built in the postwar period, and on which criticisms have been lavished but still accompanied by a sense of impotence at the necessity of the high-rise high-density concept.

Ideas and Proposals

RETIREMENT COTTAGES: AN OPTION FOR HOUSING SINGAPORE'S ELDERS WITHIN THE COMMUNITY
8 May 1999

A paper prepared with Daniel Teo in consultation with Eugene Seow for the Inter-Ministerial Committee Workgroup on Housing and Land Use Policies for an Aging Population

Elderly categories

1. Well-to-do aged sick: Requires constant medical care at home or in a special institution.
2. Elders with disabilities: Ranging from total dependency cases to partial dependency cases.
3. Able elders: Active retirement preferably within a community, near or within the family space.
4. Destitute and aged: This category requires public and philanthropic support in special institutions.

Scope

This paper focuses on category 3, the able elders.

Philosophy

The philosophy is that senior members of society, across all ethnic groups and social classes, should be regarded as a valuable national human resource rather than as a liability. Affordable and community-based accommodation should be available. The able elders form the largest group. The consensus is that it is preferable to house them within the community, regardless of ethnic or class background. It is felt that this would be beneficial to the community, to the families and to the elders themselves. Since our elders represent the collective experiential wisdom of our people, their presence in the community is especially important at this time of fundamental change.

Since the public housing environment is the de facto Singapore community space by virtue of its predominance in the social landscape this is where solutions have to be located. While there can be other solutions in terms of type, style and location for housing our seniors elsewhere, the public housing environment should be regarded as the epicentre.

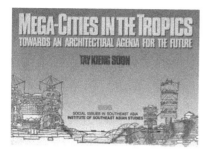

Rethinking Cities for the Tropics

In 1989, I was invited by the Institute of Southeast Asian Studies to lecture on the future tropical city concept (left). Some ideas I proposed were for an upper-level community space over the traditional ground floor commercial space (across); planting and landscaping roofs as a vital part of the urban environmental strategy (below); and reducing overall temperature and increasing wind movement to enable open living on balconies. These ideas were developed into my tropical city concept for Kampong Bugis.

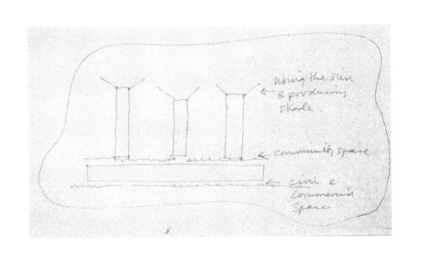

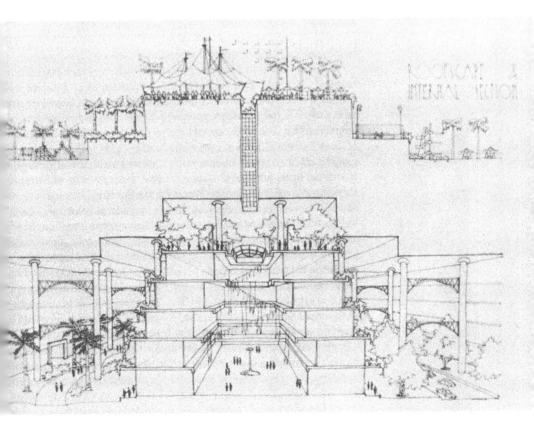

Kampong Bugis

In 1990, I led a team of architects, planners and sociologists to create a design guide plan for the sustainable development of Kampong Bugis (across top). We eventually invited architects to interpret our guidelines and were surprised by their similarly inspired designs (above and across). One feature of our plans was for narrow spaces between buildings to create shade and funnel wind (left), in contrast to the typical wide public spaces around the city.

Night Safari

I designed the entrance to the world's first nocturnal wildlife park in 1994. It welcomed visitors to a festive village where they could savour the ambience before venturing out into the dark and mysterious wilderness to spy on the animals. There was dramatic lighting to set up the mood of mystery, discovery and adventure— and even the sound of jungle drums!

The following are additional reasons for community-based housing of elders:

There is no adaptation trauma due to relocation to a new environment. Familiarity with surroundings is maintained. Friends and relations are nearby.

- There is minimum disruption of family routines, location of workplaces, schools, etc.
- Moving to a smaller apartment nearby or remodelling existing family apartments allows some economic returns to the retiree.
- Present apartments can also be re-allocated to family members, rented out or sold if there is viable alternative accommodation.
- Living within the community affords community-based part-time help. It increases effective, direct volunteerism from the community.
- Seniors can continue to contribute to the community and be valued, respected and needed by the community. This is a key human resource management strategy in a rapidly changing world.
- Accessibility to the wisdom and stability of the senior generation is necessary emotional and memory ballast in the context of rapid changes and challenges.

The following are possible spatial options:

- Reconfigure existing apartments to have a separate small granny flat within the original family space be it in private or public housing accommodation is difficult and costly. Future apartment designs should have this change planned for.
- Build special retirement villages, condominiums or blocks with partial or full medical and professional care givers on specially zoned land in the city, public housing estates or in the suburbs.
- In-fill retirement cottages in small clusters (between 5 to 15) within existing public housing neighbourhoods that

incorporate community-based caregiver-individuals and care organisations.

- Build special old-age homes run professionally.

Costs and consequences of the four categories

Granny flats

Considerable disruption to existing family during remodelling. Original apartment is divided into two. Resultant unit sizes are compromised. Disruption to building services is technically disruptive and costly. If new apartments are specially designed for easy future change, this option is a possibility. Purchase of adjacent spare space from neighbours can be instituted. Present saturation level of housing accommodation in Singapore makes this option viable, as widespread exploitation through "cubicalisation" is unlikely.

Retirement villages

New, specially designed retirement villages, condos or blocks can be built; however, land costs will be prohibitive if such housing is to compete with regular private sector housing land prices. Unless land is specially zoned, land cost will inhibit implementation. For social reasons there should be a special land-market for senior housing to achieve affordability. The higher segment of the market may prefer such accommodation for its ambiance and exclusivity. These communities, however, need the full complement of shops, recreation and health facilities.

Retirement cottages

In-fill, single-storey, retirement cottages within the public housing community can be affordable, if pro-rated public housing land costs are applied.

Old age homes

There will always be this category of elders. Society has to provide under humane and economically sustainable conditions the provision of such care facilities.

The land question

In the case where interstitial and marginal lands within public housing estates are used for housing the elderly, should not the land cost be also marginal? Obviously appropriate governing criteria for purchase and resale needs to be established.

Design of retirement cottages within public housing estates

Inherently, the retirement cottages are cheaper because there are savings in construction costs. There is no need for lifts, heavy reinforced structures or deep foundations. Land has already been prepared. Sewerage, water, electricity, telephone, TV and refuse disposal services exist. These services are simply tapped from existing lines, and therefore cheaper.

The cottages will be directly accessible, have small private gardens for every unit and are close to amenities. The cottages will provide a living environment especially suited for elderly dwellers who wish to be near family, friends and remain in the familiar community.

Being single storey, there will be minimal visual disruption to existing dwellers in the adjacent high-rise blocks. The cottages will be clustered. All the cluster sites will keep clear of existing underground services.

Locating clusters adjacent to existing apartments and well-trafficked areas attains security through informal surveillance.

The cottages would be compact, between 35 to 45 square metre in area. It consists of one bedroom with large sliding screens to separate the bedroom from the living space. A large wheelchair accessible bath is planned, a small kitchenette specially designed for maximum efficiency and easy maintenance with pull down blinds to conceal it when not in use forms part of the living space. A dining/living space with a pull-out settee bed for an occasional visitor is envisaged. A 20 square metre garden equipped with a weatherproof plastic-roof-screened-clothes-drying-yard is planned for. There is a front porch with built-in seats and the garden is provided with raised planter beds for easy tending. An optional retractable fabric awning can be fitted for family visits and other larger gatherings.

Possible locations especially in the older public housing estates

- In between public housing blocks, especially in older estates where there is more space

- Partially decked over existing open carparks
- Along road, railway, canal and highway land-margins with appropriate protective sound barrier structures
- On unused earth slopes

Demonstration project

As the concept of housing for the elders in our society is new, market survey is of limited value as a gauge of responses. To be effective, there must be real examples available. It is felt that some risks have to be taken to build various alternative models. The Studio Apartments built by HDB is one such test. This proposal is another. There could be yet others.

A full-scale demonstration of a 10-unit cluster of "Retirement Cottages" is hereby proposed. A site in Toa Payoh is suggested near Block 89. Site selection is governed by a "best chance of success" location. This is vital. The project will be initiated and executed by Daniel Teo and myself. Eugene Seow has agreed to assist in the operational concept of the project, particularly because his community welfare organisation is actually operating in the area. If the response is good, the units can be sold to the public under the same 99-year tenure terms as with typical public housing units to defray the costs. There is no monopoly in the implementation of the cottage concept. Other agencies can participate in the supply of this type of senior housing in small clusters all over Singapore, each with different features, price, finishes and style.

Prerequisites for the project

Trial proposal to be approved by Government in general and the approval of the demonstration project, in particular:
- Design to be finalised in consultation with end-user groups
- Land to be allocated to the project at public housing rates, calculated on the footprint area of each unit or even not at all. Surrounding lands are not included as they are regarded as public lands as per normal as in any public housing estate
- Building codes, where they are found to be inappropriate should be waived for this demonstration project and amended for future implementation
- Detailed technical approvals to be expedited for early realisation and launch

A New World in the Making

BUILDING LINEAR BLOCKS OVER ROADS: A PRELUDE TO
THE SINGAPORE MANAGEMENT UNIVERSITY SAGA
11 August 1999

An alternative proposal I came up with alongside my students in response to the government's plans to build the new university at Bras Basah Park.

While teaching at the Masters of Architecture (Urban Design) program at the National University of Singapore, I had set a program to consider the urban design implications of building an urban university on or around Bras Basah Park. The project exposed students to the dilemmas of the urban context, and how to intervene while preserving existing civic urban values yet provide for necessary transformation and intensification. The following were my thoughts on the matter.

Although the site selected is Bras Basah Park and its immediate surroundings, it was felt that the park should not be built on in any significant manner, as this would destroy a major spatial marker in the city. Bras Basah Park serves as a major transition point for several important city districts. Orchard Road to the north terminates at this point. The city to the south begins here. Fort Canning Hill to the west presides over the historic/civic district of the city at this point. The Selegie/Serangoon corridor to the northeast emanates from here. Bras Basah Park, as an urban space articulator, must not be lost. How to build the campus of a new urban university here then?

Expanding the conceptual field beyond the immediate site to include the entire city, one can envision other possibilities. The city could then be a living and working campus. If a structure could be found to gather all the energies of the city together, such a perspective would be a new force in the life of Singapore. This is the ambition of the plan.

Transportation systems could stitch the campus together. The Singapore River could be a major transport and spiritual resource of the campus. The Padang, the hills, the major historic parts of the city could all be stitched together into one comprehensive whole! The building of the new urban university can be seen as the opportunity to redefine the role and nature of life in the city. In the 21st century, the most important resource is knowledge, wisdom and culture. The urban university is the key to unlock such new potentials hitherto untapped.

Such a structure could take the form of a bold linear structure, like a viaduct that hovers above and thereby embraces the city. By doing so, it redefines it. It could be aligned to connect Mount Sophia to Fort Canning Hill and from there to Pearl's Hill. Here in one stroke, the hills are commandeered as spiritual resources of the city. Although the hills have languished, now is the occasion to reassert their presence. There was never an occasion to articulate such a vision in the past.

The linear structure would be 15 storeys in height with a five-storey clear colonnaded space below for visual and physical crossings of roads and rivers. From Kirk Terrace, the linear block emanates, ramping and connecting to the educational facilities on Mount Sophia. It frames Cathay Building, Singapore's first skyscraper landmark building at this location. The linear block then springs from Mount Sophia across Orchard Road to meet Fort Canning. A gateway is defined where the structure crosses Orchard Road. This resolves the urban design dilemma at this location. A direct link from the campus to Dhoby Ghaut MRT station is achieved.

The civic and cultural facilities along Bras Basah Park and the Bencoolen/Waterloo districts are accessed from the campus via an underground passage from Dhoby Ghaut MRT Station. The proposed alignment of Stamford Road, in the Museum Development Guide Plan, is swung to run parallel with Bras Basah Road rather than intersecting Bras Basah Park. This frees the park completely for a sunken water garden and park that sweeps all the way upward to Fort Canning, thereby re-establishing its original presence in relation to the city.

The linear structure of the campus can accommodate all the facilities of the campus. In addition, a campus hotel can be located where the linear structure meets Fort Canning rather than on a separate plot as shown in the Development Guide Plan. A Media Centre and communications tower completes the composition in relation to the Singapore skyline. It is anchored on the High Street axis, projected up the hill. Electric buses and bicycles can operate on the roof of the linear structure. Lifts and escalators provide access to all departments below. The roof deck level is public space. It provides public access to all the three hills, which are difficult of access. A whole new dimension is added to Singapore. Beyond Fort Canning, the linear structure hovers above Clemenceau Avenue. Not utilising urban land, the structure takes development pressure away from existing urban sites such as Bras Basah Park. The total potential floor area produced is approximately 800,000 square metres. The urban university for a student and staff population of 25,000 requires not more than 375,000 square metres. The structure can be implemented in segments. Each segment can function independently. A new image of a new Singapore comes about. A problem becomes an asset!

The principal criticism of the linear scheme was that it was a megastructure, and there is no taste for megastructures anymore. Another view expressed was surprise at the unusual approach, which has no precedent in the planning of urban universities, or in urban development in free market economies in general. The criticism against megastructures is because it lacks humanism. It was remarked that Lewis Mumford's humanism was to be preferred. Current preference seems to be for smaller piece-meal interventions. There has been a shift in tastes in this respect.

But there are many levels of opacity in the sentiments expressed that need clarification. Firstly, the sentiment against bigness is an implicit distaste for authority, for it is only authoritarian administrations that are capable of conceiving and realising big structures. But having said this, does it follow that democratic systems are incapable of realising large projects? Clearly, the difference in their inherent capability is not size but the character of the structures they create. The "walled city" of Kowloon, often cited by implicit democrats and humanists, even crypto anarchists, is an example of hugeness and incredible complexity. Surely, hugeness itself is not a fault but the lack of complexity and internal intricacy is.

In this respect, there is another essential difference. It is the difference between closed and open forms, be they towns, buildings or administrative systems. Open structures are multi-fissured, offering many alternative points of entry. This is contrasted by closed systems. Authoritarian systems typically create closed systems for hierarchical control and linear process engineering. Size in this sense makes no difference.

Closed structures depend on total consistency of all parts. They have to be implemented through a single governing vision and through one dominant design strategy. Bigness needs to be distinguished. Large open structures such as the internet, for example, are capable of indefinite intervention and openness. The protocols are not deemed oppressive. Why should large buildings be oppressive by merely being big? The fact of the matter is that largeness is not in itself a fault. Critics need to be more penetrating in their criticism.

In a situation of intense urban pressure for development, such as in Singapore, where there is need to defend existing civic urban values and where the outward spread of the city calls for a bold comprehensive approach to allocate land, megastructures have solutions to offer where small interventions may not. If large-scale concepts are ruled out simply because they are large, the palette is ruled out through default by small interventions which together may actually whittle away the civic urban values many seek to uphold. This will result in a level of uniformity distinguished only by decorative differences of the many medium-sized blocks that threaten the fabric of the city through their desperate efforts to avoid blandness.

The proposed linear structure can also be seen as both a strategy to liberate urban land through the exploitation of air space above roads and to create a coherent connectivity in the city. It need not be a wilful imposition on the city but an ally instead.

In terms of the impact on the strategic allocation of land resources in Singapore, the linear concept has beneficial effects. When applied to other suitable air spaces above some of the highways in Singapore, it can have beneficial effects on the overall planning by relieving stress on available lands and thereby protect local environmental quality. At these locations, there will be less exposure to adjacent road-induced noise, dust and pollution. Accessibility for developments at such locations will be enhanced across the highways.

A New World in the Making

PROPOSED INDO-PACIFIC CULTURAL CENTRE
AT MARINA BAY SINGAPORE
29 August 2005

Responding to the government's request for proposals for an integrated resort at Marina Bay, I proposed a companion cultural centre to raise attention to Singapore's location at the confluence of two great oceans.

The advent of casinos and integrated resorts in Singapore is a breakout event that will bring new dimensions to the country's thinking. As such, it would be a challenge and opportunity to redefine its culture, to enlarge its scope of imagination. Bringing together all the cultures of the vast, rich area in which Singapore is situated is an important way to resituate its thinking. The establishment of a huge "infotainment" facility integrated with casinos and integrated resorts that showcases all the Indo-Pacific cultures is the venue for this.

Visitors will be immersed in the created ambience. The great cultures, ancient civilisations, layered over by latter day influences, which have all left their mark here in Singapore, will be showcased dramatically in the casino and integrated resort. The Indo-Pacific Cultural Centre in Singapore is conceived as the place to celebrate this huge cultural treasure. Food, performance, shows, dance, art, craft, architecture, flora and fauna will together form the totally immersive experience expertly choreographed to portray the romance and charms of all these lands of bamboo, rice and monsoon.

Imagine dining with tigers, lions and jaguars, drifting on moonlit bamboo rafts under silken sails, and sipping coconut wine. Hear the throb of native drums from all around the Indo-Pacific. Thrill to the sounds, scents and sights of Arabia. See Polynesian hula, Madagascan flora and fauna, Balinese gamelan, Korean drums, Alaskan Inuit sculpture. Marvel at the strangely similar Mexican motifs with Chinese ones. See Maori war canoes and taste Sri Lankan curries. Witness Katakana body movements, Angkorian smiles and Chinese pavilions. Sample Singaporean fusion street food, move through bamboo structures, climb terraced rice fields, hear Filipino voices. Thai dances, Javanese gongs, Batak yodelling, Malay weaving, Chinese gongfu, Ayurvedic medicine, traditional Chinese medicine, Javanese jamu, Thai massage... These are but only some of the essences of the Indo-Pacific Cultural Centre.

The Indo-Pacific identity

Identity is not choosing some nice-looking icon; it is a total, lived experience. There are three levels to identity: at the primary level is human identity; this we can connect to within ourselves and with everyone else. Celebrating diversity with all and sundry affirms our common human heritage. At the secondary level is geography. In this age of jet travel, we only get fleeting glimpses and so we all long to partake of the beauty and "the wisdom of the inhabited Earth" in a deeper level of experience. We all want to really know our world. Let the Indo-Pacific Cultural Centre magnify this by juxtaposing all the great traces of human ingenuity across this vast space, their adaptations to the land, their bio-botanical endowment and the rich seas around them to show their collective wisdom to all of us. The third level is to be found in everyday pop culture. This is media-driven, and we are saturated in it and while entertained, we are also dulled by it. We need to connect with people and place on a more intimate and real level. More than half of humanity's shores are washed by the Indian and Pacific Oceans. Here is the cradle of the great civilisations of planet Earth. We want to be part of this! In it is the wisdom of our inhabited Earth!

The Indo-Pacific cultural centre will invigorate Singapore identity, enthral visitors, add new dimensions to living through the palette of the Indo-Pacific. This is where Singapore is unique. There is no other place that more appropriately expresses the diversity yet unity of the Indo-Pacific than Singapore can.

A forgotten heritage

The cultural reality of the Indo-Pacific is ancient but forgotten in the public imagination. Thirty years of scholarship has pieced together the story that the Indo-Pacific was traversed by an ancient Austronesian cultural expansion originating in South China and spreading to Indonesia, then spreading eastwards to Polynesia and westwards to Madagascar. Thus, these intrepid sailors who traversed the great distances by catamaran, trimaran and bamboo raft influenced the maritime cultures on the edges of the two great oceans. They have left their mark in language, ethnography, technology and genetics wherever they went. This cultural substrate, later enriched by ancient waves of Arab, Chinese and Indian globalisation evolved into present day cultures of the Indo-Pacific. And then, from the

Info-Pacific Cultural Centre

Singapore is sadly unaware of its location at the confluence of two great oceans. It is not a little China, but the cultural heart of the Indo-Pacific! In 2005, I proposed to manifest this in an Indo-Pacific Culture Centre in Marina Bay that would banish Singapore's insecurity with its identity (above). The design even included glass terrace rice fields over the museum (left).

Retirement Cottages

As part of a 1999 inter-ministerial committee workgroup on housing and land use policies for an ageing population, I proposed creating cottages to support ageing in place using two 20-foot containers. Each cottage could house a bed space, a small kitchen, toilets, bath and a sitting area that can double up for a visiting relative to sleep in. It could be placed in the green spaces between public housing blocks or above open car parks.

a retirement cottage likely to cost not more than $50,000

320 sq.ft.

building into the sea

Intensifying Southern Singapore

In contrast to traditional planning methods based on land-use and traffic, a 3D planning methodology allocates land according to densities, purposes and desired forms. This liberates green spaces and generates new possibilities. Based on the aggregate floor area of advanced economies of 50 m^2 per person for all categories of accommodation, 3D planning can accommodate two million people on Singapore's south coast at a reasonable plot ratio of 4.5:1. It would house large, connected podiums topped by a landscaped green roof. Seaward extensions would create large swimming pools that are naturally filtered by the tide.

Rubanisation

In 2008, I came up with this idea of improving living standards in rural areas through increasing economic investment, education and healthcare. Its ideal form as a one-kilometre circle minimises walking distances from residence to centralised facilities like schools, clinics and shops. The concept has since travelled to India, Vietnam, Malaysia and Puttalam in Sri Lanka.

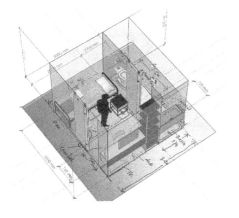

Rethinking Dormitories

Foreign worker dormitories in Singapore became major infection sources during the pandemic because of bad design and policy. Existing designs accommodated 12 persons in a room without cross ventilation and adequate communal toilets. I developed this alternative for Singapore's most crowded dormitory in Punggol that offers individual rooms, toilets and showers even while accommodating the same number of residents. This is achieved using my "grid-stack geometry" that creates wide corridors between blocks and allows cross ventilation for every room.

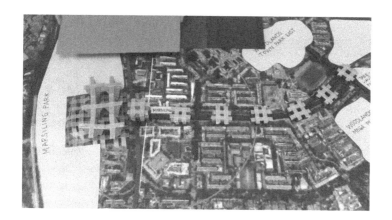

Singapore: Campus City

In 2021, my students and I reimagined Singapore as a talent hub that offers a new kind of education based on an earn-and-learn model that attracts scholars from the region (across). Every MRT station becomes an education hub. A huge, inverted pyramid is built over the tracks of Marsiling MRT as classrooms and hostels (top). A floating campus on Pulau Brani tapping off from Harbourfront MRT also serves as a park and immigration centre for a floating bridge to Batam. An eastern campus on the disused Paya Lebar Airport becomes a business park and university focused on high-tech agriculture and food processing (above).

16th century onwards, European voyages of discovery, colonisation and modernisation shaped the history and cultures in a complex interweaving of new and old. And now, globalisation linked the cultures of the western world to the Indo-Pacific in hybrid fashion. With the rise of India and China, the two major Indo-Pacific littoral states, the tapestry reaches a new stage of development. And Singapore is the centre of all of this. This is the place; it is also the time to bring together all the narratives together into one great compelling story. Singapore is the confluence of Indo-Pacific cultures. It is the place to tell this great story.

Description of the centre

It is proposed that the Indo-Pacific Cultural Centre be integrated with the casino so that tourists can be totally immersed in the panorama of Indo-Pacific diversity as they move through the spaces of the integrated resort at Marina Bay.

Integration to the city and the region

The integrated resort would be totally integrated into the city by various transport means. Of special note would be our proposed cable car that will link it to all the key downtown locations of special interest such as Little India, Fort Canning, Chinatown, Pearl's Hill, Mount Faber and finally, Sentosa. With spectacular views all over, the cable car ride will complete the experience of Singapore, the major metropolis in tropical Asia. There would also be a ferry an hour away to Sebana Cove, a marina and golf resort on the tip of South Johore, Malaysia. There, alternative low-cost luxurious accommodation would be available for casino staff and guests alike. All will enjoy unspoilt nature, wide open spaces, experience Malay village life and be able to visit fishing villages along the coast with excellent seafood as part of the total package. Tour packages will be made available to all visitors to the integrated resort at affordable prices to all attractions at Sebana and to key attractions in Singapore. This will be the competitive edge that the integrated resort will have over the competition and give it its distinctiveness.

Elements of the centre

This 20-storey "fish trap" structure will display the Bengal tiger, the Malayan tiger, the Sumatran rhino, the Bornean orang utan, plus all the iconic animals of the Indo-Pacific right next to multiple fine-dining restaurants on many different storeys. The space is also an aviary; Hornbills, parrots and lories will be everywhere.

The Omnimax theatre

Vertical zoo Within the vertical zoo structure is a full-sphere Omnimax theatre. In it, visitors will have breath-taking experiences of the great scenes of the Indo-Pacific in virtual reality. Having seen, heard and felt these, (s)he will be able to taste, smell and touch things related to the visual experiences in other parts of the centre.

Indo-Pacific ethnographic museum Specially curated, the museum will display the distinctive aspects of the different cultures but also show the similarities. This should be done comparatively in a captivating manner. The side facing the Bay is designed as rice terraces of glass with cascading water, producing shimmering light into the interior of the museum. At night, these gigantic glass terraces will be a sight to behold as a wonderful luminous waterfall. Restaurants and other related facilities are embedded within the museum exhibits so that the culture and the experience are made real and tactile.

Mount Kinabalu rock wall Towering over the rice terraces is the rock wall, which is also a noise barrier against the traffic. It is profiled after the highest mountain in Southeast Asia. It forms a fitting image. Here, rock climbing can be a dramatic way of interacting with the city.

Wedding halls On the roof of the museum, on a plateau, overlooking Marina Bay are four wedding halls. Wedding ceremonies of the different cultures of the Indo-Pacific will be enacted here in real life.

A New World in the Making

"Tree of Life" culture theatre A gigantic banyan tree, already identified growing on a beach in Singapore, will be transported by sea and transplanted onto the site next to the Esplanade to serve as a wonderful outdoor performance space beneath its boughs. Though it is a venue for Balinese dance performances, it is generic. It would also be a venue for many other cultural practices of the Indo-Pacific.

Austronesian harbour The present-day multi-hull marine craft of the Indo-Pacific are living relics of the ancient Austronesian cultural expansion. These, together with Arab dhows, Sulawesi *phinisi* and Chinese junks constitute the more recent maritime heritage of the Indo-Pacific. These are celebrated in the ambience of the harbour with appropriate waterfront facilities and the nearby Maritime Heritage Centre.

Indo-Pacific Maritime Heritage Museum The boat festival plaza is covered by gigantic bamboo structures demonstrating unique Austronesian triangular weaving not found anywhere else in the world. The covered plaza would be a venue for great maritime culture festivals of which Singapore is the epicentre. The great Belitung-Tang shipwreck collection, recently purchased by Singapore, will be most appropriately housed here and be the centrepiece of the maritime heritage of the Indo-Pacific. Together with all the iconic boats of the Indo-Pacific, it becomes the spiritual home of all Indo-Pacific cultures.

Indo-Pacific Ocean Aquarium The rich marine life of the Indo-Pacific is shown here. In particular, the unusually rich coral diversity of Singapore is shown as the mix of both oceans as it passes through the Singapore Straits.

Aquarium of Indo-Pacific River Ecologies The similarities and difference of the river life of both human settlement and aquatic life, seldom seen is here displayed in full comparative splendour.

Long house and rice fields Rice is grown in the city! The shock effect returns the mind immediately to the reality of the Indo-Pacific lands of rice, bamboo and monsoon. The long house next to it is a venue for cultural performances, a symbol of the ancient socio-cultural milieu. Its

Ideas and Proposals

bamboo floors spring underfoot to ethnic dance rhythms and music of the rainforest. Filled with the everyday artefacts of life of the tribes of the Indo-Pacific, the mind wanders and connects to an ancient stream of consciousness that unites the whole of the region.

Festival tent The large festival tent is another event space with many transient shows, food fairs and other attractions. Spaced 10 metre apart will be ice-cooled fountains to provide respite from the muggy tropical heat while sheltering from the sun.

Shopping mall Beneath the plaza is a gigantic shopping mall offering the full range of Indo-Pacific arts and crafts and other special local goods and services. Having seen, experienced and tasted the fare of the Indo-Pacific, it is time to take away souvenirs from displays chosen and curated with expert care.

Pedestrian suspension bridge A multilevel suspension pedestrian bridge links Marina Centre, the Indo-Pacific Cultural Centre and across the waterway to the casino and its other attractions. It is an opportunity to expand one's vision by connecting the past with the present panorama.

Cable car The cable car station at the top of the vertical zoo is linked to all levels by bubble elevators. It is the final node in an aerial cable-way system that connects the cultural centre to Little India, Mount Emily, Mount Sophia, Dhoby Ghaut MRT Station, then Fort Canning, Singapore River, Chinatown, Marina Bay, Pearl's Hill and on to Mount Faber and then Sentosa. This prime downtown tourism infrastructure will ensure total connectivity to all the major downtown points of interest while providing spectacular views all along the way.

SINGAPORE VERSION 2.0
27 December 2012

Singapore Version 1.0 succeeded through hosting multinational corporations (MNCs). The Singapore Version 2.0 economy has now to be more rebalanced between big corporations and small and medium enterprises (SMEs). This is both politically and economically necessary and expedient. The world has come somewhat belatedly to the end of the "free market" myth and awoken to the need to ensure job creation lost to globalisation, robotisation and the depressed aggregate demand in the rich countries for consumer goods both locally produced and imported. Total global economic growth halved from 3 per cent to 1.5 per cent. This will affect Singapore.

Singapore has to prevent MNCs located here from down-sizing, closing down or shifting out. It has to ensure jobs for locals in danger of retrenchment. This is a new policy imperative. Foreign workers can of course be sent home.

But Singapore Version 2.0 is both an economic restructuring exercise and a social opportunity. What Singapore Version 2.0 has to do is to increase the multiplier effect in the local economy. Someone's expenditure is another's income and as money circulates many times through the local economy, a higher level of well-being is generated for everyone. Since compulsory Central Provident Fund payment and lower cost housing has provided a safety net of sorts, disposable income can be more readily recycled into the local economy productively if correct policies are put in place. Essentially, a more sophisticated land-use plan has to come about to offer enterprise startups cheap rent. What is needed is to allow enterprise activities in non-market lands allocated for institutional uses. Startup SMEs can be hosted by teaching institutions. Their existing locations are not suitable as they are far from population centres.

Singapore Version 2.0 is also a social restructuring opportunity and challenge. It works by inserting a string of new social and economic facilities along a network of linked passages into all our housing estates where the bulk of the population comfortably live so long as they have the means to do so. This means jobs and exposure to new ideas and experiences that the new activities bring. To locate start-up SMEs in housing estates is ideal as they provide jobs close by. They also bring

Ideas and Proposals

more business to the traditional coffee shops, groceries and clinics thus contributing to the multiplier effect.

Because the new start-up SMEs are strung along the new network of main and branch passages linking all the neighbourhood and town centres, bus stops and MRT stations in our housing estates, a vibrant civic urban culture can come about naturally. Finally, these linkages extend outwards to the park connectors and the ex-railway line. All this will make life in Singapore more vibrant and enjoyable. This is especially so when the campuses of new and existing technical education institutes and polytechnics as well as arts, culture and civic facilities are also co-located together with the SMEs and mom and pop shops. The effect will be very enlivening for everyone.

A new level of stimulation, interaction and therefore intelligence will be brought into the routines of everyday life. This is the making of Singapore Version 2.0. The key to Singapore's future lies in the public housing estates. These are the sites for a new social and economic resurgence hitherto undervalued. By introducing a new organismic concept through inserting a multifunctional "Central Nervous System" into all the estates, a high level of social development and new economic energy can be induced. This is the basis for Singapore.

HDB version 2.0

The Housing & Development Board (HDB) changes from a housing agency to a housing authority. In this new role, it master plans and allocates land and it establishes the transactional rules. Communities wishing to implement their own neighbourhoods appoint their own consultants and design and implement their own housing communities within the Master Plan. Master plans only set out the overall density and layout geometry paying special attention to where and how the Central Nervous System (CNS) and Peripheral Nervous System (PNS) will be. The master plan defines the community plots. Each is small, of about 100 families all within short walking distances to the CNS and PNS. The mixed uses and the form of the design within each community cluster is decided by the communities themselves.

Meanwhile there should be a new differentiated pricing policy to enable young families to own flats. These are priced at zero land cost. Something along these lines: priority for young parents below the age of

35 with 2 or more children. They have to sell back to the authority at HDB price if they sell before 20 years domicile. After 20 years, they can sell at market price but not before. This is only just because it can be deemed that they had contributed to the community by being domicile all this while so they can get the capital gain. By this way, existing owners' market value is protected even as special arrangements are made for the new families that take up this scheme.

URA version 2.0

The Urban Redevelopment Authority (URA) remains the real estate agent of the slate of land vested in the Singapore Land Authority (SLA). But its role is no longer to increase land value across the board but selectively. Social equity and economic vibrancy through zoning is necessary. What is non-market community land and what is market-based land zones must be made clear. Even within each zone there can also be differentiation. This is done through the lease title unit by unit. Allocation criteria and records are not cumbersome through computerisation.

Planning methodology is now based on a dynamic system of floor space census. The statistical basis is derived from successful data gathered globally of the relations between Gross Domestic Product differentiated by type of economy and floor space per capita. This has at last uncovered the co-relation accurately. A similar census and correlation now forms the basis of the new planning methodology resulting in rational land and density allocation. Accordingly, the southern coast is defined as the predominantly international zone for intensive mix-use development thus freeing up the rest of the island for heritage, nature and local lifestyle innovation.

Town councils version 2.0

Singapore Version 2.0 is premised on actualising democracy as part of the raising of its intelligence levels. Self-government is the key. Town councils are no longer appointed but elected from the community. All key decisions are canvassed and agreed on by referendum conducted on the internet. The deficit caused by asymmetric information is solved through community radio and internet communication. Such an information culture is predicated on robust community life. Having successfully shared in building communities through the HDB Version 2.0 processes, the information deficit is thus resolved and resolvable. The role of the legislature having enacted laws that reinforce the powers of the elected town councils ensure administrative success.

EDB version 2.0

On top of attracting investors, the new version of the Economic Development Board (EDB) has an additional function, that of attracting inventors to Singapore. EDB sets up an investment and facilitation company to exercise evaluation procedures, validate claims, patent application and intellectual property (IP) protection, fund prototyping and finally match-make investors and inventors towards commercialisation. This will make Singapore an inventions IP centre leveraging off its reputation as a secure and attractive location.

SAF version 2.0

One and a half years of National Service is devoted to military aspects in the Singapore Armed Forces (SAF) and the additional year is devoted to community service. This enables better utilisation of time and resolves manpower shortages in some sectors of the economy. Young men and women will gain real-world working experience.

Community centres version 2.0

Facilities are networked into the community. They enrich the community space and also benefit from closer relationship with the other aspects of community life. Again, surveillance is by webcam.

NTUC version 2.0

National Trades Union Congress (NTUC) starts producer co-op education for its members. It provides training in co-op management and equity structure. NTUC provides startup funding for viable projects, and acts as banker where appropriate. For this role, NTUC starts community banks in every housing estate. It provides training, supervision and advice. Community banks are the bedrock of community participation and cohesion.

Schools version 2.0

Schools are spatially disaggregated and integrated into the CNSs of all housing estates. Children walk or cycle to school rooms along the slow-flow elevated passages. All school spaces are used by the community when not used by the school, thereby optimising facilities. All schools will have start-up shops, experimental and hobby workshops. Libraries are open to the public. Canteens are open to the public also. All spaces are surveilled by webcams accessible through internet by anyone. This deters vandalism.

ITE version 2.0

Presently, Institute of Technical Education (ITE) campuses are point locations far from the housing areas. Some of its teaching functions, studios, labs and workshops can be decentralised and relocated in the CNSs of the housing estates, gaining direct access and ability to connect with the community, especially in providing adult training in various skills and knowledges. Many startup shops can be provided for ITE students to start businesses in the community, which is not possible otherwise due to high rents and unsuitable location.

Polytechnics version 2.0

For the same reasons as with ITEs, polytechnics can also have greater presence in the CNSs of all HDB estates. No longer are the training institutions focused on producing manpower for jobs. The new emphasis is to train job creators.

Universities version 2.0

Some university student studios and lecture facilities located in the CNSs of the housing estates will benefit from exposure to the community and vice versa. High-level knowledge adult education classes in the community will raise the general level of thinking and reduce elitism as well. High level scientific and academic research is emphasised. The aim is to produce leaders and innovators, not just to fill manpower needs of industry, commerce and administration.

Arts version 2.0

The arts has a great leavening effect on the community as well as on the artists. Particularly when the performing arts are inserted in the community, a more relevant culture of self and community expression can be part of everyday life. Art therefore becomes life, and life becomes art. This is the way through which the general level of public aesthetic sensitivity will be raised. The arts are integrated into society not as entertainment but for enlightenment through shifting conceptual frames and rigid mindsets.

Media version 2.0

Local community radio is a must. It allows for listening while working, unlike the internet or television. Community radio is also the means for the community to truly communicate. The schools, the commercial, the cultural and the institutionally generated news will be the very stuff of community knowledge. Active programming within the community will bring about a new level of community cohesion as never before. Full time media staff in-situ drawn especially from retirees and housewives will report on activities and news in and about the community. Different community radio stations will compete with each other, and thus become the continuous national conversation. Advertising will fund the radio stations. This will also give exposure to startup businesses and be a vehicle for new ideas and new knowledge.

RUBANISATION
13 March 2012

A condensed essay for ASIA 360 on my concept of rethinking Asia's relationship with the countryside amid its dash to urbanisation.

The idea of "Rubanisation" is located in the context of contemporary dynamic change. The most important change starts with the re-conceptualisation of the urban and the rural as one space and not two. "Rubanisation" is a compound word that I had to coin from the words "rural" and "urban" as there is no equivalent.

While I appreciate the virtues of urban living, I am aware of the ever-widening disparity between the rich and the poor and between the city and the eco-system. I want to see a solution. As such, my thinking can be seen as a critique of the urbanist development model. I should not need to cite the already well-known litany of statistics that show the disparities set against the triumphal urging and applauding of undifferentiated urbanisation. As such, urbanisation has resulted in megacities in all the growth economies. Urbanisation should also mean urban aggregations in the agricultural heartlands. Since the 1800s, the accelerating exploitation of opportunities for maximising of profit has ignored the down sides of such growth and distorted the meaning of urbanisation. It is enough to note here that beyond a certain point of market-spurred growth, the heightening of profit through the processes facilitated by the present sort of urbanisation becomes immoral and dysfunctional even to its own impulse. It is necessary to critique the uncritical celebration of the virtues of the "city" as the prime human artefact and begin to address its ills and find alternative solutions. In this, I do not believe that the ills can be tackled piecemeal. A total review is necessary.

The complexity is, of course, very great, but the effects are observable. Fundamentally, it is because of the untrammelled free market that has grown beyond control. Here, radical free market ideology is at fault. Free markets cannot determine optimal growth until breakdowns occur. The urban financial system is an example. It is so interlinked and leveraged that piecemeal corrective methods cannot succeed to shore up the gigantic house of cards. The "occupy movements" are an agonising cry to draw attention to the roots of the complexity but the targets are illusive. A new consciousness is arising even as no solutions are in sight. Theoretically then, urban virtues must be seen against financial vices. The uncritical eulogising of urbanism as such will have to give way to deep review at this time of history.

Rubanisation is an attempt to reconceptualise "development" and has at its focus the form and content of human settlements. It is a critique of big city urbanisation, of the sort we see being emulated in Asia.

Rubanisation does not decry urbanism but only its distended form and its focus on big cities. Rubanisation is also a proposal for a re-integrated form of living different from the sort of urban living promoted within the middle-class in the megacities. In this aspect, Rubanisation is the counter-thesis that may amount to a civilizational shift of emphasis. It notes that healthy human life has been debased and fragmented by the urban-industrial-consumer economy. Rubanisation offers viable restorative choices to live in smaller networked urbanised settlements in the folds of nature and farms or in reformed cities. It is not an advocation to return to the mud and grime, but fast forward to a new future.

The ills and repair of existing big cities can only really take place after the reformation of the rural-urban landscape wherein Ruban lifestyles and economics have reached a certain stage of maturity starting disparately. Repair of the crises in the big cities as they reach the apogee of decay and when viable alternatives in the Rubanised landscape have been actualised. Rubanisation is a concept that arrives at this potentially transformational moment in human history. Rubanisation is not anti-city. It seeks to rebalance the current deficiencies.

Reformed cities are part of the transformation. Reformed cities have only five functions left after industrial production has been decentralised and the financial system divested of its moral hazards. The remaining roles of the big city are:

- To be the centres for the highest levels of medical research and treatment.
- To be the centres for the highest levels of knowledge production and teaching.
- To be the centres for the highest levels of inter-regional coordination and governance.
- To be the centres for the highest levels of media and arts production.

- To be the centres for the highest levels of prototyping of new technologies and scientific research.

The idea of alternative forms of human settlement has been fomenting in my mind for a long time. I was dissatisfied with Doxiadis' projection of an Ecumenopolis in which a continuous urban belt creeps all over planet Earth. My quest finally emerged at a seminar organised by the Asia Research Institute (ARI) at the National University of Singapore (NUS) in 2006 where I proposed the view that the rural/urban dichotomy should cease to be considered as two spaces but as one. In this view, all settlements are physically and electronically networked but always embedded within an agricultural continuum with nature preserves further away. Soon after this presentation at ARI, the *GlobalAsia* journal based in Seoul requested to publish my essay on rubanisation in their 2008 September issue. Since then, starting in early 2009, I was invited to Sri Lanka and to Indonesia to present Rubanisation to their respective governments and professional groups and the idea has spread even further.

Comparison to the garden city concept

While superficially a Ruban settlement is similar to the circular plan-form of Ebenezer Howard's Garden City concept of the 1930s, the differences are fundamental. Howard's Garden City for one is two kilometre in diameter whereas the maximum diameter of a Ruban settlement is one kilometre. This is why the Ruban settlement is a walking town, whereas the Garden City relies on motorised transportation. While my sentiment is similar to Howard's concern with industrialism's negative impact on human life and culture, the context and the solution to this concern is very different. Howard's Garden City was still tied to the primacy of the central city and the garden-city settlements are arrayed around it and also dependent on it. Rubanisation at its mature stage is no longer dependent on the metropolitan centre, but forms part of a network with all the Ruban settlements within a region physically and electronically to the whole world. Marshall McLuhan's idea of the "electronic cottage" was prescient. The internet, not available to Howard, was fatal to the Garden City concept. Whereas in Rubanisation, information and communications technology (ICT) is a key element that makes networked settlements possible, desirable and interconnected at the personal and institutional level, and commercially feasible at last. Finally, Rubanisation has political implications on governance. The logic of Rubanisation inevitably answers the long overdue political quest for autonomy and local democracy. The new politics and new economics have deep implications for local culture, aesthetic sensibilities and authentic value formation. The possibility of engendering new non-material satisfactions is at last possible.

The context of globalisation

The contradiction inherent in globalisation as an economic concept has reached maturity. It is between the freedom to invest anywhere and the problems that creates in the rich countries from where the investments came. Rich nations lose jobs to low cost developing countries as their corporations outsource. The middle classes in the rich countries are made poorer. They are less able to continue their consumerist lifestyle to which they have become accustomed. They are not able to buy more. This creates two crises. A political crisis of confidence in the rich countries and a decline of exports by the poorer countries. Meanwhile, the poorer countries need to divert their excess manufacturing capacity domestically, but this needs a readjustment in the wages and incomes.

It is in this context that Rubanisation comes in after adhoc changes are made. Meanwhile, there is social unrest as dislocations occur. Old grievances begin to boil over. Long-term solutions need to be initiated even as short-term handling takes place. A rebalancing of wages and incomes has to happen even as inflation cuts in. The decentralisation of jobs and investments to increase agricultural output are necessary. The relocation of light industries into smaller cities and even villages to be nearer to where people reside is needed to quell the unrest. A rethink on how all these should take place is necessary. A redeployment of human and natural capital is necessary. This involves a shift in the longer term towards more intrinsic satisfactions too if climate change and environmental degradation are to be addressed. The strategy of emphasising the central city concept that prioritises consumption and the centralising of capital and infrastructure resources to big cities is becoming bankrupt.

The urban and the rural: new geometries of environment

The question of how humans should dwell on planet Earth gets ever more important as global population grows. The mathematics of human

A New World in the Making

settlement needs to be done to clear the mind on what the dimensions of the issue really are. We need to calculate the quantities involved. There is 19 million square kilometre of net arable land. This is minus water bodies, steep hill slopes and other unsuitable topographical features for cultivation of agricultural crops. Next, we need to estimate the total floor area needed for dwellings, commercial, civic and all other spaces to compute the total impact of human needs expressed as a percentage of arable land. This is necessary because unfortunately there is no accurate census of floor area globally. Such data is vital but unavailable. The only way now is to estimate it. To do this we need a per capita gross floor area. My estimate for affluent Singapore is 50 square metre so it seems reasonable if we assume an average of 35 square metre per person globally for the world's poor. We now need the relevant population which we assume to be saying four billion poor people out of the total of seven billion. Three billion in poor rural areas and one billion poor urban dwellers we get a total of 140,000 square kilometre of gross floor area. Divided by 19 million square kilometre (net arable land), the footprint on the arable land is 0.8 per cent, assuming all buildings are single storey. If they are two-storey high on average, the land area impact would be halved to 0.4 per cent. Refinements of these calculations is vital such as to account for existing buildings and percentage of new ones, and to estimate obsolete ones and the impact of class differentials in floor space occupation. The complexity increases once we simulate the change dynamics caused by development. Still, the rough numbers raise a number of troubling questions. Does it mean that there are huge options for human settlement types? We need to add roads, drainage canals, infrastructure requirements, spacing between buildings, local parks and more. Even if we triple the footprint to account for these, the gross curtilage of settlements increases to only 1.5 per cent, which is still rather insignificant. There are other variables like building on hills rather than on flat farmlands or on stilts over water bodies, which increases the options. So, one can see that decentralised human settlement is only a function of availability of roads and other services. Clearly then, the settlement pattern will spread in small clusters outwards from the present urban areas.

Why the circle?

The form of a Ruban settlement is never more than one kilometre diameter. This is to produce a walking town so that no place is more than half a kilometre away. Why the circle? There are several considerations. Firstly, a precise boundary is necessary so that there is no ambiguity where the settlement ends, and the farms begin. Administratively, this makes things clear and precise. Although most architects hate this, it is necessary. Secondly, it ensures parity so that no one is any further than another to get to the centre where most of the commercial and civic facilities are located. Thirdly, the circumferential service road will be the shortest possible. Within the circle, there is freedom to configure the layout to suit local needs. In every case, however, the density should be the minimum that can support good schools and all children can walk to school. Compact dwellings are a norm to ensure maximum connectivity and infrastructure efficiency, such as waste collection and recycling it into compost and or algae oil and animal feed.

What facilities?

The constituent elements will vary according to the circumstances. Conceivably, they will include houses, educational institutions, library, a town hall, sports field, shopping street, restaurants, market, offices, workshops and even factories, cinema, music halls, art streets, galleries, concert hall, technical college, agricultural research, food processing, silos, cold storage, a transport centre, police station, administration offices, internet cafes, restaurants, hotel, guest houses, motor repair shops, junk store, etc.

Education

One of the main drivers for human settlement in the contemporary period is education for the children. Good schools are a pent-up demand and is the prime concern of rural and urban families. As such, the school can become the centre of the community. Quality of the education is crucial. Typically, the education system is factory-like in contemporary schools. This needs to change to a more comprehensive learning process. The Mechai Bamboo School I designed with Mechai Viravaidya in Lam Plai Mat, Buriram province, some 450 kilometres northeast of Bangkok, is the kind of school that has a transformative effect on the students and their families. The empowerment of the students and the community around it suggest that this model of education could be the key to motivate resettlement into a Ruban settlement. In the Mechai school, students learn through their own self-elected projects, which address their interests and the needs of their families. These projects are the learning context beyond books. Teachers reinforce the projects with the required curricular such as maths, science and humanities. For students, this pattern of learning is entirely engaging and relevant. The energy level applied to learning increased tremendously. The internet offers students access to the world of knowledge and information. I imagine the school to become multi-functional. It may be the site for the village bank, the village health facility, the seat of the local government, etc. This way, the forging of community cohesion and the formation of shared vision is made concrete. Architecture becomes causative, not merely decorative.

Local government

Research has to be undertaken to answer the question of density. What we know is that densities can be very high when there is social cohesion but becomes problematic when cohesion is low. This then requires more policing and draconian politics. The equation is this: Cohesion is a function of community, and this in turn is created by trust, which in turn comes from successful sharing. This suggests that the social dynamics of settling in a Ruban settlement must involve community participation from the start. This is a fundamental strategy. Local government is indispensable. Energy and food autonomy are the two critical provisions in the dynamics of political transformation. This will be resisted by centralist authorities but pursued by localist democratic interests. How this will play out will be the politics of the 21st century.

08

Afterword

In hindsight, everything seems to fit together. I can see the roots of my ideas of Rubanisation even in early childhood when I started building tiny houses out of scrap materials. Active play and reading—out of boredom, mostly, starting with Arthur Mee's *The Children's Encyclopaedia*, progressing through *Reader's Digest* and *National Geographic* and on to *The Communist Manifesto* and Bertrand Russell's *In Praise of Idleness*— these gave me a grounding in what is now called comprehensive design thinking.

I grew up in the days of Malayanisation, of decolonisation. This induced a sense of being Malayan. The nation-building ethos of the then new People's Action Party government inspired my design approach of social purpose and focus on building a new Singapore. And I was lucky to have my Southeast Asian consciousness inspired by my first-year architecture tutor Lim Chong Keat, who opened my eyes to the Malayan landscape and vernacular architecture.

But I wonder if this all would happen had I not been compelled to study in Singapore.

After five decades of practice, dogged by politics, I always wondered why I felt very different from my colleagues trained in Australia, Britain and America. This was doubly puzzling because we all read the same books, admired all the same buildings and absorbed the same architectural philosophies. Why did I strive to find a different aesthetic, as described by Robert Powell in *Line, Edge and Shade*? He tried to describe why and in what ways my work departed from the posture of taut, sheer-edged rectangularity taken by most high-achieving architects to be emblematic of "modernity". How had I become more eclectic and erratic? And why?

A New World in the Making

I always thought of design at many different scales concurrently. Architecture was never for me about creating an isolated art object. A house or a building or indeed a city was never an art object nor a machine for living in. It was and still is only a microcosm of a socio-psychological environmental spatial system. Low-cost housing embodied a conception of convivial and creative living. A hospital was to be navigable despite the terror of its spatial complexity. Architecture was always a humanising project, but its engineering had to be socially and aesthetically coherent as well as consistent and dynamic. For that, I had to formulate the epistemology of aesthetics to free design thinking from its preconceived cultural and ideological constructs.

Architecture is spatial and complex organisational design at every scale. Thus, it engages rising scales from urban design to urbanisation, and then to regionalism. This led me finally to Rubanisation and the desire to dissolve the rural-urban dichotomy altogether. Today's megacity is the product of industrial and financial capitalism gone riot. Its days are numbered, together with its stylish protagonists! Instead, the future is a network urbanisation enabled by a web of economic and informational matrices.

Over a decade since I first articulated Rubanisation, the concept is gradually being concretised. I was recently introduced to Indonesia's foremost industrial estate developer after Singapore's former ambassador to the country had read of my ideas on Rubanisation and felt it would be useful to the developer, who had been tasked by his president to build 100 new towns. A different chance meeting in Singapore in early 2022 led to a request for me to propose a prototype Green Township to be built in Central Java. These encounters set off a dynamic that coincided with an earlier proposal I had made in 2020 to turn all of Singapore's university campuses into enterprise zones. By co-locating enterprises, start-ups and financial institutions along with education facilities, a new learning culture can be created amongst professors and research students at higher education institutions. This would transform Singapore into an Enterprise City, and not simply just a cog in the global supply chain.

In response to Singapore's Urban Redevelopment Authority's (URA) recent call for new planning ideas, I sent in my Enterprise Campus proposal. It was well received. I guess the authorities had to listen. My 1970s Golden Mile Complex had just been designated by URA for conservation, and I

Afterword

had been an adjunct professor at the National University of Singapore's architecture school for several years. I ended up having a long meeting with the relevant minister on the proposal, and I also discussed my encounters with Indonesian developers to build new towns. Coincidentally, Singapore and Indonesia signed a joint agreement in March 2022 to tackle climate change together. This has created some powerful incentives for creating new Green Townships as part of my vision for an Eco-Regional Economy with Singapore playing the central catalytic role. The country's triple A credit rating enables us to raise a trillion-dollar green bond to finance the greening of the regional economy. But administrating it will require entrepreneurial and managerial skills, and that's where my idea to develop enterprise campuses in Singapore comes in.

Education has long been a major concern of mine having put so much of my time and thinking into being an educator. Several years ago, I had proposed a new Super School Concept to replace Singapore's existing primary and secondary school system. It was presented at a 2014 conference organised by Singapore's Institute of Policy Studies and there was strong buy-in from the attendees which included former school principals and teachers. After many constructive meetings with the Ministry of Education, the idea was eventually rebuffed. I later realised that even if implemented it could only produce results in 12 to 24 years. Too long! I shifted my focus onto higher education, looking at our campuses, planned and conceived in the 1970s and 1980s. This was how I arrived at the idea of enterprise campuses which can produce results within four to eight years. Much better! This idea and the Green Township concept have also become particularly relevant as the global economy on which Singapore totally depends on today is beginning to falter.

Realising the Eco-Regional Economy will need a new kind of leadership in business and policy. Design thinking thus extends into leadership and enterprise, that is the design of the whole system of life. The "total scope of architecture" as envisaged by Walter Gropius has now to be seen as obsolete. The final statement attributed to Le Corbusier that "architects are wrong, and nature is right" resounds! This is where the trajectory of my career as an activist-architect has led me. There is a new spatial design approach that must be aesthetically coherent, consistent and dynamic at the primal level and yet culturally, ideologically and politically cogent. This is the new challenge. This type of design thinking has, out of necessity, gone well beyond the conventional concept of architectural design thinking as defined and practised. We are entering a whole new and different world. We have to if we are not all to perish...

A new world in the making requires new architecture design thinking!

List of Images

Family Portrait	6
Parent's Wedding Portrait	18
Braddell Heights	19
Cameron Highlands	19
Young Scout	20
Wolf Cub Brothers	20
Building Bamboo Kitchen Gadgets	21
Showing Thesis Project to Dr Toh Chin Chye	32
Model of Tourist Information Bureau	50
Studying Architecture at Singapore Polytechnic	50
Sketches of Tourist Information Bureau	51
Modern Kampong House	51
Nanyang University Convocation Stage	52
Exterior of proposed National Theatre	54
Interior of proposed National Theatre	55
Logo of Singapore Polytechnic Architectural Society	56
Drawing of Low-Cost Furniture for Flats	56
Various actualised Low-Cost Furniture for Flats	57
Interior of Barker Road Methodist Church	58
Exterior of Barker Road Methodist Church	59
Blank Altar-Wall at Barker Road Methodist Church	59
Thesis Proposal of Fine Arts Centre	60
Visit to Java and the Bandung Institute of Technology	61
Young Biker at Ponggol Marina	72
Cover of SPUR Publication	88
SPUR Study on Implications of Airport Proposals	89
South Sea Lagoon Project by SPUR	90
SPUR Environment Exhibition	90
Toa Payoh Neighbourhood Plan	92
8-Storey Plan for Toa Payoh Neighbourhood	92
13-Storey Plan for Toa Payoh Neighbourhood	93
5-Storey Plan for Toa Payoh Neighbourhood	93
Individual Gardens in the Cheras Housing Project	94
Shaded Breezeways at Cheras	94

List of Images

Interior of a Home at Cheras	95
Model of Back-To-Back Clusters at Cheras	95
Illustration from *Transport dilemma in Singapore*	116
Landscaped Tower for the Kampong Bugis Design Guide Plan	186
Cover of *Mega-Cities in the Tropics*	230
Planting and Landscaping Roofs for a Tropical City	230
Upper-Level Community Spaces for a Tropical City	231
Models for Kampong Bugis Design Guide Plan #1	232
Models for Kampong Bugis Design Guide Plan #2	232
Kampong Bugis Design Guide Plan	233
Models for Kampong Bugis Design Guide Plan #3	233
Night Safari	234
Model of Indo-Pacific Cultural Centre at Marina Bay #1	246
Model of Indo-Pacific Cultural Centre at Marina Bay #2	246
Proposal for Cottages	247
Intensifying Southern Singapore, a Proposal	248–9
Rubanisation Proposal	250
Rethinking Dormitories	251
Model of Marsiling MRT, Singapore: Campus City	252
Model of Eastern Campus, Singapore: Campus City	252
Model of Singapore: Campus City	253

Index

Abdul Sannie, 78

administration, Western concepts of, 150

adolescence, life of, 38–9

adult education, 262

aeromodelling, passion for, 37

aeronautics, 37

aesthetics
   Chinese, 84
   development of, 147
   insecurity, 147
   and intellectual integrity, 65
   of low-cost housing, 207–8

affiliation, territorial concepts of, 1

age-induced learning, 13

air pollution, elimination of, 143

airport planning, international standards for, 199

air raid shelter, 17, 22, 100

Alpha Gallery, 78

altruism, 41

American B-29 Superfortress bombers, 31

American International Assurance Company (AIA), 9

Ang Kheng Leng, 48–9, 52

Anglo-Chinese School (ACS), 13, 35, 39, 42
   Lee Kuo Chuan Auditorium, 42
   school chapel service, 35–6

Anson Road stadium, 9

anti-backwardness, 155

anti-communism, 154

anti-gangsterism, 154

anti-pornography, 154–5

Arabisation of names, 180

arche-typology, 217

Architects Collaborative, The, 75

architecture, pursuit of, 47–62

architecture school, 64

arts version 2.0, 263

Asian cities, future of, 122–8

Asian City of Tomorrow, 122

Asian Seamen's Club, 64

Asian values, campaigning of, 182

Asia Research Institute (ARI), 266

authentic aesthetics, development of, 147

authentic national architecture, 148

"Baby Water" business, 24

Bandung Institute of Technology (ITB), 61, 69

Bank Rakyat Building, in Penang, 80

Barker Road Methodist Church, 15, 42, 44, 46, 58

Bartlett School of Architecture, in London, 66

Basoeki, Raden Abdullah, 87

Battle of Tarawa, The (movie), 22

Bauhaus of Weimar Germany, 63

Beach Road market, 9

Bedok reclamation area, 129

Belitung-Tang shipwreck, 256

bilingualism, 110

Board of the Methodist Church, 42

boat festival plaza, 256

Index

"Boh Sua Tian" (Hokkien for wireless), 181
Boh Tea Estate, 19, 24
Boon Lay Road police station, 41
Boston City Hall design, 81
"boutique" restaurants, 71
Braddell Heights, 12, 19
    adventures in, 36–8
    Boys' Club, 41
    early life in, 36
    farms and waste land, 37
    neighbourhood gang, 37
    suburban housing estate, 37
Bras Basah Park, 166, 240–2
Breuer, Marcel, 63
Brewer, Frank, 42
Brighton Polytechnic, 62
British Army, 24, 40, 42
British imperialism, 113–14
British law and order, 31, 152
British liberalism, 110
British Malaya, 31
    currency, 24
British Trade Union Congress, 77
Bugis Street, 155, 178
building construction, 47, 62
Bukit Timah Road, 29, 179
bus transport system
    fare hike, 144
    ownership of, 143

cable cars, 254, 257
Cameron Highlands, 22–4, 27
    life in, 27–9
    memories of days in, 27
Campus City, 252

capital accumulation, 123, 174
carparks, multi-storey, 130
Central Business District, 130, 175
Central Medical Hall, Singapore, 24
Central Provident Fund, 258
Changi Airport, 198–200
changing values, development and its impact on, 133–8
Chapman, Spencer, 31
"charismatic" literalism, 44
Chen Voon Fee, 75, 80
Cheras Housing Project (Kuala Lumpur), 95, 98
Chia, Kenneth, 80
Children's Encyclopaedia, The (Arthur Mee), 271
Children's Society, 204
Chinatown, 56, 120, 254, 257
Chinese aesthetics, 84
Chinese backwardness, problems of, 114
Chinese Chamber of Commerce, 154
Chinese chauvinism, 180
Chinese dialect, 26, 180
Chinese-educated political leaders, in Singapore, 179
Chinese identity, 26
Chinese junks, 256
Chinese-language schools, 25–6
Chinese, Malay, Indian and Others (CMIO) formulation, 180
Chinese Ministry of Foreign Affairs, 26
Chinese-ness, concept of, 27
Chinese religious practices, 10
Chng Jit Koon, 179
Choe, Alan, 57

Chong Yoke Choy, 209
Christian ethics, 35–6, 41
Christianity, 12, 15
Christ, Jesus, 43
Church of England Zenana Mission
    Society (CEZMS) School,
    Singapore. *See* St. Margaret's
    School
Chwee Heng, 52, 64, 67, 85
civic and environmental
    consciousness, 131
civil society, contribution of, 162–4
class and culture difference, 10
Clementi Park, 196
cluster link houses, 97, 207, 209
coffee processing factory, in Tanglin
    Halt, 81
cognitive development, 13
colloquial values, of Singapore, 183
Collyer Quay's 12-lane coastal
    superhighway, 129–32
    effect on environment, 131
Colombo Plan scholarships, 81
colonial administration, 150
Committee on Quality of Life in
    Singapore, 224
communal sentiments, 154
communication networks, 220
Communist Manifesto, The, 41, 271
community-based house-help
    services, 172
community centres version 2.0, 261
community festival, 171
community welfare organisation, 239
comprehensivity, concept of, 66
Confucian ethics, 182
congested city, 126

corporate capital, 174
creches and kindergartens,
    development of, 195
cultural capital, creation of, 167–8
cultural consciousness, 181
cultural insecurity, 147
    phenomenon of, 147
Cultural Revolution, 179
culture refinement, characteristics
    of, 147

decision making
    centralisation of, 134
    process of, 140
delinquency, problem of, 141
democratic modernism, 108
Design and Build Scheme (DBS), 100
*Design and Territoriality in Public
    Housing in Singapore* (Michael
    Walter), 202
Design Partnership, 97
    expulsion from, 101–4
desire lines, 127
Development Bank of Singapore, 172,
    197
Development Guide Plans (DGPs),
    223–4, 241
Dhanabalan, S., 99–100, 223
Dhoby Ghaut MRT Station, 241, 257
diesel fuel tax, 143
dignity and purposefulness, sense
    of, 110
Doraisamy, Michael Robert, 36
dormitories for foreign workers, 251
Doxiadis' projection of an
    Ecumenopolis, 266

Index

DP Architects (Pte), 97, 103
draftsman-based local practices, 81
Duke of Edinburgh, 62

East/West traffic, 130
Economic Development Board (EDB)
   version 2.0, 261
economic integration, process of, 175
Eco-Regional Economy, 273
education, quality of, 269–70
efficient cities, development of, 123
electric trams, 12
electronic communication systems,
   220
electronic cottage, idea of, 266
Electronic Information Systems, 221
Elizabeth Walk, 130–1
End of Empire and the Making of
   Malaya, The (Tim Harper), 31
energy optimisation, strategy of, 219
English education, 107, 109
English-language schools, 25
Enlightenment, 110
entrepreneurial capital, 173
European Town, 137

Faber Hill, 196
face-to-face communication, 220
family, 9–13
family life, quality of, 201
family structures, 194
Ferrie, James, 76
festival tent, 257
financial burdens, of the family, 9
financing, of housing projects, 197

Fine Arts Centre, 61
Fitzpatrick Supermarket, 76
Force 136 (British intelligence
   organisation), 31
Force 136 (Tan Chong Tee), 31
foreign worker dormitories, 251
Fort Canning, 55, 151, 241
Foster, Joyce, 42
Foster, Robert, 42
Frankel Estate, 193
freedom and liberation, culture of,
   103
freedom fighters, 108
free enterprise economy, 123
"free market" myth, 258
free speech, meaning of, 2
Fuller, Buckminster, 65
fund prototyping, 261

Gamer, Robert, 140
garden city, concept of, 266–7
Garden of Gethsemane, 43
generation gap, 134
GlobalAsia journal, 266
globalisation, impact of, 267
global supply chain, 272
Goh Hood Keng, 36
Goh Keng Swee, 167, 182
gotong royong spirit, 96
government's sale of land, 196
Grand Hotel Preanger, 69
Great Asian Streets
   event-space in relation to
   capitalist transformations,
   176–7
   future of, 177

Index

inter-relationships and conflicts, 175

lively streets for the users, 175

operator's points of view, 175

power structure of, 176

social and spatial ecology of, 174

Symposium, 3rd, 173–7

urban spaces and streets, 174–5

Greater East Asia Co-Prosperity Sphere, 28–9

Green Township, 272–3

grid-stack geometry, 251

Gripe's Baby Water, 23

Gropius, Walter, 63, 75, 273

Gross Domestic Product, 260

Guangzhou, 26

guided democracy, 69

Guthrie's (trading house), 67, 82

Hall, Elmer, 42

"hanyu pinyin-isation" of place names, 179

hanyu pinyin movement, 180

Harbourfront MRT, 252

Heritage Committee, 181

heritage conservation

current situation of, 157

and demolition of historical buildings, 153

as "glue" of society, 149

growth of consciousness on, 156

listing buildings for preservation, 153

nature conservation, 155–6

negative factors in anti-backwardness, 155

anti-communalism, 153–4

anti-communism, 154

anti-gangsterism, 154

anti-pornography, 154–5

political and social implications of influx of immigration, 151

law and administration, 150–1

multicultural heritage, 152

place, 151

priorities, 149

race relations, 152

political power and, 152–3

politics of, 158

positive aspects of, 156

recommendations of the Committee on, 157–8

in Singapore, 149

Temasek (ancient Singapore), 151

Western heritage of laws and administrative criteria, 150

heritage, of Indonesia, 70

heroic nation-building themes, 87

high-density living, consequence of, 203

higher education, in Malaysia, 110

high-rise high-density (HRHD) housing, 206

high-rise slab blocks, 216

historical buildings, demolition of, 153

Ho, Charles, 85

Hock Ann Brickworks, 37

Hock's Baby Water, 23

Hokkiens, 10

Ho Kok Cheong, 97

Ho Kwong Yew, 39

Holland Court, 82

Index

home industries, development of, 174

Ho Pak Toe, 49, 85

hot-housing cultural capital formation, 167

housing co-operatives, 196

Housing Developers Association (HDA), 98

Housing & Development Act (1975), 102

housing, for industrial centres, 193–7

"Housing, Identity and Nation-building" paper (1968), 87

housing shortage, 37

Howard, Ebenezer, 266

Howe Yoon Chong, 78–9

Hume Industries, 82

ikan daun (leopard bush fish), 28

ikan kawan, 28

Illinois Institute of Technology, 78

immigration, influx of, 151

Imperial Japanese Army Air Service, 22

incrementality, problem of, 220

independence movement, in Singapore, 25, 107, 115

India, independence of, 31

Indonesia, independence of, 31

Indonesian revolution, 68

Indonesia Raya, 68, 69

Indo-Pacific Cultural Centre, Marina Bay Singapore, 244–57
bio-botanical endowment, 245
campus city, 252
cultural reality of, 245
day cultures of, 245

description of, 254

dormitories, 251

elements of, 255

"fish trap" structure, 255

forgotten heritage, 245–54

Indo-Pacific identity, 245

"infotainment" facility, 244

integration to the city and the region, 254

maritime heritage of, 256

Omnimax theatre, 255–7

Indo-Pacific littoral states, 254

Indo-Pacific Maritime Heritage Museum, proposal for, 256

Indo-Pacific Ocean Aquarium, 256

industrial and urban centres, in Singapore, 196–7

industrial dormitories, 197

industrialisation
demands of, 128
process of, 125
programmes, 133

industrial production, 265

industrial restructuring, 225

Industrial Revolution, 123, 133, 221

industrial workers, housing for, 196

industrial working-class cities, 127

information and communications technology (ICT), 220, 266

information-intensive system, 220

information technology (IT) revolution, 163

In Praise of Idleness (Bertrand Russell), 271

Institute of Technical Education (ITE) version 2.0, 262

integrated tropical urbanism, 100

Index

intellectual property (IP) protection, 261

intelligent tropical city
architectural precedents, 217
artistic and lifestyle possibilities of, 220
climate, 217
concept of, 218
information content, 220–2
new and architectural responses for, 219
problem of incrementality, 220
problems of environmental and aesthetic equilibrium, 222
social and cultural responses, 217–19

International Indo-Pacific Ocean University, 170

International Union of' Public Transport, 143

inter-racial family, 13

Jalan Besar stadium, 9

Japan
cultural values, 147
defeat of the British by, 110
economic success of, 147
Meiji Period, 147
occupation of Singapore, 23

Japanese Romanisation system, 179

Java, student trip to, 61, 67–71

job opportunities, creation of, 119, 125

jobs and investments, decentralisation of, 267

Jogjakarta gamelan, 70

Johnson's Baby Water, 23

Jungle is Neutral, The (Spencer Chapman), 31

Jurong Park, 40

Kahn, Louis, 77

Kallang Airport, 49

Kampong Bugis case study, 223–8, 232
East Coast Dike, 226
"grid stack" model, 227
high-density building prototypes, 226
space allocation, 226
strategic land use review, 225–8

Kampong Bugis Design Guide Plan, 188

Kandang Kerbau
hospital project, 62, 100
market, 179
police station, 23

Kepes, György, 63

kiasuism, strategy of, 148

Kie Hock Shipping, 67

Kim (Rudyard Kipling), 40

Kim Hao House, in Saigon, 50

Kim's Game, 40

Kirk Terrace, 241

Kitchener Road, 30

Koh Seow Chuan, 79, 97

koleks, 11

Konfrontasi, 68

Korean War, 36, 179

Kranji River, 40

kretek (a type of Indonesian cigarette), 69–70

Index

Kuala Lumpur administration, 98
Kuok, Robert, 99
Kwan House, 50

Labour Front party, 79
laissez faire ownership, of land, 128
Land Acquisition Act, 223
land for housing development,
    releasing of, 196
land resources, strategic allocation
    of, 243
land zones, market-based, 260
language/class divide, 25–7
Lavender Street, 23, 30
Le Corbusier, 273
    Unité d'Habitation, 76
Lee Boon Yang, 224
Lee Kip Lin, 66
Lee Kuan Yew, 80
    meeting with, 87–97
Le Mayeur, Adrien-Jean, 71
Leong C.C., 201
Leo Properties, 99
"liberation" of Malaya, 31
life in Singapore, 169–72
Lim Chong Keat, 43, 58, 63, 65, 75,
    76, 83–4, 97, 271
    versus William Lim Siew Wai,
    78–81
Lim Chuan Hoe, Richard, 79
Lim, Peter, 42
Lim Siew Wai, William "Willy", 43,
    75–80, 84–6, 97
Lim Swee Ee, 11
lineal city, idea of, 127

Line, Edge and Shade (Robert Powell),
    1, 271
Li Zehou, 84
local firms, rise of, 81–3
local government, 77, 270
local trading houses, 82
London Airport, 199
Low Keng Huat, 97
low-rise high-density (LRHD)
    housing, 201–16
    aesthetic problem, 207–8
    alternative housing forms, 205–7
    case of, 209–13
    in Cheras, Kuala Lumpur, 201,
    209–10
    children living in, 202
    children's play spaces in, 211
    City Hall in Kuala Lumpur,
    Malaysia, 209
    complaints with regard to, 210
    development for larger sites, 211
    future of, 209
    options for housing forms, 204–5
    other general aspects of, 214–16
    policies and designs of, 208
    recommendations for, 213
    respondents' confidence
    in forming of a community
    association by racial group, 212
    in Rizal, Philippines, 203
    Sambahayan condominium
    project, 203
    size of the toilet in, 214
    territoriality, issue of, 214
    in Toa Payoh, 92–4
    ventilation and heat, 213

Index

weather proofing, 213–14
Lynch, Kevin, 208

MacDonald House, 68
Malayan aesthetics, 83
Malayan Architects Co-Partnership
(MAC), 43, 58, 75–7
   competition for the Singapore
   Conference Hall and Trade Union
   House, 76
   "Malayan" identity, 83
   real estate development, 82
Malayan Chinese-educated
   intelligentsia, 109
Malayan Communist Party (MCP), 31
Malayan consciousness, evolution of,
109
Malayan culture, 109, 114, 115, 165
Malayan Forum, 108
Malayan generation, tribute to, 107
Malayan identity, 83, 113–15
Malayan Malay intellectual class
   under British colonial rule, 109
Malayan nationalism, 110, 111
Malayan-ness, decline of, 112
Malayan People's Anti-Japanese
   Army (MPAJA), 31
Malayan personality, 110–11
Malayan Project, 114
Malayan values, 107–9
Malay kampongs, 96
Malaysia
   affinity, affiliation and allegiance,
   113
   British values, 112
   cities and town of, 112

   English education background,
   107
   establishment of law and order by
   the British, 110
   formation of, 83
   higher education in, 110
   independence movement, 107
   landscape and pastimes, 111–13
   nationalism, 110
   opening of English-medium
   schools in, 110
   per capita income, 123
   political ideologies, 108
   political leadership, 108
   process of nation-building, 110
   relation with Singapore, 80
   Singapore's separation from, 83,
   107, 111
Manchester University, 76
Mandarin language, 26
   significance of, 181
Maphilindo, 68
MARA Institute, 209
Marine Parade Promenade, 189–90
maritime culture festivals, 256
market rates, 223
Marx, Karl, 164
Massachusetts Institute of
   Technology (MIT), 62, 76, 221
Mass Rapid Transit (MRT) system,
   126, 140–1, 144
Master Plan Review, 224–5
May & Baker, 24
May Fourth Movement (1919), 42
McLuhan, Marshall, 266
Mechai Viravaidya, 269
media version 2.0, 263

Index

medium rise high-density (MRHD) housing, 206

Mee, Arthur, 271

Meier, Richard, 142

Melaka Malay kampong houses, 65

Melbourne University, 49

Methodist Girls' School, 39

Methodist mission, at Cairnhill, 42

middle-income housing, 196, 197

middle peasants, 10

modernisation, process of, 133

Moholy-Nagy, László, 63

monopolistic bureaucratic system, 100

Monsoon (magazine), 78

moral bankruptcy, 133

moral decay within society, dangers of, 135

moral righteousness, 16

mortgage insurance, to underwrite loans, 197

motorcar ownership, 144

motorised transportation, 266

Mount Kinabalu rock wall, 255

Mount Sophia, 241

multinational corporations (MNCs), 160, 258

multiracial culture, 153

multi-racialism, 153

Mumford, Lewis, 242

Nanyang University
Convocation Stage, 52–3
library, 154
Students' Union House, 76

National Geographic, 271

National Heritage Trust, 157

national identity, evolution of, 119

nationalism, development of, 120

National Monuments Board, 153

National Museum Development Committee, 178

National Museum of Singapore, 155

National Parks Board, 155

National Theatre competition, 55, 77

National Trades Union Congress (NTUC), 144, 261

National University of Singapore (NUS), 179, 240, 266, 273

National Wage Council (NWC), 144

nation-building press, 2

nation building, process of, 119, 131

nature conservation, 155–6

Nee Soon, 181

New Asia International University Learning Zones, 172

new towns, development of, 195

New World Amusement Park, 24, 30

New York Airport, 199

Ng Keng Siang, 39, 52

Nicoll Highway, 131

Night Safari, 235

"night soil" carrier, 30

Ni Pollok, 71

"nominally democratic" society, 16

non-market community land, 260

North Atlantic hegemony, 2

North Bridge Road area, 137

Obiang-ism, strategy of, 146–8

occupy movements, 264

Official Receiver, 102

Omnimax theatre, 255–7
Ong Eng Guan, 85
Ong Teng Cheong, 97
open architectural competition, in Singapore, 77
Orang Asli bamboo fish trap, 27–8
Orang Laut, 151
Orchard Road, 13, 68, 76, 190, 240–1

Palmer and Turner Prize, 78
Pang Swee Keng, 9
park developments and garden estates, 127
Pasir Panjang beach house, 39
Pasir Ris, 131
patriot of the will, 4
Pax Japonica, 29
Paya Lebar Airport, 198–9
    expansion programme, 200
pedestrian suspension bridge, 257
People's Action Party (PAP), 15–16, 62, 76, 79, 271
    self-renewal, 97
People's Park Complex development, 97
Peripheral Nervous System (PNS), as an urban design concept, 259
persons per acre (ppa), 203
petty trader capitalism, 173, 176
place identity, 151
plot ratio, of HDB housing, 206
Poetics of Space, The (Gaston Bachelard), 47
political affiliation, 2, 26
political culture, 2, 86, 108, 150
politicisation of faith, 41

Polytechnic Architectural Society, 56, 67
polytechnics version 2.0, 262
Pont, Henri Maclaine, 70
population density, 203
pornography, 154
Portland cement, 82
Port of Singapore Authority (PSA), 140
Post Office Savings Bank (POSB), 143
Prince Edward Road, 62–3
Progressive Architecture magazine, 81
Pruitt-Igoe apartments in St. Louis, USA, 227
public entertainment, 171
public gardens, creation of, 227
public housing, 100, 197
    accommodation, 236
    neighbourhoods, 236
public transport, 101, 130, 139, 141–2
Public Utilities Board (PUB), 143
Public Works Department (PWD), 77, 112, 140

quality of life, 108, 134, 201, 224
quality of living, 136
Queen's Scholarship, 48

race relations, problems of, 152
racial conflict, 153
Raffles, Stamford, 69, 107, 150
Rahim Ishak, 91
rapid industrialisation, preconditions for, 123
rate of return, 143
Razak, Tun Abdul Hussein, 97

Index

Reader's Digest, 271
real estate development, 82
real estate valuators, 192
reasoning, process of, 101
recession of 1985, 10
recreational and civic amenities, 196
"Red House", Federal Dispensary,
　Battery Road, 23
regeneration, cycle of, 127
regional culture, 167
regional economy, greening of, 273
regional fraternity, 68
Registry of Vehicles (ROV), 140
reinforced concrete, development of,
　126
religiosity, power-dimension of, 45
remote working, 220
retirement cottages, 229–39
　affordable and community-based
　accommodation, 229
　community-based housing of
　elders, 236
　costs and consequences of
　　granny flats, 237
　　old age homes, 237
　　retirement cottages, 237
　　retirement villages, 237
　demonstration project, 239
　design of, 238
　elderly categories, 229
　housing and land use policies, 247
　in-fill retirement cottages, 236
　land question, 238
　locations in the older public
　housing estates, 238–9
　night safari, 235

philosophy of, 229
prerequisites for, 239
within public housing estates, 238
Studio Apartments, 239
ribbon development, problem of, 127
rice bowl politics, 2
Road Transport Advisory Committee,
　139
road transportation, 194
Romanisation of Chinese, 179
Romondt, Vincent Van, 61, 69
roster and night duty shifts, 195
Rotary Club, 139
Royal Air Force, 198
rubanisation, idea of, 250, 264–70
Ruban lifestyles and economics, 265
Ruban settlement, 266, 269
Rumah Miskin Police Station, 23
rural/urban dichotomy, 266
rural-urban drift
　causes of, 124
　to seek employment, 128
Russell, Bertrand, 271

SAA Architects, 80
Sands of Iwo Jima (movie), 22
satellite towns, construction of, 125
Schoemaker, Wolff, 69
school boy "apostles", 41–4
School of Architecture, NUS, 99
schools version 2.0, 262
Science and Economic Development
　(Richard Meier), 142
Scout Camp, in Jurong, 40
scouting days, 39–41

Index

seaward extensions, 248

secular institutions, importance of, 108

sedition, laws of, 180

Selegie/Serangoon corridor, 240

self-rule, notion of, 110

Selvadurai, Pathmanaban, 99

Sennett Estate's roads, 179

sense of freedom, 103

Seow, Eugene, 76, 239

Serangoon Garden Estate, 193

Serangoon Road, 22–3, 35, 179
    return to, 29–31
    two-storey row house, 30

Shell Sports Club, at Paya Lebar, 38

Shenton Way, 62, 66

shopping mall, 257

sibling rivalry, 13–17

Silicon Valley, 221

Sime Darby, 67, 82

Sim Lim Group, 82

Singapore
    town of, 112
    under colonial administration, 150
    cultural and intellectual development of, 83
    cultural role of, 119–21
    founding of, 150
    Japanese Imperial atrocities in, 179
    Minister of Communications, 143
    Ministry of Education, 273
    Ministry of National Development (MND), 85, 99
    nationalism, 1–2

paradoxical paradise, 184

pedestrian and traffic segregation, 120

per capita income, 123

population of, 120

relation with Malaysia, 80

separation from Malaysia, 83, 107, 111

strategic land use issue in, 224–5

Street and Building Names Board, 178

as trading outpost of the East India Company, 150

transport dilemma, 139–40

US Embassy in, 102

Singaporean corporate sector, 160

Singapore Armed Forces (SAF), 261

Singapore Botanic Gardens, 155

Singapore Bus Service (SBS), 142

Singapore Conference Hall, 63

Singapore Constitution Exposition (1959), 49

Singapore Cricket Club, 9

Singapore Herald (newspaper), 102

Singapore Heritage Society, 156

Singapore Housing & Development Board (HDB), 56, 101, 125, 140, 195, 201, 223
    high-rise concept, 99
    public housing designs, 225
    Urban Renewal Department of, 129
    version 2.0, 259–60

Singapore Improvement Trust (SIT), 215–16

Singapore Institute of Architects (SIA), 48–9, 99, 223
   professional development committee, 99
   publication committee, 85
Singapore Land Authority (SLA), 260
Singapore Management University (SMU), 23
Singapore: Past, Present & Future, 101
Singapore Parliament Review Committee, 99
Singapore Planning and Urban Research Group (SPUR), 85–7, 88, 101, 122–8, 132, 198
   imagining future Singapore, 91
Singapore Polytechnic, 43, 48, 50, 55, 62, 75, 77
   Polytechnic Architectural Society, 67
Singapore River, 240
Singapore society, multi-racial basis of, 152
Singapore Tourism Board, 178
Singapore Version 2.0, 258–9
slums, 208
small and medium enterprises (SMEs), 160, 258
smaller households, proliferation of, 197
sociability of housing, 201, 204
social engineering, 218
social equity, 260
social health, 136
Socialist Club, 41, 85
social restructuring, 258
social transformation, 152

social unrest, forms of, 133
Society of Malayan Architects (SMA), 48
society–state power dynamics, 1
socio-psychological environmental spatial system, 272
Southeast Asian cultural museum, 167
South Sea Lagoon Project
   brief description, 189
   cost benefit of, 192
   at East Coast reclamation, 189–92
   economic benefit of, 190
   financing of, 191
   reclamation land value, 190
   recreational facilities, 190
   social benefit of, 189–90
   technical feasibility of, 191
   tourist attraction, 190
   urgency of action, 191
Speak Mandarin campaign, 26, 181
spiritual experience, 44–7
Sri Vijaya (Srivijaya), 151
St. Andrew's School, 37, 42
start-up SMEs, 259
state corporate sector, 161
State Scholarship, award of, 48
St. Joseph's Institution, 9
St. Margaret's School, 9
stock market crash of 1929, 9
Straits Times, The, 142
street camps in HDB estates, organisation of, 204
street economy, 173
suaku, 146
Sulawesi *phinisi*, 256

Index

Sungei Road Thieves' Market, 11
Sun Yat Sen Memorial Library, 10
Swatow, China, 9

Taiwan, 26–8
    American orientation, 27
Tanah Merah, 40
Tan Ah Tah, 9
Tan, Augustine, 97
Tan Chin Nam, 98
Tan Chong Tee, 31
Tanglin Halt, 81
Tan Jake Hooi, 85
Tanjong Pagar Railway Station, 63
Tan Swan Beng, 100
Tan Teck Khim, 97
Tay Cheng Kui, 11
Tay Eng Soon, 13–7
Tay Meng Hock, 9
tea money, 25
Teh Cheang Wan, 85, 99, 223
Tekka Market, 11, 23
Temasek (ancient Singapore), 151
Temasek (magazine), 78
Teochews, 10
Teoh, Jim, 41
Thio Chan Bee, 36, 41
Thompson, George, 87
Thumboo, Edwin, 179, 181
Tio Seng Chin, 77
Toa Payoh Neighbourhood II, 207
Toh Chin Chye, 64, 79
Tojo, General, 28
Tokyo University, 66
tongkang (barge) business, 11

tourist information bureau, 50
Town and Country Planning Acts,
    219
town councils version 2.0, 260–1
town planning, 190, 193, 218–19
Trade Union House, 63, 76–7, 80
traffic congestion, 139, 190
transportation, in Singapore
    air pollution, elimination of, 143
    diesel fuel tax, 143
    fuel cost in total systems
        accounting, 142–3
    Mass Rapid Transit (MRT)
        system, 126, 140–1
    operating cost, 142
    ownership of, 143–5
    planning for, 139
    problem-solving, 142
    process of reorganisation of, 143
    public transport, 139
    Singapore Bus Service (SBS), 142
    social problems of, 141–2
"Tree of Life" culture theatre,
    proposal, 255–6
tree planting programme, of
    Singapore, 155
Tropical Architecture Conference of
    1954, 76
tropically-styled buildings, 219
twilight zones, 127

UMNO (Malaysia's ruling party), 80
United Chinese Bank. See United
    Overseas Bank (UOB)
Unite d'habitation housing, 227
United Overseas Bank (UOB), 82

Index

universal bilingual education, 150
Universitas Gadjah Mada, 70
Universitas Indonesia (UI), 68
universities version 2.0, 262
University of California, 142
University of Malaya, 209
University of Melbourne, 79
University of Singapore
    Bukit Timah Campus, 61
    Freshmen Orientation Week on
    "Cultural Subversion", 103
    School of Architecture, 101–2
    Students' Union, 103
urban and rural lands, 133, 223
urban and the rural environment,
    267–8
urban centres, economic life in, 202
urban-industrial-consumer economy,
    265
urban land reform, 128
urban living, 265
    virtues of, 264
urban planning, 100
    politics of, 140
Urban Redevelopment Authority
    (URA)
    Golden Mile Complex, 272–3
    version 2.0, 260
urban renewal programme, 121, 125,
    129, 178, 193
    government's sale of land under,
    196
    slum clearance, 152
urban renewal schemes, 223
urban renewal sites, 129
urban universities, 240, 242

vernacular dilemma, 109–10
vertical zoo, 255
Vickery, D.J., 48
Victorian industrial housing, 208
Vietnam, protests against US
    bombing of, 97, 102
virtual reality, 255
visual order, 208

wages and incomes, 267
"walled city" of Kowloon, 242
Walter, Michael, 202
Weber, Max, 164
wedding halls, 255
Wee Cho Yaw, 82
Wee Chwee Heng, 52, 64, 85
Western imperialism, 31
western industrialised societies,
    evolution of, 195
wholeness, sense of, 46, 65–6
"winning hearts and minds", 2
Wolf Cubs (Club Scouts), 20, 39
Wong Fook Kay, 78
Woodhull, Sydney, 77
World War II, 5, 17–25, 42, 122, 218
    air raid shelters, 17
    American B-29 Superfortress
    bombers, 31
    Japanese bombing of Singapore (8
    December 1941), 22
    Pacific War, 22
Wright, Frank Lloyd, 67
Wu Qing Rui, 182

Index

Yaacob, Datuk Latiff, 98
Yap Pheng Gek, 179
Yeo, George, 84
Yio Chu Kang Road, 181
Yong Nyuk Lin, 48

Young Men's Christian Association (YMCA), 9, 171
Youth in the Army (C.C. Leong), 146, 201